WOMEN, POWER, and CHANGE

WOMEN, POWER, and CHANGE

Selected Papers from
Social Work Practice in Sexist Society:
First NASW Conference on Social Work
Practice with Women,
September 14–16, 1980,
Washington, D.C.

Ann Weick and Susan T. Vandiver, Editors

National Association of Social Workers
NASW PRESS Washington, DC

International Standard Book No.: 0-87101-092-5
Library of Congress Catalog Card No.: 81-83429

Printed in U.S.A.

FOREWORD

Successful social services for women must move beyond accepting the status quo of society or the life situations of individual clients. Attempts to change the individual must also include actions to change the social system. This approach to social services for women offers rich opportunities for the profession because, unlike other helping professions, social work incorporates a person-in-situation orientation. The needs of women are not unique; their needs parallel those of all human beings to see and understand themselves and their situations in the context of the broader social environment and to have options for growth and self-actualization. Although the profession's efforts to incorporate approaches to changing both individuals and society have sometimes been less than successful, they have nonetheless been a major tenet of its mission.

The First National Conference on Social Work Practice with Women: Social Work Practice in Sexist Society was an important development in the profession's interest in women's issues. Before the conference, the profession's focus was on exposing and addressing the sexism that exists in the profession and in the social service system. Generally, these efforts involved a broad array of affirmative action activities to increase the opportunities for women to move into positions of power and leadership. The conference signaled an important new interest in women's issues by social workers: how the social service system and the social work profession can identify and understand the unique social service needs of women and the intervention strategies and delivery systems necessary for meeting these needs.

The recurrent theme of the papers presented at the conference and in the articles in this volume is the growing awareness by social workers of the sense of powerlessness that women feel, individually and collectively, because society's sexist attitudes keep them stereotyped and without power. An even greater concern is the emerging awareness that many of society's attitudes have permeated the organization of the profession and the theories and methods used by social workers. The overriding message of the conference was that effective social service programs for women must be directed toward the individual and collective empowerment of women. The goal of empowering women offers unique opportunities for social workers, the most important of which is to devise strategies for themselves and for clients. Thus, the interests of social workers, who are predominantly women, and those of their clients, who also are predominantly women, are the same. The profession's earlier efforts to improve the status of women in the profession and in social service programs through affirmative action programs are now being broadened to include a like concern for improving the position of female clients in the social service system and in the larger society. In attempting to improve services for women, social workers may profit from the lessons they learned in working to enhance the position of women in the profession itself.

As the second woman to be elected president of the National Association of Social Workers (NASW) in the association's twenty-five-year history, I became increasingly aware of the struggle of women to achieve positions of power and leadership in the profession. I was especially proud to be involved in the planning and convening of this conference and to share the keynote address with Mary Ann Mahaffey, who in 1975, the twentieth year of the association, became the first woman president of NASW.

Why did a profession dominated by women allow its leadership positions to be transferred to men? The shift to male leadership began after World War II when men started to enter the profession in greater numbers. It paralleled the profession's clear effort to achieve greater status in the male-dominated society by emulating the normative patterns of society that called for men to assume leadership positions, both as staff and volunteers. The recent women's movement has motivated female social workers, like women everywhere, to reevaluate their positions and to regain their preeminent position. Now the question is this: How can a profession that is numerically dominated and led by women achieve status in society? The issue of the profession's status, compared to other professions and society as a whole, is indeed complicated. One major factor is the relative and shared powerlessness of women and of social workers, who are also mainly women. This shared powerlessness has caused social work to become less influential in the policy-making of the social service system. Recently, the profession has critically shifted its emphasis in order to increase its status and power.

Social work's quest for social status has never been aimed merely at improving the position of the profession. Rather, it has incorporated the desire to use a position of influence to improve the situation of clients. In short, empowering social workers in the larger society would permit social work to make a significant contribution to the empowerment of women, particularly female clients. Social workers can influence the effort to reverse and overcome the effects of the sexist attitudes that are pervasive in society as a whole only if they have the power to determine the policies and preferred strategies of intervention. Accordingly, social work's quest for status and the search for intervention strategies to empower women are closely related.

Political action is an important strategy. Direct participation in the political process may well offer a new means for social work to achieve status and influence in the decisions that determine the nature and quality of the social services, and NASW has steadily increased its participation in political action in the last decade. A position of influence can be achieved by the direct participation of social workers in the political process as well as by supporting candidates who are favorable to the concerns of social work. The women's movement also has increased its participation in politics through its efforts to win passage of the Equal Rights Amendment (ERA) and through political caucuses. Thus, political action seems to be a realistic means not only to bring about the empowerment of women and clients, but also to improve the status and influence of social workers, individually and collectively, female and male.

To achieve the objectives of the conference, the event itself as well as this book must be seen only as the springboard from which serious and concentrated efforts are directed toward understanding the social empowerment of women as clients and professionals. The interests and needs of women— regardless of their position in society—have much in common.

NANCY A. HUMPHREYS, *President*

June 1981   *National Association of Social Workers*

Conference Planning Committee

Positions are those held at the time of the conference (September 1980)

Ann Weick, Ph.D. *(chairperson)*, Associate Professor, School of Social Welfare, University of Kansas, Lawrence

Katharine Ostrander, MSSW, Director, Social Work Program, Newport College—Salveregina, Newport, Rhode Island

Judith Pierson, MSW, Project Director, "Moving Women Up," Highland Park, New Jersey

Susan T. Vandiver, MSW, Chairperson, NASW Committee on Women's Issues, and Director, Foundation for Children with Learning Disabilities, New York, New York

> Carol J. Sheffer *(staff)*, Senior Staff Associate for Women's Issues, National Association of Social Workers, Washington, D.C.

Conference Book Committee

Positions are those held at the time of the conference (September 1980)

Ann Weick, Ph.D. *(chairperson)*, Associate Professor, School of Social Welfare, University of Kansas, Lawrence

Jeanne M. Giovannoni, Ph.D., Professor, School of Social Welfare, University of California, Los Angeles

Dolores G. Norton, Ph.D., Associate Professor, School of Social Service Administration, University of Chicago, Chicago, Illinois

Elaine Pinderhughes, MSW, Associate Professor, School of Social Work, Boston College, Chestnut Hill, Massachusetts

Betty Sancier, MSW, Professor, School of Social Welfare, University of Wisconsin, Milwaukee

Susan T. Vandiver, MSW, Chairperson, NASW Committee on Women's Issues, Director, Foundation for Children with Learning Disabilities, New York, New York

> Beatrice N. Saunders *(staff)*, Director, Department of Publications, National Association of Social Workers, New York, New York

Contributors

Positions are those held at the time of the conference (September 1980)

MARTHA BAUM, Ph.D., Associate Professor, School of Social Work, University of Pittsburgh, Pittsburgh, Pennsylvania

EVELYN LANCE BLANCHARD, MSW, Community Development Specialist, Indian Health Service, Portland, Oregon

RUTH A. BRANDWEIN, Ph.D., Director, School of Social Work, University of Iowa, Iowa City

MARIE CASSELLA, MSW, Social Worker, Dorchester House Multi-Service Center, Dorchester, Massachusetts

JOAN M. CUMMERTON, DSW, Professor, Department of Social Work Education, San Francisco State University, San Francisco, California

JANICE M. DE LANGE, Ph.D., Assistant Professor, School of Social Work, University of Washington, Seattle

CHERYL ELLSWORTH, MSW, Coordinator, Project on Women and Mental Health, School of Social Work, University of Washington, Seattle

STEPHANIE FALLCREEK, MSW, Research Associate and Project Director, School of Social Work, University of Washington, Seattle

MARTHA MOLINA FIMBRES, MSW, Lecturer and Psychiatric Social Worker, Department of Psychiatry, College of Medicine, Arizona Health Sciences Center, University of Arizona, Tucson

BETSY MCALISTER GROVES, MSW, Adolescent Social Worker, Dorchester House Multi-Service Center, Dorchester, Massachusetts

DEBORAH M. HENSON, MSW, Special Education Social Worker, Orleans Parish School Board, New Orleans, Louisiana

KATHLEEN SPANGLER HILL, MSW, Chief Staff to the Job Club, Champaign Consortium for CETA, University of Illinois, Urbana-Champaign

NANCY HOOYMAN, Ph.D., Associate Professor and Director, Projects on Aging, School of Social Work, University of Washington, Seattle

JANE JACOBS, MSW, Clinical Director, Mental Health Program, Dorchester House Multi-Service Center, Dorchester, Massachusetts

CAROL H. MEYER, DSW, Professor of Social Work, School of Social Work, Columbia University, New York, New York

RUTH ANN RUFF, MSW, Planner, Summer Youth Employment Program, Division of Youth Services, Seattle Department of Human Resources, Seattle, Washington

ANGELA SHEN RYAN, MSW, Lecturer, School of Social Work, Hunter College of the City University of New York, New York, New York

ESTHER SALES, Ph.D., Assistant Professor, School of Social Work, University of Pittsburgh, Pittsburgh, Pennsylvania

BETTY SANCIER, MSW, Professor, School of Social Welfare, University of Wisconsin, Milwaukee

JANET L. SCHINDERMAN, BA, Program Director, Crescent House, New Orleans, Louisiana

BARBARA K. SHORE, Ph.D., Professor, School of Social Work, University of Pittsburgh, Pittsburgh, Pennsylvania

BARBARA BRYANT SOLOMON, DSW, Professor, School of Social Work, University of Southern California, Los Angeles

SUE BAILEY STAM, MSW, Health Educator and Planner, Wallingford Wellness Project, Seattle, Washington

JOAN HUDYMA TUCKER, MSW, Program Developer, Womansphere, Seattle, Washington

ANN WEICK, Ph.D., Associate Professor, School of Social Welfare, University of Kansas, Lawrence

JANICE WOOD WETZEL, Ph.D., Associate Professor, Smith College School for Social Work, Northampton, Massachusetts

BARBARA W. WHITE, MSW, Instructor, School of Social Work, Florida State University, Tallahassee

NATALIE JANE WOODMAN, MSS, Associate Professor, School of Social Work, Arizona State University, Tempe

ACKNOWLEDGMENTS

The National Committee on Women's Issues of the National Association of Social Workers (NASW) made this book possible. Their guidance and consultation resulted in the First National Conference on Social Work Practice with Women: Social Work Practice in Sexist Society, held in Washington, D.C., September 14–16, 1980. That such a conference was needed in the profession was confirmed by the attendance of some seven hundred social workers, mainly women, who came from all parts of the country to examine the theoretical bases of the field in relation to women's issues and to share ideas about new models of nonsexist practice. The articles in this volume were selected from over one hundred presentations at the conference. The Conference Book Committee, working with staff of the NASW Department of Publications, reviewed the papers and recommended those to be included in this volume. Their collective wisdom and judgment are reflected here.

Special thanks for the countless hours of volunteer work put into the entire project go to Katharine Ostrander and Judith Pierson, members of the Conference Planning Committee, and to Jeanne M. Giovannoni, Dolores G. Norton, Elaine Pinderhughes, and Betty Sancier, who served on the Conference Book Committee.

All NASW staff assisted with the project, but several in particular share credit for the achievement: Carol Sheffer and Georgianna Carrington, of the national office, for their efforts on the conference; Wendy Almeleh, senior editor, Department of Publications, for her editorial assistance; and Beatrice Saunders, former director, Department of Publications, for her invaluable publications consultation and support, which extended to the day of her retirement and beyond.

The editors express their appreciation of the Ford Foundation for its grant in support of the overall effort. The foundation's generosity made it possible to encompass both theoretical and practical materials in the conference and in this volume.

A.W. and S.V.

CONTENTS

INTRODUCTION

Power and change are themes of strength and hope for women. Centuries-old customs and laws have permitted women to occupy only a narrow place in society. However, there has also been spirited protest challenging the status quo. In myriad ways, women have struggled alone and in groups to express the fullness of what it means to be human. Key to this struggle has been a recognition that conditions can be changed—that there is nothing immutable in any societal design. Being able to see the promise of better forms even while living with existing ones is the generative force underlying the hopes of women for experiencing a different life. Current patterns exacerbate powerlessness by making change unthinkable; development of new patterns creates a situation of risk in which creative adaptations can become part of the human repertoire.

Social work cannot be seen apart from the dynamics of the larger society. Societal values shaped the formation of the profession and continue to influence its practice. Although social work values flow from the democratic principles on which society is based and share the same radical message embodied in calls for equality, these values, like the larger social values, are burdened with dilemmas and conflict. Tolerance and enjoyment of difference (valuing the uniqueness of individuals), awareness of the impact of larger social and economic forces (person-in-environment), and the dignity that comes from the freedom to choose (self-determination) become distorted when they are applied from a sexist perspective. In large measure, the indictments made against social work practice are directly related to the failure to understand and apply the social work values and views to which all social workers presumably subscribe.

Between the challenge of ideals and the realities of daily life is a creative tension that provides energy for a renewal in social work practice. The First NASW National Conference on Social Work Practice with

Women: "Social Work Practice in Sexist Society" was a national expression of this energy. Hundreds of women from across the country came together to share their concerns about the effects of sexist attitudes and practices on the provision of services to women. This sharing of concerns was bolstered by the exchange of ideas about how to make services more responsive to women's needs.

Among the wealth of ideas presented at the conference, power and change emerged as central subjects. They were chosen as themes for this book because they immediately prompt a reexamination of the values and principles that ground social work practice. It is in practice with women that the profession's quality of understanding of and commitment to these principles is more clearly revealed. Work with women is a mirror that reflects all the ways in which we social workers compromise, subvert, and ignore professional values. Our response to women as clients epitomizes the quality of our responses to all clients. Whatever prompts us to minimize women's needs and options leads us to shortchange both our clients and ourselves. Whatever leads to sound creative practice with women accrues to the good of all.

The study of social work practice with women has two important lessons for social work. By assessing the quality of services to women, one can see that the profession's theory and practice are plagued by the same limited view of women which exists in the larger society. In spite of its professed beliefs about personal dignity, human potential, and self-determination, the profession's programs, policies, and services all too often impose the same restrictions on women as does the larger society. Rather than acting on our professional values as a buffer against society's harsher views, our practice too often becomes a conduit for further oppression. In this way, our actions reinforce the powerlessness of women.

Focusing on women as clients tells something else about social work practice. That is, the social work role of facilitator of change is frequently clumsy when applied to women. Because women's lives are now, perhaps more than ever before, subject to social and personal challenges, our knowledge of the process of change and the nature of our role in this process is also subject to challenge. As we social workers interact with women clients, we often disregard or diagnose away the larger social understanding that makes change possible. Instead we focus on the microcosm of a single personality, choosing to ignore the societal forces that helped shape the individual.

To see these dynamics at work, social workers must be willing to look deeply into practice with women. This examination is important because it helps us to understand the convoluted nature of the problem. But, more than that, the examination becomes the crucial stepping-stone for revitalized practice with women. Although a study of the problems highlights the predicament of women, a study of the solutions will enhance all social work practice. This book is dedicated to that premise.

The articles in this book were originally presented at the First NASW National Conference on Social Work Practice with Women. They represent a sampling of the many subjects and issues raised at the conference that are still being addressed as women social workers struggle to understand the problems affecting practice with women. The articles are instructive regarding the dynamic of powerlessness in women's lives. They speak to the many ways powerlessness is experienced. They also speak to the intricate relationship between the social forces that contribute to and reinforce powerlessness and the personal vulnerability of women in the face of these forces.

This complex interrelationship is exemplified by the dynamics of victimization. The social conditions that permit battering, rape, and all forms of abuse burden women who are victims of this violence. The victim must deal not only with the assault but with the guilt and emotional pain of society's message that she is somehow at fault.

But victimization is not restricted to the arena of physical violence. In their economic roles, women endure discrimination in job mobility and the ignominy of jobs in the secondary labor market or face the greater stigma of public welfare. Women of color deal with the double jeopardy of race and sex, insuring that they will be subject to oppression on both counts. Lesbians face the punishing attitudes of a society that condemns differences in sexual orientation. Is it any wonder that the emotional toll from coping with such conditions is often diagnosed as depression? Depression is vulnerability turned in on itself. The circle of societal and personal interaction is maintained; women continue to feel powerless, and society continues to fuel their powerlessness through its rigid responses.

This inactive loop would be a matter of despair were it not for the inherent potential of human beings to reassess their situation and imagine that things could be different. The courage of this imagination is the first step in hewing a path of change. And social work, perhaps more than any other profession, is based on the belief that human beings have the potential to change themselves and their world.

A key question, then, is how to intervene in situations of powerlessness so women come to know and experience the strength of their own power. The authors move beyond an analysis of the problem toward prospects for this type of change. They show how important it is to make a radical reappraisal of and reconfirm social work values as the foundation of change. Respect for diversity comes from a belief in the nature of human dignity; the assumption of homogeneity among women of any group ignores each woman's uniqueness. However, along with diversity are deep ties of history and culture. The commonality inherent in the experience of being female can form a cohesive bond among all women. Shared encounters with racism and oppression form an additional bond among women of color.

Social work also has a special view of human struggles. Although the profession is dedicated to helping people change life conditions that hinder their desire or ability to grow, it recognizes that growth is also a struggle. Rather than making narrow assessments at one point in time, social work views personal change as a continuous, developmental process with many complex shadings. The task of social workers is to advocate for the conditions that allow people to engage in the struggle for growth and human fulfillment and to provide direct services to maximize their ability to choose for themselves.

Recognition of the conditions of change requires the large environmental view that has been the hallmark of social work. Social workers understand that the conditions of people's lives are not understood solely in a personal context and that to make an adequate professional assessment, the larger social forces impinging on people's life choices must be taken into account. The constraints imposed by the economic and political structures, by deeply ingrained patterns of prejudice, by narrow role-oriented socialization, and by inflexible institutions conspire to lessen and at times snuff out the faint glimmerings of hope for a better life. The profession's focus is on the personal as well as the political realities of people's lives, but somehow that focus has become blurred. Without this emphasis, the professed belief in self-determination is a delusion.

Understanding how to facilitate change by helping clients find and use their positive power is a central goal of professional social work practice. Linked with that goal is the need for each social worker to assess his or her professional power and to use it to alter social conditions that militate against a dignified life. Each task requires a clarity of insight and sureness of resolve that match the highest demands of the profession. Social work can be the profession that asks, in the face of change, Why not? When confronted with shortsightedness, we social workers can inquire: Become adjusted to what? And we can turn our energies to the risks and challenges inherent in changing society and empowering those with whom we work.

ANN WEICK AND SUSAN T. VANDIVER

June 1981

1
Vulnerability and Power

REDEFINING CONCEPTS OF MENTAL HEALTH

Janice Wood Wetzel

It is not by chance that an article entitled "Redefining Concepts of Mental Health" is included in this volume. Sixty-three percent of the social work profession are women, the majority of whom are in low-echelon clinical positions. Female social workers supply at least 50 percent of the psychosocial treatment provided to all clients in private and public hospitals, clinics, and social service agencies. Furthermore, two-thirds of all clients are also women, as are three-fourths of nursing home residents served by social workers.[1] Thus, it is obvious that women as a group have a vested interest in preventing mental illness and promoting mental health.

In this article, the author discusses the basic social work principles regarding mental health and how they may be reconceptualized to fulfill the needs of women. She then goes on to describe the mental health problems that women face and to offer suggestions for dealing better with them.

SOCIAL WORK PRINCIPLES

Psychosocial interventions used by social workers generally are based on three ostensibly distinct concepts of mental health: psychoanalysis, behavior modification, and humanism. In their orthodox forms they appear to be separate modalities.[2] Although the efficacy of these concepts is still being debated, none of the models seems to have remained a single entity. For example, contemporary psychoanalytic theory has incorporated the principles of ego psychology, and behavior modification has adopted cognitive theory, as have the fields of biophysics and biochemistry.[3]

The cross-germination of ideas is also evident in psychoanalytic developmental psychology. A leading construct of ego psychology, which embodies the theory of object relations, psychoanalytic developmental psychology has incorporated the symbolic interactionist perspective of sociologist Mead and the humanism of psychiatrist Rank.[4] Rank, it may be remembered, influenced social workers Taft and Robinson, the founders of the controversial functional school of social work that evolved as a counter to Freudian ideology.[5] Taft and Robinson espoused the importance of human attachment, separation, and individuation today held dear by object relations theorists. And who are more surprised than scientifically based behaviorists to learn that their methods of reconditioning perception to alter behavior are exactly those methods used by philosophically oriented advocates of holistic health who have been influenced by Eastern, Judaic, and Christian sects as well as twentieth-century existentialists?[6] Clearly, then, seemingly disparate minds are reaching similar universal conclusions. It is neither appropriate nor vital to argue in favor of a single conceptual framework for mental health. It is only the degree of eclecticism that is debatable.

Whatever the professional mode of practice, it is generally agreed that all methods should be soundly based on shared social work values and ethics. Some values are formally written into the Code of Ethics of the National Association of Social Workers (NASW); others have evolved through common practice. They have been both disputed and defended, and social workers even advise one another to be wary of an overzealous application of principles that do not conform to the realities of practice.[7] As members of a comparatively new profession, social workers have tended to tread cautiously, emphasizing what they do not know empirically. They have been painfully aware that the profession is based on the "soft" social sciences and therefore lacks scientific detachment. It is as if social workers imagine that the world outside social work operates on the solid facts, expertise, and wisdom they have yet to acquire. Yet, whenever they come to know a subject well, social workers often find they are the experts. The realm of mental health and the prevention of mental illness are a case in point.

Social workers must accept that they are leaders. They must accept subjective experience as valid knowledge and hence not reject social work research and its application to clients because such research necessarily lacks neat experimental designs mistakenly believed to result in objective, uncontaminated "truth." No longer can social workers afford the luxury of a low profile, modestly claiming they are "too young to know." Social workers must respect the strengths of the profession, beginning with the principles they value.[8]

Social workers take pride in their ability to synthesize knowledge from many disciplines; let this synthesis be done on behalf of women. Social workers recognize the intrinsic worth, dignity, and importance of all human beings; let this principle be applied specifically to women. Social workers affirm that there are human needs common to all persons, yet understand that each person is different; let women be included in this affirmation. Social workers assert that the realization of the full potential of each individual is an essential attribute of a democratic society, together with a sense of social responsibility gained through active participation in society; let these values be operationalized in the lives of women.[9] Social workers claim responsibility for providing ways in which obstacles to self-realization can be overcome and prevented; let this claim be applied to women. Social workers avow their belief in the prevention and elimination of discrimination in rendering service, in work assignments, and in employment practices; let them translate this belief into action on behalf of all women.

EPIDEMIOLOGICAL VIEW

The first step toward actualizing the values of social work is to take an epidemiological view of both social problems and mental illness.[10] In taking such a view, the following questions need to be asked:

- What are the major social problems?
- Which persons are most likely to experience the problems?
- In whom is the incidence of the problems increasing most rapidly?
- What are the common characteristics of the at-risk population?
- What are the common denominators of the problems?

Social workers are in a unique position to answer these questions, since they, more than any other professionals, come in daily contact with a myriad of contemporary social problems. It is social workers who are most able to delineate the at-risk populations and where the new cases are emerging. It is social workers who can provide the global perspective necessary to locate the common characteristics of clients and to identify common denominators found in their problems and environments.

The report of the President's Commission on Mental Health—a document that will influence the next decade of mental health planning—concluded: "Although there has been an explosion of new information about women in the last decade, very little has been incorporated into training programs for mental health service providers."[11] Mental health clinicians have not been given the knowledge and training necessary to serve the needs of women. Despite mandates of NASW and the Council on Social Work Education, on the whole, social work educators, clinicians, and administrators continue to resist the inclusion of courses on and services for women in social work education and practice.[12] Sexist attitudes have much to do with the lack of recognition of the vastness and far-ranging implications of the problems of women. It is essential that all social workers are cognizant of the scope of the problems that place women at risk vis à vis their mental health. A summary of these problems and the social conditions that cause them follows.

DEPRESSION AND SUBSTANCE ABUSE

Depression—the nation's leading mental health problem—affects at least eight million people annually. Three times as many women as men are likely to become severely depressed, and one out of every six women becomes clinically depressed in her lifetime. Although causes are not known and theories vary, empirical evidence indicates that women's powerlessness, their controlled place in society, their socialization to dependence, and the lack of support in family and work environments are variables.[13] Most clients of social workers, psychologists, and psychiatrists are depressed women.

Reasons cited for alcoholism in women parallel those cited for depression. Although over 40 percent of the alcoholics in the United States are women, all but a few of the alcoholism research programs and treatment services are for men. The same holds true for drug addicts, 20 percent of whom are women.[14] Since the majority of drugs are prescribed for women, women's abuse of drugs may be considered iatrogenic.

POVERTY

It is not by chance that 79 percent of the poor people in this country are women. Poverty is a condition primarily of women. Poor women are hit harder by nearly every social problem and mental health concern. Some subgroups of poor women are outlined below.

Elderly Women

The condition of elderly women is a case in point. Three out of four poor persons over age 65 are women. Single or widowed elderly women living alone are more likely to be poor than are any other group of elderly persons. As for minority women, half the aged black women earn less than $2,000 annually, and aged Spanish-speaking women earn even less. Women aged 65–69 have median incomes that are less than half those of men of corresponding ages. Seventy-five percent of all the elderly persons in institutions are women, most of whom are white, poor, and alone in the world.[15]

Working Women and Dual Careers

The transformation of women's place in the workforce has had an enormous impact on this society. Forty-eight percent of the women aged 16 and over are employed outside the home. Eighty percent of these women are concentrated at the same low-level jobs at which women have been working for decades. Although minority women are on the lowest rung of the employment ladder, white women are not far above them.[16] Thus, despite their new roles, women continue to be financially dependent. Moreover, women's earnings have actually decreased from 63 percent to 57 percent of men's earnings in the last two decades.

Traditional housewives who do not work outside the home have the highest rate of mental illness, and the risk of their becoming mentally ill increases if they have small children. It is interesting to note that married men have the lowest incidence of mental illness—a fact that led sociologist Bernard to speak of "his and her" marriages.[17]

The 47.4 million married women who work outside the home, however, are literally not home free. Although they have taken on new roles, they continue to bear the responsibilities of housewife and mother with little or no help from their husbands. Their burden is stressful and their mental health is often in jeopardy.[18]

Women as Single Parents

By 1978, eight million families were maintained by women living without a spouse—a 44 percent increase over 1970. Over eleven million children were living with their mother, as compared with one million who resided with their father.[19]

Female-headed families with children under age 18 represent the highest poverty-risk group in the nation. Over 46 percent of all such households live in poverty, as do 50 percent of all minority female-headed households. In fact, 95 percent of the recipients of Aid to Families with Dependent Children are women and their children. To be even more explicit, more than half the families receiving public assistance in 1977 were still living below the official poverty line after receiving benefits.

Although more than one-fourth of all welfare mothers work outside the home, they do not earn enough to support their families. Included in this group are more than one million 15–19 year olds and thirty thousand girls under age 15 who become pregnant each year, two-thirds of whom are without husbands and 94 percent of whom keep their babies. The suicide rate for single teenage mothers is ten times that of other teenagers.[20] The facts are staggering. The mental health of teenage mothers and the children they bring into the world is at risk.

Displaced Homemakers

A displaced homemaker can be defined as a middle-aged or older woman who has worked in the home for a substantial number of years giving unpaid service to the family, is not gainfully employed, has no marketable skills, and is no longer supported by income from another family member (owing to widowhood, divorce, or separation) or from federal assistance. There are an estimated two to three million displaced homemakers in this country.[21] The middle-aged displaced homemaker is in the worst position. If she has never worked, she does not qualify for unemployment compensation. If she is widowed before age 60, she is not entitled to widow's benefits. And unless she is physically disabled or has children under age 18, she is not eligible for federal assistance. If she is divorced after fewer than ten years of marriage, she does not qualify for social security benefits through her ex-husband's earnings and she loses all rights as a beneficiary to her ex-husband's pension and health plans.

According to some estimates, more than 50 percent of all single women aged 60 and over live at or below the poverty level. Widows represent one of the largest poverty groups. By 1976, there were 12 million surviving spouses in the country, with five widows for every widower. The rate of remarriage for widows over age 65 is eight times less than that of widowers. The suicide rate of widows is twice that of married women.[22]

The divorced, too, are in crisis. Nationally, divorce increased by 91 percent between 1970 and 1978, with the most dramatic increase among adults aged 30–44.[23] Like widows, divorced women are far less likely to remarry than are their ex-husbands. As single women, they and those women who are separated exhibit many more symptoms of mental disorders than do single women who have never married—the group of women least likely to experience mental illness.

VICTIMS OF VIOLENCE

Battered Women

A battered woman is generally considered to be any woman who is assaulted by a man with whom she has a significant relationship. According to 1979 statistics of the Federal Bureau of Investigation (FBI), the number of reported wife beatings is three times that of reported rapes, or three in every nine minutes. However, because the majority of incidents are not reported, the reported incidents, according to FBI estimates, represent less than 10 percent of the actual number occurring.[24] Thus, it would be a conservative estimate to say that every eighteen seconds at least one woman is beaten by her husband. Battered women, it is not surprising, are high risks for mental illness. They are usually dependent and controlled housewives who lack self-esteem and assertiveness, much like severely depressed women. Indeed they are often one and the same.

Rape

Rape is the nation's fastest growing major crime. According to FBI figures, it is not unreasonable to assume that of the over 100 million women in this country, at least 250,000 will be raped in a given year.[25] The chances are greater than one in fifteen that a woman will be raped at some point in her life. The emotional repercussions of rape often last a lifetime. The impact on the lives of all women who live with the threat of potential violence is less often addressed.

The aforementioned social problems do not exhaust the list, and neither they nor the symptoms of so-called mental illness that accompany them should be viewed as single entities. It is not by chance that women are the leading mental health risks, the greatest poverty risks, and the major victims of personal violence. The statistics are a predictable reflection of dysfunctional societal norms that create barriers to personal growth and perpetuate destructive environments.

Social workers have been consistent proponents of the person-environment approach to understanding human behavior. It is time to operationalize that construct with the vast resource of social work knowledge that already exists. The mysteries can be unraveled surrounding the identification by social workers of dysfunctional personality characteristics and common environmental denominators that have an impact on mental health. To do so, social workers have only to stop viewing each client in a vacuum and each social problem as unique.

DEPENDENCE VS. INDEPENDENCE

Social workers regard the psychological development of individuals as essential knowledge to be integrated into practice. Social scientists agree that all human beings need to become independent to develop and survive. Whether the determinant of independence is biologically innate, culturally learned, or a combination of the two varies according to the theorist.[26]

But what about the client who likes to be dependent? What of the transcending cultural values that caution social workers to delimit the development of independence in women? For years, social workers have struggled with these questions, believing that self-determination is a value to be protected. However, what appears to be an enriching principle may be an abusive practice. That is, research indicates that maturational processes are not sufficient for the development of independence, which must be acquired through learning and must be nurtured.[27] Thus, self-determination applied to dependent people may be a dishonest principle; by supporting self-determination, social work may be perpetuating their vulnerability to mental illness. This statement is as true for women as it is for men. It is true for poor women regardless of environmental limitations. It is true of minority women regardless of cultural pressures to the contrary. It is true of wives and mothers, regardless of the opinions of their husbands. It is especially true of women who are verbally and physically abused. That battered women return, ostensibly voluntarily, to be battered again too often is a reflection of dependence and of identification with the oppressor—a defense mechanism seldom recognized in women.

The fundamental needs of women have been deemed different from the basic needs of men. Independence has not only been ignored, it has been disallowed as a female attribute. Women have been socialized to dependence and submissiveness, according to social science research. Longstreth, for example, interprets the development of dependence in women as following the principle of least cultural resistance—that behavior which causes a minimum of opposition. His conclusions were the result of a national longitudinal study concerning the social development of girls and boys.[28]

According to Horney, dependence and submissiveness are destructive states whenever they exist, resulting in disguised, but equally negative, reactions when they cannot be overtly expressed.[29] The observations of social scientists corroborate her position. For example, dependence has been found to result in a submissive loss of freedom, a lowered level of aspiration, insecurity, a lack of self-worth, and the undermining of one's knowledge and reasoning powers, which results in the ability to be easily persuaded—a common female attribute.[30] After an extensive review of empirical studies of the psychology of women, Sherman concluded that dependence is a maladaptive trait leading to inadequate functioning in such roles as wife, mother, and sexual partner.[31] Dependence, defined as being easily influenced by others, has also been found to be highly correlated with depression in cross-cultural research.[32]

The implications of these just-stated findings can no longer be ignored. Feminist theory, which affirms the development and advancement of women, has left the realm of ideology and entered the arena of social work ethics and values. Therefore, social workers must enhance and support the competence, independence, and aspirations of women and must respect and encourage women's knowledge and reasoning powers. Self-respect, self-confidence, and the ability to be self-sustaining are necessary for independence. As women develop autonomy and independence, they will be less easily influenced and less affected by adverse environments. Then the long-held principle of self-determination can be operationalized without fear of abuse.

Social workers are familiar with the concepts of power and control. Power has been defined as having control over another, derived from the other's dependence.[33] Women's powerlessness is perpetuated, but independence alone is not the answer. Controlling work environments were found to be correlated with depression, regardless of one's dependence or independence, in recent cross-cultural research, and the majority of women in low-level jobs are most likely to be in controlling work situations.[34] However, it appears that no one thrives in controlling environments. This information is not new. The literature on job satisfaction and business and health care management and national governmental studies have long indicated such an awareness. Social workers must vigorously apply this knowledge to social work schools and to their work settings in health care and social services. And they must make it their responsibility to consult with management and labor on behalf of clients.

Everyone needs emotional support. According to research, lack of support from family members and colleagues at work is highly correlated with mental illness. The report of the President's Commission on Mental Health, recognizing the universal need for mutual support, has called for a revolution in mental health to be focused on prevention, which it defined, in part, as the establishment or strengthening of informal natural helping networks, as well as formal community support systems and linkages.[35]

The mandate of the commission is admirable and insightful. However, if the family is to become a natural helping network for women, many essential changes must be made and painful issues confronted. One such issue is the traditional family's emotional, physical, and financial destructiveness to many women.[36] Although the statistics are new, the dynamics are not, for the family has always been a microcosm of the larger culture.

ANTIFEMALE ATTITUDES

Hatred of women has been pervasive for generations. Freud, while denying his own misogynist tendencies, found the prevalent antifemale attitudes held by both sexes to be perplexing.[37] Contemporary research on sex roles has found that attributes labeled as feminine are demeaned by men and many women and hence are less socially desirable to both sexes.[38]

Mead and Kaplan's cross-cultural studies extended the phenomena even further. It is not what women do that is demeaned, they observed, but the fact that women are doing it.[39] If an activity is downgraded, it is relegated to women; if it is esteemed, it is taken over by men. When human attributes, socially defined as feminine, are recognized in men, they are rejected as shameful traits to be shed or carefully hidden from public view. Hence, in men and boys, aggressiveness is encouraged and nurturing, supportive qualities are discouraged as women and girls are negated.

Chetwyne and Harnett found that, in the American culture, the debasement of female adolescents by males is deemed normal. That battering and rape are most likely to occur in the home and that nurturing of women in families is an infrequent attitude is predictable, given the facts. It is interesting to note that Hovland and Janis correlated dependence (the approved female trait) with a greater need for nurturance. It is a paradox that those who are socialized to be dependent are also socialized to nurture, but no one is taught to nurture them beyond childhood. The point is not to downgrade nurturing qualities. It is only to insist on teaching boys and men to develop these qualities too. Both women and men can be socialized, as Miller put it, "to serve and yet not be subservient."[40] Social workers must include these principles in their teaching, consultation, and practice. Then natural helping networks as tools of prevention will have credibility.

WOMEN'S STRENGTHS

The social work profession values its health perspective—its focus on clients' ego strengths rather than weaknesses and on their coping abilities, not only on their problems in functioning. By including the strengths of women in this principle, social workers can learn much about the components that foster mental health and prevent mental illness. The supportive, nurturing qualities of women are a case in point. Emotional support probably does much to prevent mental illness in men. The fact that married men have the lowest rate of mental illness and single men have a higher rate speaks to the point. Research indicates that single, divorced, and widowed men are much less able to live alone without emotional disturbance than are women. Their remarriage rate is eight times that of women, and their decisions to remarry are often ill conceived and hasty.[41]

Why is it that women who have never married have the lowest rate of mental illness? By studying the lives of healthy women who live alone, one can learn a great deal. Some of these women surely are lesbians. The lesbian community is just that—a community. Theirs is a natural helping network often extending quietly from community to community, city to city, and state to state.[42] Despite societal stigma and rejection, their community support system may be the central reason for what appears to be their comparatively low rate of mental illness.

That women outlive men and the gap in longevity between men and women progressively widens decade after decade cannot be overlooked. Nor can it be ignored that women appear to become more mentally healthy as they get older, despite the double standard of aging in this country.[43] Perhaps women's supportive qualities, their ability to relate to others, their flexibility in adapting to ever changing roles, and their development of independence later in life help make the difference. It may even be that their home maintenance skills enhance their well-being. For example, Bikson and Goodchilds found that elderly widowed men living alone would often rather die than learn the women-identified homemaking skills necessary to care for themselves.[44] Thus, it can be seen that this society's mores are dysfunctional for all.

Social workers must reeducate themselves and, in turn, educate others, thereby helping to promote mental health and prevent mental illness. As a profession, social work must affirm a single-standard system whereby one sex does not have power over the other but all human beings have power: the power to be oneself and the power to become fully developed responsible human beings. There is no scarcity of such power. Thus, it need not be threatening, for what one gains will not be taken away from another.[45] There must be a new-found congruence between social work values and social science knowledge, on the one hand, and clinical practice, education, and policy on the other. Women long have been at risk in our society. By redefining their concepts of mental health, social workers will have the wherewithal to turn history around. They must do so because women are in crisis and the profession's values and ethics are at stake.

REFERENCES

1. *Membership Survey* (Washington, D.C.: National Association of Social Workers, 1975); *Annual Report of Membership Statistics* (Washington, D.C.: National Association of Social Workers, 1978); *Register of Clinical Social Workers* (Washington, D.C.: National Association of Social Workers, 1979); "Alcohol, Drug Abuse, and Mental Health," *National Data Book* (Washington, D.C.: U.S. Department of Health, Education & Welfare, January 1980); and *Facts about Older Americans, 1976* (Washington, D.C.: U.S. Department of Health, Education & Welfare, 1976).

2. *See* David Mechanic, *Mental Health and Social Policy* (Englewood Cliffs, N.J.: Prentice-Hall, 1969); and Mechanic, *Politics, Medicine and Social Science* (New York: John Wiley & Sons, 1974).

3. *See*, for example, Gertrude Blanck and Rubin Blanck, *Ego Psychology* (New York: Columbia University Press, 1974); Aaron T. Beck, *Cognitive Therapy and the Emotional Disorders* (New York: International Universities Press, 1976); and Harold Morowitz, *The Wine of Life and Other Essays on Societies, Energy, and Living Things* (New York: St. Martin's Press, 1979).

4. *See* Margaret S. Mahler, Fred Pine, and Anni Bergman, *The Psychological Birth of the Human Infant* (New York: Basic Books, 1975); Gertrude Blanck and Rubin Blanck, *Ego Psychology II* (New York: Columbia University Press, 1979); George Herbert Mead, *Mind, Self, and Society* (Chicago: University of Chicago Press, 1934); and Otto Rank, *The Practical Rearing of Psychoanalysis* (New York: National Committee for Mental Hygiene, 1927).

5. Jessie Taft, "The Relation of Function to Process in Social Casework," *Journal of Social Work Process*, 1 (1937); and Virginia P. Robinson, *The Development of a Professional Staff: Selected Writings* (New York: AMS Press, 1978).

6. *See* Aaron T. Beck et al., *Cognitive Therapy of Depression* (New York: Guilford Press, 1979); and Kenneth R. Pelletier, *Mind as Healer, Mind as Slayer* (New York: Delta Books, 1978).

7. Scott Briar and Henry Miller, *Problems and Issues in Social Casework* (New York: Columbia University Press, 1971).

8. "Profession of Social Work: Code of Ethics," *Encyclopedia of Social Work*, (17th issue; Washington, D.C.: National Association of Social Workers, 1977), Vol. 2, pp. 1066–1067.

9. Briar and Miller, op. cit.

10. Brian McMahon and Thomas F. Pugh, *Epidemiology Principles and Methods* (Boston: Little, Brown & Co., 1970).

11. *Report to the President from the President's Commission on Mental Health* (Washington, D.C.: U.S. Government Printing Office, 1978), Vol. 3, p. 770.

12. "Report of the Committee on Objectives and Strategies to the 1973 Delegate Assembly" (Washington, D.C.: National Association of Social Workers, 1973) (duplicated); and *Manual for Accrediting Standards for Graduate Professional Schools of Social Work* (New York: Council on Social Work Education, 1971).

13. Myrna M. Weissman and Gerald Klerman, "Sex Differences and the Epidemiology of Depression," *Archives of General Psychiatry*, 34 (January 1977), pp. 98–111.

14. Naomi Gottlieb, ed., *Alternative Social Services for Women* (New York: Columbia University Press, 1980).

15. U.S. Commission on Civil Rights, *Women Still in Poverty* (Washington, D.C.: U.S. Government Printing Office, July 1979).

16. "Money Income and Poverty Status of Families and Persons in the United States: 1978 (Advance Report)," *Current Population Reports*, Series P-60, No. 120 (Washington, D.C.: U.S. Bureau of the Census, 1978).

17. Jessie Bernard, *The Future of Marriage* (New York: Bantam Books, 1973).

18. Anne E. Fisher, ed., *Women's World: NIMH Supported Research on Women* (Washington, D.C.: U.S. Department of Health, Education & Welfare, 1978).

19. "Marital Status and Living Arrangements: March 1978," *Current Population Reports: Population Characteristics*, Series P-20, No. 338 (Washington, D.C.: U.S. Bureau of the Census, May 1979).

20. Alan Guttmacher Institute, *11 Million Teenagers: What Can Be Done about the Epidemic of Adolescent Pregnancies in the United States* (New York: Planned Parenthood Federation of America, 1979).

21. Fisher, ed., op. cit.

22. *National Policy Concerns for Older Women: Commitment to a Better Life* (Washington, D.C.: Federal Council on the Aging, 1976).

23. "Marital Status and Living Arrangements: March 1978."

24. *Uniform Crime Reports* (Washington, D.C.: Federal Bureau of Investigation, 1979).

25. Ibid.

26. *See*, for example, Robert W. White, "Motivation Reconsidered: The Concept of Competence," *Psychological Review*, 66 (1959), pp. 297–333; *Report to the President from the President's Commission on Mental Health*; Henry Z. Minton,

"Power and Personality," in James T. Tedeschi, ed., *The Influence Processes* (Chicago: Aldine-Atherton, 1972), pp. 100-150.

27. *See* James Alexander, "On Dependence and Independence," *Bulletin of the Philadelphia Association of Psychoanalysis*, 20 (January 1970), pp. 49-57; and White, op. cit.

28. Langdon E. Longstreth, "Passivity, Dependence, and Aggression," *Psychological Development of the Child* (2d ed.; New York: John Wiley & Sons, 1974), pp. 237-262. *See also*, Janice Wood Wetzel, "Depression and Dependence Upon Unsustaining Environments," *Clinical Social Work Journal*, 6 (Summer 1978), pp. 75-89.

29. Karen Horney, *Feminine Psychology*, Harold Kelman, ed. (New York: W. W. Norton & Co., 1973).

30. *See* R. M. Emerson, "Power-Dependence Relation," *American Sociological Review*, 27 (1962), pp. 31-41; Henri Parens and Leon Saul, Jr., *Dependence in Man* (New York: International Universities Press, 1971); and Carl Hovland and I. L. Janis, *Personality and Persuasability*, Vol. 2 (New Haven, Conn.: Yale University Press, 1959).

31. Julia Sherman, *On the Psychology of Women: A Survey of Empirical Studies* (Springfield, Ill.: Charles C Thomas, 1971).

32. Wetzel, op. cit.; and Wetzel and Franklin C. Redmond, "A Person-Environment Study of Depression," *Social Service Review*, 54 (September 1980), pp. 363-375.

33. John W. Thibaut and Harold H. Kelley, *The Social Psychology of Groups* (New York: Wiley Press, 1959), pp. 100-125.

34. *See* Wetzel, op. cit.; Wetzel and Redmond, op. cit.; Wetzel, "The Work Environment and Depression: Implications for Intervention," in John W. Hanks, ed., *Toward Human Dignity* (Washington, D.C.: National Association of Social Workers, 1978), pp. 236-245; and Wetzel, "Mental Health, Working Class Women and Their Work," *Journal of Applied Social Sciences*, 5 (Fall-Winter 1980-81), pp. 1-13.

35. Wetzel and Redmond, op. cit.; and *Report to the President from the President's Commission on Mental Health*.

36. "To Form a More Perfect Union . . ." *Justice for American Women* (Washington, D.C.: National Commission on the Observance of International Women's Year, 1976).

37. Sigmund Freud, "Some Psychical Consequences of the Anatomical Distinctions Between the Sexes" (1925) in *Collected Papers*, Vol. 5 (London, England: Hogarth Press, 1950), pp. 186-197.

38. Helen S. Astin, ed., *Sex Roles: A Research Bibliography* (Washington, D.C.: National Institute of Mental Health, 1975); and Inge Broverman et al., "Sex Role Stereotypes: A Current Appraisal," *Journal of Social Issues*, 28 (Spring 1972), pp. 488-495.

39. Margaret Mead and Frances B. Kaplan, eds., *Report of the President's Commission on the Status of Women* (New York: Charles Scribner's Sons, 1965).

40. Jane Chetwyne and Oonagh Harnett, eds., *The Sex Role System: Psychological and Sociological Perspectives* (Boston: Routledge & Kegan Paul, 1978); Hovland and Janis, op. cit.; and Jean Baker Miller, *Toward a New Psychology of Women* (Boston: Beacon Press, 1976), p. 71.

41. *See* Bernard, op. cit.; and Leslie Van Gelder, "An Unmarried Man: Report on a New American Syndrome," *Ms.*, 8 (November 1979), pp. 51-52, 73-75.

42. Sissi Loftin, "Lesbian Support Networks." Unpublished doctoral dissertation, University of Texas at Austin, 1981.

43. Gail Sheehy, "The Happiness Report," *Redbook* (July 1979), pp. 29, 54-60; and Inge P. Bell, "The Double Standard: Age," *Trans-Action* (November-December 1970), pp. 75-80.

44. T. K. Bikson and J. K. Goodchilds, "Old People and New Ideas: Receptivity and Rigidity" (Santa Monica, Calif.: Rand Corp., August 1979).

45. Dorriece Pirtle, Christine A. Dougher, and Janice Wood Wetzel, "Feminist Theory and Social Work Practice," paper presented at the Fiftieth Anniversary Conference of the George Warren Brown School of Social Work, St. Louis, Mo., 1976; and Wetzel, "Prevention of Mental Illness through Existential Principles," *Journal of Religion and Health,* 19 (Winter 1980), pp. 268-274.

DEPRESSION IN WOMEN: EXPLANATIONS AND PREVENTION

Janice M. De Lange

The current high rate of depression among Americans, particularly women, is of concern to mental health workers. Studies have found that in every age group two to three times as many women as men, whether hospitalized or in the general population, report they are depressed.[1] Why is depression more frequent in women than in men? The purpose of this article is to explore explanations for the differential sex ratio of depression and to discuss prevention and the therapeutic needs of women based on such explanations.

EXPLANATIONS

More Women Report Depression

One explanation of the differential sex ratio of depression is that women report depressive symptoms more readily than do men because they have been trained to express feelings and because society permits women to admit to such symptoms, whereas men are more reluctant to do so.[2] So far, evidence to substantiate this hypothesis has been scant. The larger number of depressed women cannot be accounted for by the explanation that more women seek help, either medical or psychological, because the same sex ratio holds true in community surveys of women and men selected randomly, apart from involvement in clinics or agencies. Weissman and Klerman concluded that the higher rate of depressed women is real; more women than men simply are depressed.[3]

Hormonal Changes

A second explanation is that the female endocrine system or the hormonal changes that women undergo during menstruation, menopause, pregnancy, and childbirth, are responsible for the higher rate of depression in women than in men. Some evidence of increased rates of depression has been found with the use of oral contraceptives and from premenstrual tension. However, Weissman and Klerman concluded in their summary of findings that the effects of these two factors are probably of small magnitude and not enough to account for the large difference in rates of depression between men and women. Menopause, which has been blamed for a variety of changes in mood and behavior, has been found to have no effect on increasing the rate of depression. Winokur hypothesized that depression found at the time of menopause may be associated with other factors, such as age. Bart stated that cross-cultural studies rule out the possibility that depression in menopausal women is caused by hormonal changes.[4]

The postpartum period is the only time at which increased rates of depression have been linked with changes in the endocrine system.[5] Therefore, although a controversy still exists over the role of the female hormonal system in affecting depression, results are insufficient to conclude that hormones are primarily responsible for the higher rate of depression in women.

Different Symptoms

A third explanation is that men and women may react with different symptoms when under emotional strain. Phillips and Segal found that women present more psychological symptoms and men more physiological ones.[6] For instance, women tend to have emotional problems while men tend to get heart attacks, ulcers, and the like. Such differences in the symptoms experienced under stress may, in part, be due to the greater biological weakness and susceptibility of men to physical disease and mortality and in part to sex-role training in which men and women learn to experience and act on stress differently. Also, under stress, women tend to display self-depreciatory and self-critical attitudes that can result in depression and anxiety, whereas men tend to act out in such aggressive and socially deviant ways as robbery and rape. Thus, one may conclude that men and women react differently under stress and that women have a greater tendency toward depressive symptoms. What effect these differential tendencies have on the sex ratio of depression is as yet unclear.

Women's Role

A fourth explanation is that the typical role of women in society—that of wife and homemaker—creates stresses that are likely to lead to depression, whereas the role of men, with its emphasis on achievement, winning, and competition, is likely to lead to anxiety.[7] If their role has a major effect on the increased incidence of depression in women, then the rate of depression should be higher in married women than in married men and unmarried men and women. Studies have found this to be the case, although the facts are more complex. For example, in a review of studies, Gove found that, within the same age categories, married women had a higher rate of mental illness than did married men.[8] The reverse was true for single people; that is, single, divorced, and widowed men had a higher rate of depression than did single, divorced, and widowed women. Radloff's community survey of over 2,500 persons found that married, divorced, and separated women were more depressed than the same category of men; among the never married or widowed, men were more depressed than women.[9] Controlling for age, income, and education did not reduce the effect. Unemployment (defined as not working but looking for work) was the only condition under which married men were more depressed than married women. Furthermore, the findings that married women have higher rates of depression than married men and that single men have higher rates of depression than single women support the idea that depression in women is not primarily based on hormonal changes.

In the findings just reported, one needs to keep in mind that selective factors may be involved in determining what roles a woman will choose. That is, women who are more dependent and who identify with the characteristic feminine traits may be more likely to choose the traditional roles of wife and mother; women who are more independent and self-sufficient may choose to remain single or have careers. The latter group may already be less prone to depression regardless of the status of their roles.

Gove and Tudor hypothesized that women have a higher rate of mental illness because traditionally, men have two roles (husband and breadwinner) and therefore two sources of gratification, whereas women are more often restricted to one role—and a devalued one at that. Their hypothesis suggests that working women would demonstrate less depression than housewives. Some studies have shown that employment prevents depression. For example, Mostow and Newberry, in comparing lower-class working women to lower-class housewives, found that given the same acuteness of depression at the beginning of treatment, the working women recovered faster and were significantly less impaired than the housewives at a three-month follow-up. Radloff found that both working wives and housewives were more depressed than working husbands. However, when she controlled for the rating given for happiness with marriage and happiness with job (for housewives, homemaking), housewives were significantly more depressed than were working wives.[10] The dual-role hypothesis is partially supported in this finding, but it does not explain the higher rate of depression in working wives than in working husbands.

The kind of work involved in homemaking and child care may be partly responsible for depression in women, particularly since all women seem to carry the role of homemaker regardless of their job status. The overriding factor may be satisfaction with homemaking. For example, when housewives were separated into those wanting to work and those not looking for work, the housewives who wanted to work were the worst off. In addition, the presence of small children has been associated with a higher rate of depression, with the highest scores for women with children under 6 years and the lowest scores for women with children over 12 years. In studying the "empty-nest" syndrome among women aged 40–59, Bart found that those who heavily identified with the feminine role and who had an overprotective and overly involved relationship with their children were more likely to be depressed when the children left. She hypothesized that this depression was related to the women's loss of role.[11]

Relational Deficits

Bernard offered another explanation for the higher rate of depression in women.[12] The female way of being social emphasizes close and intimate ties, communication, affection, and attachment. Regardless of whether one thinks this tendency is based on biology or socialization, women are rendered more vulnerable to stress and depression when deprived of such ties. In the past, women gave each other mutual help in times of birth, family illnesses, marriages, and other rituals. However, this world of women came to be seen as inferior. Gradually bonds of affection between women weakened and were replaced by sociability with men. Now women are often in isolated households and, at an early age, see other women as competitors for the attention of men and the social position to be gained through men.

Replacing relationships with women with those with men has been a poor substitution, according to Bernard. Men are not socialized to relate to others in an intimate way, as women are, and to share joys, sorrows, and anxieties; therefore, women experience a "relational deficit" that makes them vulnerable to depression. Weissman and Paykel's finding that depressed women report many more problems in marital intimacy and communication with husbands gives credence to this hypothesis.[13]

Low Self-esteem

Although Freud and other early psychoanalysts related depression to narcissism and object loss, later psychoanalytic theorists emphasized that the loss of self-esteem is a precipitating factor in depression. Beck, a cognitive therapist, associated depression-precipitating situations with those that often lower a person's self-esteem. Research has demonstrated a correlation between low self-esteem and depression. For example, Coleman had college women read and concentrate on positive and negative self-statements, which induced either positive or negative attitudes about the self, and found that the lowering or raising of self-esteem by this method had a significant effect on the production of depression or elation, respectively.[14]

Depression, then, can be the affective response to a loss in self-esteem or to circumstances that threaten a person's positive self-evaluation and evoke negative self-attitudes. Kaplan hypothesized that because of sex-role training, women in self-devaluing circumstances are less likely to use mechanisms that deflect the blame away from themselves and are more likely to use self-rejection responses.[15] He assumed that aggression is a mechanism for deflecting blame onto others and for restoring or maintaining self-esteem. He thought that women do not use this mechanism because of their greater dependence on others for their own identity and because they have been socialized to inhibit hostile, aggressive, or even assertive responses. Kaplan's findings indicated that women do not generally use this mechanism. He concluded that, as a result, women would experience a loss of self-esteem and consequent depression in self-devaluing situations.

Given the link between low self-esteem and depression, it may be that there is a generalized low esteem in women which contributes to the high incidence of depression. It also seems likely that the low esteem in which women are held in this society affects individual women's self-esteem and thus increases women's vulnerability to depression. Thus, a situation that would threaten anyone's self-esteem is more likely to result in depression in women whose self-esteem is already shaky.

There is ample evidence for a generalized low self-esteem among women. Studies have found that both men and women show a systematic preference for men and male characteristics. Rosenkrantz et al. found that people rated fewer of the typically female qualities and more than twice as many of the typically male qualities as desirable. In addition, women tended to incorporate the negative qualities into their self-concept.[16]

There are many other indications of the preference for males in our society. For example, according to Chesler, among others, both men and women prefer male professionals and other experts. Furthermore, when Goldberg asked college women to evaluate articles in six fields, the women gave significantly higher ratings to the articles they thought were written by men. Not only did they do so for articles in the typically male fields of law and city planning, but, contrary to Goldberg's expectation, they even judged male authors to be better in the typically female fields of dietetics and elementary school teaching. Using similar procedures Pheterson, Kiesler, and Goldberg asked college women to evaluate paintings. When the women were told that the painting had won a contest, it made no difference whether the painting was supposedly done by a woman or man;

if, however, women were told that the painting was being entered in a contest, so it was uncertain how "good" it was, they rated the painting higher when it carried a man's name than when it carried a woman's name.[17] Such studies suggest that women expect men to be more successful than women and give credence to what most women feel—that society does not think highly of women in general.

Further indications of the low self-esteem that individual women have of themselves are found in studies which show that, given equal performance, women tend to evaluate their performance more poorly than do men and that women predict and expect less success than do men and underestimate what they will be able to accomplish on a specific task. Studies further indicate that women reinforce themselves less than do men (that is, they make fewer positive statements and pay themselves fewer tokens for their performance) and that when women achieve success, they are more likely than men to attribute their success to chance rather than to their abilities or efforts.[18] Such tendencies have dire consequences for women. Self-confidence is a necessary ingredient for the realization of one's potential.

Learned Helplessness

The theory of learned helplessness, developed by Seligman and supported by research on animals and human beings, is increasingly being recognized as a credible explanation for depression in women. Simply stated, learned helplessness is the belief that one has no control over events—that one's actions have little or no effect on consequences, either rewards or punishment. Hence, one acts passively in the face of trauma—even in the case of controllable events. According to Seligman, the manifestation of learned helplessness is reactive depression.[19]

The sex-role training of women may increase their susceptibility to learned helplessness. Being kept dependent and protected; given little opportunity to explore and gain mastery over new situations; being told that one's accomplishments and achievements are not what counts; and being relegated to a lower paying, lower prestige job than an equally or less competent man contribute to women learning that their responses have little to do with what happens to them.

The powerlessness that women feel when they know their responses will have no effect on a discriminatory situation also increases their susceptibility to learned helplessness. An example of such a situation is the repeated promotion to managerial positions of men who have less seniority and no more skills than the women who are being passed over. This type of situation and those in which women are kept from decision-making positions increase women's vulnerability to learned helplessness. Radloff and Rae found that single women who live in their own households and thus, it may be assumed, are more in control over what happens to them have a lower incidence of depression than do single women who live with or are dependent on parents, relatives, and others.[20]

PREVENTION

How can vulnerability to learned helplessness and depression be lessened or eradicated in future generations of women? First, role restrictions owing to sex need to be removed so role is not assigned at birth. Second, to counteract the current training for learned helplessness, girls and women need experience in gaining mastery over and controlling their environment. Whereas boys are encouraged to explore and master their environment, girls are protected from risk and kept closer to their parents. For example, boys are allowed to cross the street and go further from home at an earlier age than girls, despite the fact that girls mature earlier than boys. Seligman stated that a life without mastery may produce a vulnerability to depression.[21] Women need equal opportunity to experience power in society and to control their own lives. Independence and the expectation of success need to be reinforced.

Third, the data on low self-esteem indicate that on the individual and societal levels, people, especially women, must be taught to respect the world of women (women's work and female characteristics) and to eliminate negative talk and put-downs of women, which have a devastating effect, especially on young children.

Fourth, women's relationships with other women must be cultivated and treasured so they provide a model of sisterhood for little girls. Cooperation among women and the feeling of sisterhood are particularly important at puberty and the early years of dating when pressures to conform to sex roles may be the greatest.

Fifth, the lack of data associating the endocrine system with depression indicates that little girls and women should no longer be taught, as a matter of course, to expect to experience menopausal blues and depressing days prior to and during menses, since one tends to get what one expects.

Such changes are merely a beginning of what can be done to help decrease women's vulnerability to depression. In the end, all individual and societal actions and expectations must be analyzed for their effect on women's mental health.

TREATMENT GOALS AND APPROACHES

According to Beck, depression reoccurs at a high rate.[22] Therefore, it is important to think of a treatment approach that changes habits and, particularly for women, that raises self-esteem and decreases the vulnerability to future depression. Examining the factors involved in increasing women's susceptibility to depression points the way to treatment goals. The following are therapeutic goals for women to accomplish and counselors to facilitate: (1) to gain control over and experience mastery in their own lives, (2) to experience success and achievement on all levels, from household chores to education or careers, with an accompanying feeling of competence, (3) to decrease negative thinking about the self, and (4) to increase the giving of reinforcement to the self (in the form of positive statements about and tangible rewards to themselves), which can only occur when one has self-respect.

The behavioral approach views the cause of depression as the lack or loss of reinforcement (in general, pleasurable or rewarding events) and the receipt of a high rate of punishment. Lewinsohn proposed that it is not the amount of reinforcement that is the problem, but the low rate of reponse-contingent reinforcement, that is, the extent to which an individual's behavior is followed by positive or negative reinforcement.[23] His interpretation fits in with the theory of learned helplessness—that one needs to experience and develop the belief that one's behavior affects outcome.

The cognitive approach to depression has been developed primarily by Beck. In Beck's view, depression is a primary thought disorder from which the behavioral and affective components result.[24] Thus depression is the consequence of a maladaptive belief system; distorted thought patterns result in the misinterpretation of events which elicits depression.

Both the behavioral and the cognitive approaches can be used to give women positive and reinforcing experiences and to change their thinking about themselves. The behavioral approach concentrates on increasing positive experiences, completion of tasks, and self-reinforcement. The cognitive approach can help to raise self-esteem and change thought patterns by using techniques such as thought-stopping and cognitive restructuring.[25] Using reinforcement techniques can enable women gradually to gain some control over their lives.

Since depression includes a diverse set of symptoms that differ among individuals, no one intervention or one set of interventions is likely to work for everyone. Therefore, a combination of techniques is needed. Individual women may work better with one approach than another. Whatever approach is used, the goal remains the same: to decrease the vulnerability of women to depression and to enable them to enjoy life to the fullest.

REFERENCES

1. *See,* for example, Howard B. Kaplan, "Gender and Depression: A Sociological Analysis of a Conditional Relationship," in William E. Fann et al., eds., *Phenomenology and Treatment of Depression* (New York: Spectrum Publications,

1977), pp. 81–113; Lenore Radloff, "Sex Differences in Depression: The Effects of Occupation and Marital Status," *Sex Roles,* 1 (May–June 1975), pp. 249–266; and Myrna M. Weissman and Gerald L. Klerman, "Sex Differences and the Epidemiology of Depression," *Archives of General Psychiatry,* 34 (January 1977), pp. 98–111.

2. Derek L. Phillips and Bernard E. Segal, "Sexual Status and Psychiatric Symptoms," *American Sociological Review,* 34 (February 1969), pp. 249–266.

3. Weissman and Klerman, op. cit.

4. Weissman and Klerman, op. cit.; Francis J. Kane, "Iatrogenic Depression in Women," in William E. Fann et al., eds., *Phenomenology and Treatment of Depression* (New York: Spectrum Publications, 1977), pp. 69–80; George Winokur, "Depression in Menopause," *American Journal of Psychiatry,* 130 (January 1973), pp. 92–93; and Pauline Bart, "Depression in Middle-Aged Women," in Judith M. Bardwick, ed., *Readings on the Psychology of Women* (New York: Harper & Row, 1972), pp. 134–142.

5. Weissman and Klerman, op. cit.

6. Phillips and Segal, op. cit. *See also* Phyllis Chesler, "Women as Psychiatric and Psychotherapeutic Patients," *Journal of Marriage and the Family,* 33 (November 1971), pp. 746–759.

7. Jessie Bernard, "Homosociality and Female Depression," *Journal of Social Issues,* 32 (Fall 1976), pp. 213–238.

8. Walter R. Gove, "The Relationship between Sex Roles, Marital Status, and Mental Illness," *Social Forces,* 51 (September 1972), pp. 34–44.

9. Radloff, op. cit.

10. *See* Walter R. Gove and Jeanette F. Tudor, "Adult Sex Roles and Mental Illness," *American Journal of Sociology,* 78 (January 1973), pp. 812–835; E. Mostow and P. Newberry, "Work Role and Depression in Women: A Comparison of Workers and Housewives in Treatment," *American Journal of Orthopsychiatry,* 45 (July 1975), pp. 538–548; and ibid.

11. *See* Radloff, op. cit.; Bernard, op. cit., p. 226; George W. Brown, Marie N. Bhrolchain, and Tirril Harris, "Social Class and Psychiatric Disturbance among Women in an Urban Population," *Sociology,* 9 (May 1975), pp. 225–254; and Bart, op. cit.

12. Bernard, op. cit.

13. Ibid.; and Myrna M. Weissman and Eugene S. Paykel, *The Depressed Woman: A Study of Social Relationships* (Chicago: University of Chicago Press, 1974).

14. *See* Robert M. A. Hirschfeld et al., "Dependency—Self-Esteem—Clinical Depression," *Journal of the American Academy of Psychoanalysis,* 4 (July 1976), pp. 373–388; Aaron T. Beck, *Depression: Clinical, Experimental, and Theoretical Aspects* (New York: Harper & Row, 1967); Ronald E. Coleman, "Manipulation of Self-esteem as a Determinant of Mood of Elated and Depressed Women," *Journal of Abnormal Psychology,* 84 (December 1975), pp. 693–700; and James Battle, "Relationship between Self-esteem and Depression," *Psychological Reports,* 42 (June 1978), pp. 745–746.

15. Kaplan, op. cit.

16. *See* John P. McKee and Alex C. Sherriffs, "The Differential Evaluation of Males and Females," *Journal of Personality,* 25 (March 1957), pp. 356–371; and Paul S. Rosenkrantz et al., "Sex-Role Stereotypes and Self-concepts in College

Students," *Journal of Consulting and Clinical Psychology*, 32 (June 1968), pp. 287–295.

17. *See* Chesler, op. cit.; Phillip Goldberg, "Are Women Prejudiced against Women?" *Transaction*, 5 (April 1968), pp. 28–30; and Gail I. Pheterson, Sara B. Kiesler, and Phillip Goldberg, "Evaluation of the Performances of Women as a Function of Their Sex, Achievement, and Personal History," *Journal of Personality and Social Psychology*, 19 (July 1971), pp. 114–118.

18. *See* Virginia C. Crandall, "Sex Differences in Expectancy of Intellectual and Academic Reinforcement," in Charles P. Smith, ed., *Achievement-Related Motives in Children* (New York: Russell Sage Foundation, 1969), pp. 11–45; Kay Deaux and Elizabeth Farris, "Attributing Causes for One's Own Performance: The Effects of Sex, Norms, and Outcome," *Journal of Research in Personality*, 11 (March 1977), pp. 59–72; Irene H. Frieze et al., *Women and Sex Roles: A Social Perspective* (New York: W. W. Norton & Co., 1978); John Kosa, Leo D. Rachiele, and Cyril O. Schommer, "The Self-Image and Performances of Socially Mobile College Students," *Journal of Social Psychology*, 56 (April 1962), pp. 301–316; Eleanor E. Maccoby and Carol N. Jacklin, *The Psychology of Sex Differences* (Stanford, Calif.: Stanford University Press, 1974); and Fred Vollmer, "Determinants of Expectancy of Examination Results," *Scandinavian Journal of Psychology*, 17 (1976), pp. 238–245.

19. *See* Martin E. P. Seligman, *Helplessness: On Depression, Development, and Death* (San Francisco: W. H. Freeman & Co., 1975); Seligman, "Depression and Learned Helplessness," in Raymond J. Friedman and Martin M. Katz, eds., *The Psychology of Depression: Contemporary Theory and Research* (New York: Halstead Press, 1974), pp. 83–107; Carol E. Hooker, "Learned Helplessness," *Social Work*, 21 (May 1976), pp. 194–198; and Radloff, op. cit.

20. Lenore Radloff and Donald S. Rae, "Susceptibility and Precipitating Factors in Depression: Sex Differences and Similarities, *Journal of Abnormal Psychology*, 88 (April 1979), pp. 174–181.

21. Seligman, *Helplessness: On Depression, Development, and Death.*

22. Beck, op. cit.

23. Peter M. Lewinsohn, "A Behavioral Approach to Depression," in Raymond J. Friedman and Martin M. Katz, eds., *The Psychology of Depression: Contemporary Theory and Research* (New York: John Wiley & Sons, 1974), pp. 157–178.

24. Beck, op. cit.

25. Michael J. Mahoney, *Cognition and Behavior Modification* (Cambridge, Mass.: Ballinger Publishing Co., 1974).

THERAPY WITH BATTERED WOMEN

Deborah M. Henson
Janet L. Schinderman

Wife battering is a phenomenon of our culture.[1] Its prevalence reflects the consciousness of our sexist society, which casts women in contradictory roles and punishes them for failure to actualize the contradiction. The battered woman is reminded of her failure to meet the expectations of those who constitute her immediate society: husband, children, relatives, church members, and co-workers. According to Pagelow, a sociologist, the battered woman tries to meet the requirements of the female role while her husband plays the stereotyped male role.[2] Often, she receives minimal support from the people with whom she associates on a day-to-day basis.

Wife battering is not a comfortable subject. Lacking feedback from a support group of friends or family, the battered woman learns not to believe in herself as the batterer erodes her self-concept with repeated beatings and verbal abuse. No matter what she tries, she still gets beaten and thus develops a sense of hopelessness about her ability to affect her own life. Some call this phenomenon "learned helplessness." Hooker and Walker explained this concept in detail.[3]

NEED FOR THERAPY

The subject of therapy or counseling with battered women is controversial in feminist circles. Resisting the myth of the battered woman as sick, masochistic, and crazy, many women's groups scorn inclusion of a therapeutic component when designing services for this target group. They stress advocacy and community education as essential in helping battered women learn to protect themselves and to prosecute their abusers and at the same time to change community attitudes about wife abuse.

The authors think, however, that therapy does not connote sickness, but rather healing and education. Battered women have emotional bruises, if not severe scars.[4] The majority of women who seek assistance from shelters for battered women welcome some form of therapy, if only for a short time. The response of battered women who come to nonresidential clinics is different because such women feel isolated and confused and thus have difficulty in setting priorities for themselves. Battered wives need to sort out their confusion between loving their husbands and loving themselves in all the many manifestations this issue presents. They need education about human relationships and encouragement to make, what is to many, the most difficult decision of their lives.

Therapy with a battered woman must first provide the safety she needs to think, to reason, and to feel. To experience another human being valuing her, listening to her, and caring for her without demands sometimes begins to penetrate the walls of emotional distance that the battered woman has erected out of fear. The walls have the self-protective function of separating her from the awful pain of her crushed dreams and of her failing marriage juxtaposed against the myth of the happy American family. They have been invaluable to her survival. However, if she decides to change her life, the walls become obstacles to developing a closeness with others.

The emotional distance of the battered woman is experienced by the therapist who has the capacity and desire for closeness and who uses that ability as a primary healing tool. The therapist must address the effect of distancing while giving the client the message that the walls were at one time crucial to her survival. That is, the therapist can validate the battered woman's past coping methods while encouraging her to learn new behavior that will be more satisfying in the present.

The primary reasons for offering ongoing therapy to battered women are twofold. First, by providing the battered woman with safety and acceptance, the therapist can help her disentangle her identity, wants, and needs from her husband's or partner's so she can make decisions about her life. Second, the battered woman needs assistance in learning or relearning how to be close. She needs to build a support system and will eventually seek another primary love relationship. It will probably be frightening to let go of the distancing defenses she has practiced for self-protection. Trust is only gradually rebuilt through practice with another human being. The therapist can greatly enhance this process by role modeling closeness with the client and encouraging her to risk intimacy in and outside therapy. This is often a lengthy process, but crucial to the client's long-term adjustment.

INITIAL BEHAVIOR PATTERNS

During two years of direct service and supervisory experience in a metropolitan nonresidential program for battered women, the authors identified three major patterns of initial behavior in the battered women they saw: passivity-ingratiation, manipulation-anger, and decisiveness. These patterns overlap and are not to be substituted for a careful assessment of the individual's dynamics. They are offered as a framework and, with suggested treatment strategies, will enable therapists to move beyond their clients' distancing defenses as soon as possible and thus enhance the therapeutic relationship.

Passivity-ingratiation is frequently the first pattern seen in a battered woman who seeks help. The client may be polite, friendly, and adulate the therapist for being knowledgable and caring. If the therapist suggests such options as prosecution of or separation from the abusive man, the client seems to consider them and may agree they are the best solution. Such a client may also say little to the therapist who, at the end of the session, feels exhausted from doing 90 percent of the work. She may go along with the overeager worker who arranges a place for her to stay, makes plans to go to court with her, and contracts for more therapy sessions. However, after the initial session, the therapist may never see the client again.

A woman exhibiting this pattern needs to get in touch with her feelings, which are buried below years of second-guessing others. Helping her to acknowledge her anger is one way to aid her in becoming motivated to change. The client may feel angry about the years she spent in pleasing others and sacrificing herself for them and anger at herself or her mother for teaching her false ways to survive. Hence, it is important to teach her survival tools based on self-definition and self-expression. Later, when she is truly motivated to learn new ways, a behavioral approach provides her with practice in a nonthreatening environment.

To get the client to the point where she sincerely wants to change, the therapist must address her overwhelming feelings of emptiness and sadness. Who is she deep inside after years of thinking first of others? She will need to grieve for the true childhood she never had or for the slow death of an earlier self who had an identity. However, she may feel overwhelmed by this grieving; thus, the therapist must explain that grieving is an important step in building her new self or in rediscovering her old self. It will take her a long time to figure out what she wants at any given moment. The therapist can assist her by being patient and encouraging her to know herself without rushing to reassure her or make suggestions.

The second pattern is *manipulation-anger*. The therapist may initially perceive this pattern as motivation to right the wrongs inflicted by men. However, the client's anger soon may be directed toward the therapist if the client thinks she is not the therapist's sole object of attention. The client may attempt to call the therapist ten times a day; when the therapist has not produced a magical solution to her problems, she may turn to another staff person for similar assistance. Soon several staff members will feel drained by the client's constant demands. Although one can applaud the client's tenacity, she actually alienates helpers, which results in her getting bypassed or referred.

Such a woman needs to be confronted gently, preferably face to face, with her ineffective behavior. At the same time, her anger and persistence can be affirmed. She needs to learn to channel her demands appropriately to make systems work for her rather than to alienate those who could help her. For example, once her needs are addressed and supported, this type of woman often can perform a social-change role in an agency, perhaps volunteering at first to advocate for other battered women. She must learn to ventilate her anger rather than displace it to allies and, in some cases, her children. Underneath the anger, she may feel deprived and sad. By practicing with the therapist and in a group, she can learn to ask others to nurture her, rather than manipulate them, and to begin to nurture herself.

The third pattern is *decisiveness*. The decisive client knows what she needs to do in a general way. She needs honest information about the effects of family violence on her children, her legal options, the chances of her abusive partner changing, the difficulties to be encountered in starting over, and the importance of continued support while she is making major life changes. She may need to understand her guilt feelings and need encouragement to be gentle with herself.

PRACTICE MODELS

Several practice models can serve as a theoretical framework when designing services for battered women. They are crisis intervention, feminist therapy, and an eclectic combination of insight therapy and behavioral modification.

Crisis intervention provides a basic model of responding to the battered woman. By the time the battered woman calls for help, the coping mechanisms that previously carried her through the day-to-day life of sporadic battering have failed. It is helpful for the crisis counselor who handles the initial call to find out what precipitated the call. Perhaps the last beating was different from the others. It may have caused severe injuries or she may have thought she would die. The fear of being killed causes many women to decide to seek help. The undeniable reality that she could die cuts through the wishing, hoping, and praying for the abusive man to change that sustained the relationship for so long. It also brings with it the realization that the children will be alone with their abusive father or perhaps will be abandoned. Embarrassment, shame, and fear for her life or her children's safety may also propel the battered woman to seek help after the man hits their child for the first time, beats her in front of others, or locks her out of the house for the first time.

Because all crises are time limited, the battered woman must receive immediate attention. If she feels supported and accepted when she calls for help, the chances of her following through at some point are greater. If she can be scheduled for an appointment within a day, so much the better. During this crisis period, her defenses are floundering. Thus, information that others care about her and that she deserves a safe life plants the seed for later decision-making.

The basic tenet of feminist therapy is that power differentials between the client and therapist must be equalized. Therefore, the client is treated as an equal and reminded that it is her life and her right and responsibility to make her own decisions. The therapist supports the client's strengths, provides information about alternatives, and helps her gain a perspective on her relationship with the man that is broader than the issue of wife battering. The therapist explains and discusses society's perpetuation of the problem through its condoning of male privileges and women being treated as their men's property.

Feminist therapy also emphasizes the value of support groups for women because such groups help women overcome their guilt and acknowledge their anger. In the group, the women discover they have a common plight, and the resources each woman possesses to help herself and others are validated. However, a support group is beneficial for a battered woman after she has developed a one-to-one relationship with a therapist. It is hard for a woman who is isolated to handle the stimulation of a group at the beginning in a nonresidential facility. In a shelter, a support group is not as threatening because the battered woman already knows the participants.

In the eclectic combination of approaches, the therapist tries to be flexible enough to adapt herself and the therapeutic plan to the needs of the particular woman. Components of the eclectic approach may include individual insight-oriented therapy, group therapy, and behavioral therapies. One procedure would be to begin with group intake with two to four clients and one to three staff members; the aim would be the assessment of basic needs. Individual therapy, group therapy, or, in many cases, advocacy and referral for emergency services might follow the intake. The most successful cases are those in which a woman engages with a therapist for at least several individual sessions and then either remains in individual therapy for several months to a year or begins group therapy.

SHELTER AS THERAPY

There are many characteristics of a shelter specifically geared to battered women. The primary characteristic, however, is that it allows the battered woman to put her violent experience in a perspective larger than herself.

The battered woman who wishes to leave her abusive situation but who does not have an option such as a shelter faces tremendous difficulty. Her husband's possessiveness may not allow her to go for regular counseling. The isolation and low esteem that she feels contributes to her inaction. Furthermore, many battered women are ignorant about transportation and other available community resources. Without knowledge of day care facilities and their eligibility requirements, the battered woman must look for a job and housing with her children in hand.

The shelter offers a woman the opportunity to work on both short-term and long-term plans. Before she can arrive at a stage at which she can make such decisions, she must first feel she has the right and ability to devise her own plans. The battered woman's isolation inhibits movement. Coming from a home with no peer ally, she lacks the support and encouragement necessary to value her own opinion or hear that it is valued by another person. The shelter offers a base of comparison, a time for sharing stories, and an opportunity to receive feedback about herself.

Each resident comes to a shelter with her own history. Although locale, severity of abuse, and occasion may differ for each woman, common feelings unite them as a group. Suddenly, there is more than one battered woman. When a woman sees that abuse is not confined to her neighborhood, religion, or race, she can begin to expand her experience. With increased awareness, she learns how prevalent domestic violence is on the state and national levels as well as locally. This wider perspective is a step on her journey toward growth. The shelter allows her space for turning the personal experience into the reverberation of the group's reflection and learning. The synergistic result of the group enhances the individual experience and so the process spreads.

During her stay at a shelter, the battered woman goes through a three-stage experience. The three stages are arrival, body of stay, and separation. Regardless of her length of stay, the shelter experience is a journey through each stage.

Arrival

The battered woman and her children most often arrive at the shelter in various states of confusion and isolation. The battered woman is filled with guilt and shame at her plight and a sense of responsibility toward her marriage and children, but not toward herself. She comes to the shelter having been controlled and is afraid that an ill-chosen action may result in violence.

During the first days at the shelter, she tends to be withdrawn and to stand at the outer edge of the group. She may take time to feel the space around her by remaining physically outside the mainstream of activity. During a house rap session or group therapy, she may face the wall or excuse herself entirely. She may remain physically present but nonverbal, entering a room after the group has settled or excusing herself before the group ends. When this occurs, it is important for staff and residents to continue to reach out to her. Her self-exclusion may result from a lack of practice in participation or a feeling of worthlessness. Staff can assist her by pointing out that, as a house member, her participation is vital to the shaping of the whole group.

Staying out of the mainstream may be acted out in different ways. Some women are afraid to stay in their rooms apart from everyone. At the same time, they may be reluctant to open up to fellow residents or staff about their abusive situations. This is a time for listening. Hearing is keen, and a woman may sit in the same well-positioned chair for hours to gain a sense of the flow of the house.

In an effort to please and to stay busy, some women occupy themselves immediately with housework. It is a familiar role for most: that of homemaker, caretaker, cook, and cleaner. Although the women may not be assigned a list of chores until their third or fourth day at the shelter, becoming involved in housekeeping at an earlier point allows them to feel familiar in their new environment. By setting up a structure that affords residents privacy and inclusion, the shelter offers something for every mood.

Central to the phase of arrival is a skepticism about the choices that lie ahead. The battered woman may hear others discussing plans for getting a job and housing, but she does not conceive of these as possible options for her. Even a woman whose abusive situation has been short lived rarely believes she has alternatives. This skepticism is a result of the lack of skills necessary to view a situation from a problem-solving approach. The battered woman believes that problems are to be accepted, not challenged, and that situations do not change because there is no better alternative. In a shelter, however, a resident sees women in roles as diverse as counselor, household coordinator, and administrator. She may begin to ask the staff questions about the way in which women work cooperatively. For most, it is the first time they have seen women working together noncompetitively.

Body of Stay

By the time a woman begins to ask questions about the way things are run at the shelter, she has entered the second stage. At this point, she begins to step outside herself into the world around her for comparisons with her own experiences. As she comes to feel part of the house, she takes a more active role in its daily activities. A major component of a woman's stay at the shelter is her ambivalence and how she acts it out. By exploring the ambivalence, she learns to solve her problems. When a name is put on the confusion she feels and she is told that it is a natural part of her emotions, she feels liberated. She may use her ambivalence as a springboard for outlining options. She may feel she needs permission from the staff and from other residents to sort out her confusion about the love she may feel for her husband if she also wants to leave him.

In the second stage, the battered woman sees women who have been at the shelter longer than she, but also begins to welcome the new arrivals. This adds to her perspective. It is a time for talking and participating in the decision-making of the shelter. For example, when a resident asks why the menu offers only certain foods, she is offered the opportunity to attend meetings for planning the menu and to do some cooking herself. As her suggestions are heard and put into effect, she may feel for the first time that she has worth and that her opinions are valued.

As her perspective enlarges, a resident tends to participate more in informal discussions as well as formal therapy sessions. A frequent topic is society's contribution to the problems of domestic violence through the depiction in the media of women as victims. Strong familial expectations about the permanence of marriage and the family are also discussed.

During the second stage, a woman enacts most of the plan she has developed for herself and her children with the help and encouragement of counselors as advocates, sounding boards, and resources about community services. A battered woman's needs may include legal, law enforcement, or medical services. To obtain the services she will need, she must venture outside the shelter for the first time, which is often a frightening experience. Moreover, she must deal with various agencies in the areas of housing, employment, and child care and, in so doing, may make as many as twenty stops in one day. This is such a new way of life for some that even asking a stranger for the time of day or directions may be a new-found option.

Separation

As the time for leaving the shelter approaches, the residents enter the third stage—separation. Although all residents find separation difficult, each woman acts out her fears differently. Some are openly sad about leaving the shelter and are able to talk about their mixed feelings of fear and excitement about moving on. Often they seek approval from other residents to gain assurance that their plan is solid. They express interest in becoming a therapist at a shelter for battered women or ask if it is possible to remain permanently as a staff member.

Some residents may display their anger in such acts as violating the curfew or failing to do chores they previously agreed to do. They may suddenly become unwilling to cooperate in the household and complain about things as varied as the quality of meals and the general lack of privacy. Some residents who participated most during the second stage now begin to complain frequently. Some do not resolve their anger while still at the shelter and leave without saying good-bye.

Residents often express ambivalence about leaving the shelter by participating less with others in the house. As a result, they may choose to leave the shelter early each morning and return late at night to slacken attendance at house rap or group sessions. Such behavior is interpreted as a signal to the group to help these residents explore their feelings about separation.

The resident must come to feel her own power in the process of separation. Part of this strength comes from the ability to form attachments and to grow close to others in a short time. However, the resident also feels sad at the prospect of losing this feeling of closeness and of leaving those she has grown to love. During termination, these concepts are discussed with the departing resident to help her integrate what she has learned at the shelter.

STRATEGIES FOR CHANGE

Some basic strategies for helping a battered woman decide to change apply regardless of the practice modality used. The first and most important is role modeling by the therapist. The therapist who likes and respects herself and who takes care of herself increases the benefits of therapy. The therapist who arrives at a session tired or preoccupied, gives the client the confusing message of "I'll help you learn to value and care for yourself, but I don't practice these ideas."

Most abused women accept the stereotypical role of selflessness and consider others' needs first. Thus, they need to have a role model who is self-caring and self-nurturing. It is enlightening for them to learn that a woman can take good care of herself and also be strong and warm with others. From such a role model, they receive nonverbal permission to love, value, and trust themselves and yet remain able to care for others. Furthermore, the therapist must like herself to prevent the battered woman's depression, pain, and anger from spilling over into her own life. One strategy is for the therapist to empathize with the client's pain and immediately switch to a pleasurable thought to care for herself. Later, the therapist can teach the client to do the same.

Another strategy is aimed at helping the battered woman develop her sense of identity. This is accomplished by gently refocusing the client's conversation back to herself when she wanders onto the topic of the abusive man's "problems." The therapist can explain that no one can change him except himself. She can help the client focus on her feelings, needs, and wants that are separate from the abusive man. However, she must approach this topic with sensitivity because the couple is often symbiotic and the client may be threatened by these suggestions or consider them as criticisms. The client needs reassurance that the therapist accepts her worried feelings about the abusive man even though she does not focus on him in the session.

It is essential for the therapist to address the woman's feelings of ambivalence when the client brings up the possibility of leaving her abusive mate. There is a fine line between helping the client explore her positive feelings for him and implicitly encouraging her to stay with him. Taking the woman's decision to leave at face value is unwise. When the therapist gets excited about and supports the client's decision to leave the abusive man, the woman who returns to her husband often feels guilty about disappointing the therapist and will not return to the center.

A battered woman may return to her husband many times before making the final decision to leave him. Therefore, the therapist should let the woman know that she understands the complexity of the situation and that going back to him in no way means she is unacceptable or cut off. The client may have warm feelings for him when he is not beating or verbally abusing her and may be confused by her feelings that her children need a father. In these instances, a problem-solving approach is useful; in such an approach the client practices making her own decisions by assessing the problem, planning possible solutions, anticipating obstacles, and evaluating the results. This process emphasizes the identification of alternatives.

It is beneficial to discuss strengths and joys with the client, rather than always focus on "the problem." It is productive for the therapist simply to be with the client without either of them feeling a need to develop a solution. The therapist's respect for the battered woman begins to undo the woman's assumptions about her basic unworthiness. Respect is demonstrated by being on time for appointments; not interrupting her; valuing her statements, however meek or unassertive; and talking with her in her own language. For example, if the client does not relate to "How do you feel about that?" she may respond to "How do you see it?"

After the initial relationship is formed, two other strategies can be used to enhance the process of change. One is to help the battered woman develop a sense of personal power through understanding her responsibility for the choices she makes. Because of the woman's low self-esteem and tendency to blame herself for the failure of the relationship with the abusive man, the therapist should use this approach with caution. The therapist should differentiate between the concepts of blame for failure of a relationship and of the conscious decision to take responsibility for one's life. In essence, there must be a balance between the intrapsychic view and the view that society is solely responsible for the woman's continued abuse. If society is totally responsible, then the implication is that the woman is truly a helpless victim. The acknowledgment of society's ills alone does not help the woman gain a sense of personal power, which will short-circuit the response pattern of learned helplessness.

To change, one must have hope. However, the therapist should not offer the battered woman empty promises of protection because the social institutions do not respond efficiently to wife abuse. What can the therapist offer her? Herself.

The central task for survival is self-discovery—the development of self-love and self-trust. The battered woman can learn that she makes choices and with her choices she can save herself. She can seek support from friends, counselors, and other battered women until she decides to leave the abusive man or until the situation is otherwise resolved. Slowly, with this support, she can build up her courage to begin the journey toward a safe life, learning to believe that she has the internal resources to care for herself.

The therapeutic process necessitates a mutual journey for both client and therapist. To delve into unknown parts of the self, the therapist and client face the terror of feared discoveries. The therapist must provide a safe environment for the battered woman and resist pushing her. The anger and sadness that the therapist feels while working with the battered woman involves her own early pain. Close supervision or therapy for the therapist is advisable to provide support, permission to ventilate, and assistance in working through her own feelings. The result is increased choices and hence freedom for both.

REFERENCES

1. Diana E. H. Russell and Nicole Van de Ven, eds., *International Tribunal of Crimes Against Women* (Millbrae, Calif.: Les Femmes Publishing, 1976).

2. Mildred Pagelow, "Kitchens, Cultures, and the Feminist Movement," *Aegis Magazine on Ending Violence Against Women,* published by National Communication Network (May–June 1979), pp. 4–8.

3. Carol Hooker, "Learned Helplessness," *Social Work,* 21 (May 1976), pp. 194–198; and Lenore Walker, *The Battered Woman* (New York: Harper & Row, 1979).

4. *See* Andrea Dworkin, "The Bruise that Doesn't Heal," *Mother Jones* (July 1978), pp. 31–36.

RAPE CRISIS THEORY REVISITED

Martha Baum
Barbara K. Shore
Esther Sales

For some years, crisis theory has been the central focus of social work in planning and developing programs. Crisis theory is based on assumptions about the time-limited nature of the responses to a stressful event and thus helps guide the pacing, timing, and sequence of activities in intervention. Briefly stated, crisis theory posits a peak of reaction immediately following a stressful event after which there is a gradual return to an equilibrium or a steady state.[1] However, data from the authors' recent study of the reactions of rape victims to the rape event and the longer-term consequences to the victims indicate that some modification of crisis theory may be in order. In this article, the authors discuss previous studies of rape victims in relation to crisis theory, report the findings of their study, and draw implications for social work practice.

RELEVANT STUDIES

Crisis theory suggests that the stress produced by a crisis for which one does not have suitable or effective coping responses creates initial emotional and behavioral disorganization.[2] If the crisis is not resolved in a reasonable time, more major and permanent disorganization may result. Generally speaking, however, crisis theory centers on an immediate reaction that may be brief or prolonged, but which is followed by a gradual return to "normalcy" as the crisis recedes into the past or the disorganization declines.[3]

Research on which this article is based was supported by Grant No. R 18-MH 30315 from the National Center for the Prevention and Control of Rape, National Institute of Mental Health.

Rape is a crisis in the sense that it is a traumatic event with which a woman is not prepared to cope. Rape victims have been studied in this context, and the results appear to support the crisis model.[4] Although researchers do not necessarily agree on the exact phases the victim undergoes after the assault, the overall findings from the studies are consistent. The reactions of rape victims generally include an acute period of disorganization often accompanied by regressive tendencies and physical disability, even though few victims are seriously injured. Victims then undergo a period of reorganization that is accompanied by residual symptoms of phobias, nightmares, and anxiety. During this period, the victims may also attempt to alter their residences or their routine activities to avoid repetition of the incident or reminders that the rape occurred.[5] The period of reorganization, then, is characterized by a lessening of psychoemotional symptoms and by the victim's attempts to alter their life-styles and to defend themselves from further attack or the revival of terrifying memories. This interim phase leads to subsequent readjustment, which is viewed as a stable state in which the victims no longer need special intervention.

The studies just cited examined the short-term reactions of victims, for no more than a few months. However, Kilpatrick, Veronen, and Resick's study followed victims and a matched comparison group of nonvictims over a period of six months, during which time both the victims and nonvictims were interviewed four times.[6] Although the crisis theory approach was not used in that study, the results obtained may be considered in this framework. At six to ten days and at one month following the attack, the victims differed significantly from the nonvictims on all the test batteries in the study: a pathological symptoms checklist, a mood states scale, a modified fear survey, and state-trait inventory. The results indicated that the trauma had greatly disrupted the victims' functioning. By three months, however, the victims had recovered much of their equilibrium. The scores on global indexes of pathology and mood disturbance declined, and the scores of victims no longer differed significantly from those of nonvictims. Nevertheless, a core of distress remained that reflected the victims' focalized fear and anxiety. At the six-month interview, the range of stress symptoms had narrowed further but was still greater than that of the control group within the remaining areas.

Although Kilpatrick, Veronen, and Resick's carefully designed and controlled study found evidence of a longer duration of assault-caused stress than other studies cited, the results are in line with the expectations of crisis theory: (1) an immediate psychoemotional reaction of major proportions, (2) reorganization at three months, and (3) further reduction of symptoms at six months, although not to the level of functioning displayed by the matched nonvictims. The downward path of the cycle over the six-month period resembles a crisis theory trajectory.

THE PITTSBURGH STUDY

In the previous studies cited, the focus was primarily on psychoemotional responses to stress. The focus of the authors' present research was psychosocial in that it applied a conceptual framework of social stress and documented the social resources available to support vulnerable rape victims as well as the victims' ability to cope with the traumatic event. This section describes the study format, the study sample, the scales used to measure the stress levels exhibited by the victims, the patterns of symptomatology over time, and the relationship of environmental responses to the patterns found in the psychoemotional data.

Format and Sample

To approximate a longitudinal design, two strategies were implemented. First, a cohort format was used to collect data from women at different intervals, ranging from one month to more than three years since the rape occurred so changes over time could be observed. Second, in a panel study, a follow-up interview was conducted with a subsample of victims who closely matched the total sample on salient background characteristics. In the panel study, the women could, in effect, act as their own controls by comparing their responses at the first interview with those in the second interview six months later.

The sample of victims was recruited primarily from two major rape crisis centers in Pittsburgh, Pennsylvania, in 1977–79. To augment and broaden the sample, victims were also recruited through advertisements in the mass media. A total of 127 adult victims cooperated in face-to-face, in-depth interviews to yield the study data. Seventy-seven of the women were interviewed a second time for the panel study. Although the authors had no means of collecting a random sample of victims, the victims in this study strongly mirrored characteristics of samples reported in other studies. Most of the victims were under age 30 and unmarried, and black women were significantly overrepresented in terms of what would be expected from population statistics for Pittsburgh.[7]

Scales

In the first interview, the 127 victims were asked to report on three time periods: (1) just prior to the assault, (2) immediately after the assault, and (3) at the time of the first interview. Six months later, the subsample of 77 victims who matched the total sample closely in age, race, marital status, and education were interviewed a second time, yielding a fourth time period. Three scales were administered to the victims to measure stress: one labeled "Problems" (such as nightmares, inability to concentrate, feeling a need for help with emotional problems), one labeled "Fears" (such as fear of being home alone or fear of going out on the street), and one labeled "Avoidances" (such as avoidance of going out alone or avoidance of specific areas or places). The Problems, Fears, and Avoidances Scales contained twenty, eight, and five items respectively. The data showed that each scale had high interitem reliability. Since each scale was designed to tap a different indicator of stress, but all were intended to measure stress as the central concept, intercorrelations between scales were made to establish validity. All correlations were significant at the 0.001 level.

Table 1 shows the median scores on the three scales at the four time periods. The first three rows under each scale represent the data obtained during the first interview. The pattern in these rows closely follows what would be anticipated from crisis theory. As can be seen in Rows 1 and 2 of each scale, the median scores on all three scales rose sharply immediately after the assault. By the time of the first interview (Row 3), when victims reported on their current state, the symptoms of stress had subsided sub-

Table 1. Median Scores on the Problems, Fears, and Avoidances Scales[a]

Scales	Median Scores
Problems (range 0–20)	
Before the assault	1.4
Immediately after the assault	8.4
First interview	3.6
Follow-up interview	4.1
Fears (range 0–8)	
Before the assault	0
Immediately after the assault	4.0
First interview	2.8
Follow-up interview	3.9
Avoidances (range 0–5)	
Before the assault	0
Immediately after the assault	2.8
First interview	1.6
Follow-up interview	2.2

[a] Median scores are for the total sample in the first three time periods and for the follow-up sample in the fourth time period.

stantially although not to the reported prerape level. A period of reorganization seems to have occurred. Unexpectedly, however, from a crisis-theory
perspective, results from the follow-up interview, displayed in Row 4 of
each scale, show that stress symptoms from all three scales increased rather
than continued to decline. This increase was not a function of a change in
the sample, since when the median scores of the follow-up sample were
extracted from the total sample for the three prior periods, they mirrored
the median scores of the total sample, producing the same pattern time
period-by-time period.

Symptomotology

Consistent patterns of social relationships and activities emerged for the
first three time periods. Few victims were isolated; most had been embedded
in a network of family and friends prior to the incident. Immediately after
the rape, the network showed signs of disturbance. Some ties, especially
with husbands and intimate male friends, were broken and never repaired.
However, by the time of the first interview, the ruptures seemed to be
healing, and broken ties often had been replaced by new ones. Engagement
in work, educational endeavors, and volunteer activities had not returned
to the preincident levels by the first interview, but the discrepancy was
decreasing.

At the time of the second interview (the fourth time period), the
victims' psychological and social states were no longer consistent. The
women's social activities had returned to preincident levels and volunteer
activities seemed to have increased. Similarly, their social relationships
seemed to have been restored, if not enhanced. More women were married,
more had children, and some had increased their circle of friends. However,
the women's psychological state had not been restored, as evidenced by the
rise in problems, fears, and avoidances. One can only surmise that the
risk-taking necessary to become reinvolved in social activities and in trusting others, especially men, had reactivated some of the rape-induced stress.

Since the victims as an aggregate were at different time points from the
incident, one could hope to discern specific patterns only by dividing them
up into time-interval cohorts. This technique could only be used for the
data from the first interview because subgroups from the second interview
were too small. The 127 victims interviewed initially could be divided into
five almost equal groups in terms of time interval since the rape took place:
one to three months, three to six months, six to twelve months, thirteen to
thirty-six months, and thirty-seven or more months.

The time-interval groups proved to be similar in composition; there
were no significant differences in age, race, marital status, or educational
level. Furthermore, there were no significant between-group differences in
the way the victims described the rape incident and their reactions to it.

There were also no between-group differences in scores on the Problems, Fears, and Avoidances Scales for the victims' descriptions of themselves just prior to the incident or immediately after the incident. Thus, whether the rape experience was recent or had occurred as much as several years in the past, the recall of the victims tended to be similar.

For the purposes of this article, however, the data from the first interview are most important, for it would be at this point that distance in time from the incident should have been reflected in a pattern of diminishing stress as the incident receded into the past. However, the data from this study did not show any clear trend in that direction. Among all the items from the Problems, Fears, and Avoidances Scales, only five of the total thirty-three items revealed significant differences broken down by time-interval groups. These few significant differences, together with several supporting trends that did not reach significance, revealed a shadowy pattern which represented a distorted normal curve. That is, the proportion of victims exhibiting stress symptoms was high among the one-to-three-months group, dipped to its lowest level among the four-to-six months group, rose to a peak among the seven-to-twelve-months group, and gradually tapered off in the last two groups. (See Fig. 1.)

The two sets of data (panel and cohort), then, are consistent in demonstrating the tendency of symptoms to revive after a period of quiescence. That the one-to-three-months group did not show the highest level of symptoms and the four-to-six-months group exhibited little stress conforms to the findings of Kilpatrick, Veronen, and Resick's longitudinal

Figure 1. Stress Symptoms Curve, by Time Intervals

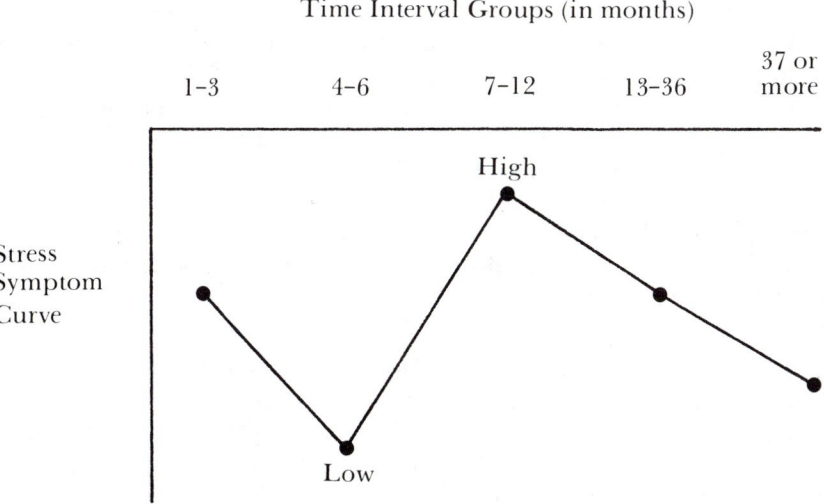

Time Interval Groups (in months)

| 1–3 | 4–6 | 7–12 | 13–36 | 37 or more |

study.[8] That study found that although stress symptoms were prevalent six to ten days and one month after the incident, they had receded substantially by three months. By contrast, the authors' approximations for examining long-term effects through cohort and panel data indicated that symptoms arise again at a later time. Again, the data on social relationships and activities may help to explain the results. The seven-to-twelve-months group did not differ from other groups in terms of occupational or educational involvement. In the aggregate, the victims were somewhat less likely to be employed at this point than prior to the incident, but decreased involvement was reflected equally in all groups.

However, some differences in the profile of the seven-to-twelve-months group are worth reporting. For example, that group was significantly less likely to be attending church or engaging in volunteer activities of any kind. More interesting still, members of that group were by far the most likely of all to be unmarried and living alone. None of these differences appeared in the profiles of the members of the groups when they described their lives before the rape. In relation to the other groups after the incident, then, the women in the seven-to-twelve-months group seemed to be in a state of withdrawal. Their state may be contrasted to members of the four-to-six-months group, who were in a period of apparent psychological calm and were more actively engaged in volunteer activities and more likely to be married and sharing a household with others.

Since members of all the time-interval groups were similar in background characteristics and in self-reports of their lives prior to the incident, the authors thought they could be treated as though they were respondents in a true longitudinal study. Looked at this way, the data seem to indicate that in the earliest time interval, the victims tended to be disorganized, both psychologically and socially. As the immediate trauma began to wear off, they started to recover and to resume the activities in which they had customarily been involved. But in the relief of putting the assault behind them and beginning to feel better emotionally, they seemed to overtax themselves by getting involved in social situations that may have revived memories of the rape or fears of another attack. Accordingly, stress symptoms increased, and victims sought relief in a period of withdrawal at about the seven-to-twelve-months time interval. Gradually, however, this revival of the earlier stage also subsided, and the women again were more active and less fearful and anxious.

The cohort data offered a somewhat different interpretation than was found for the aggregate data from the four time periods in which the rise of symptoms at follow-up appeared to be a reflection of increased social engagement and attendant risks. The authors suspect, however, that the patterns in their data simply indicate that although women who were raped eventually regain their equilibrium to a large degree, they are not, for a long time, at home in their social world. Whether increased activity is directly related to the revival of stress or indirectly related via a period of withdrawal, the women in the sample did not demonstrate a straight-line recovery pattern. Rather, the pattern was one with peaks and valleys that, to the limits of the inquiry, never returned to the preincident level of adjustment.

IMPLICATIONS FOR THEORY AND PRACTICE

The results of the research suggest a number of implications for crisis theory and for social work practice. Crisis theory was useful as the organizing frame of reference for the study. However, as it is generally promulgated, it presumes that tension, as reflected in anxiety or depression, diminishes over time. Whether the results of this study were looked at in panel or cohort patterns, it was clear that stress symptoms did not recede in a straight-line fashion over time but actually tended to rise again over the relatively long term. Crisis theory, then, at least as applied to rape victims, needs some modification to account for this type of pattern.

Another conceptual problem is that the relationship between the level of stress, as measured by the Problems, Fears, and Avoidances Scales, and behavioral functioning was not consistent. After the crisis seemed to have passed, the victims returned to a previous level of functioning or even an accelerated level of functioning that may be what is expected of victims or may be what victims expect of themselves. But it is apparent that this renewed activity may have occurred at the expense of increases in symptoms of stress. In addition, the women reported changes in how they related to the social environment. Although they tended to regret these changes, the women found they had become less trusting, less open, and less comfortable with others. Therefore, it seems necessary to consider whether a trauma as severe as rape results in permanent psychological damage.

To discover more about whether the trauma of rape is permanent or temporary, both behavioral and attitudinal measures need to be used in all studies of crisis. Further, more sensitive measures need to be developed to discover the more subtle nuances of the relationship between the psychological and social dimensions. In this study, it was possible to pinpoint a relationship in the victims between heightened tension and involvement in court proceedings. However, court proceedings affected only a small number of victims at various points over time. There may well be a number of experiences and events in victims' lives that affect their psychological states. By looking for more explicit links between subjective reactions and social happenings, it will be possible to understand more thoroughly the aftermath of crisis.

Table 2. Rape Crisis Center Services Used by Victims,
by Time Since Rape[a]

Time	Number of Victims Using Service (N = 126)	Average Number of Visits per Person
1-3 months	39	4.2
4-6 months	14	3.4
7-12 months	27	3.3
13-36 months	22	2.3
37 or more months	24	1.5

[a] $F = 3.45$, $4/122$ df, $p < 0.05$.

There are numerous practice implications of the study findings, only some of which will be identified here. First, the data show that victims need support for a much longer period than crisis theory has led one to believe. The relationship between the assumptions of crisis theory and what is happening in practice is reflected in Table 2, which shows that the number of rape crisis center services being used by victims diminishes as the time since the incident increases. Probably, it is not the intention of those who offer services to victims to discourage them from continuing to seek aid for as long as they feel they need it. But it is apparent, at least in the data available, that most of the services concentrate on the period immediately after the rape. It may well be that the victims themselves feel they should discontinue or diminish their service demands in favor of those who ostensibly are suffering more.

It is important, however, that those who work with rape victims recognize that although they may appear to be functioning well, the emotional price they are paying continues to be high and thus longer-term support would be valuable. It is also important to note that the experience of the incident becomes a part of future activities and relationships. Social workers must help rape victims deal with the consequences of fluctuating tension states and a disvalued sense of self as untrusting persons. In this way, social workers can help these women to feel they have more control over their lives and to accept their "new selves" in much the same way that social workers help young children to develop the capacity to be cautious in dealing with a strange and complex world, yet not feel unduly mistrustful of others. It seems that rape victims, like others who undergo severe crises, can benefit by learning that appropriate self-defense, self-preservation, and survival tactics, which are realistic in terms of their experiences, can be combined with an open and warm relationship to people.

It is also clear that practitioners have to be careful not to force people into conformity with useful theoretical models. Theoretical models need constant feedback and elaboration so they do not lead social workers unintentionally to distort reality. Social work practice must always be open to a modification of models based on new facts learned from clients. In this case, the authors are not arguing for a long-term or short-term perspective on the crisis of rape. Rather what is salient for practice is a differential assessment and differential application of appropriate models, depending on the victim, her reactions, and the social environment in which she operates. On the basis of aggregate data, it can only be said that many if not most victims need responsive care for a much longer period than would have been predicted. This may be true only for rape victims, but it would seem important to study patterns of response to other crises to assess similarities and differences.

Furthermore, it is important to note that the findings of this study indicate a substantial difference between behavior and feelings. Social work practice has tended to believe that either feelings precede and control behavior or that behavior shapes feelings. The data show that there is no necessary congruence between behavior and feelings and that social workers need to reassess assumptions about how behavior and feelings work together and where and under what circumstances disparities occur between them. This will lead to a more differentiated assessment of the victims' strengths and weaknesses and their total functioning. By being more sensitive to such disjunctions, social workers can help people cope with current crises and prepare for future crises in a more substantive way than has been done.

CONCLUSION

Overall, several observations need to be stressed. First, insufficient attention is being given to the long-term psychological effects of rape. In this connection, victims should be encouraged to seek help for their felt needs as long as they experience them and to return to social work agencies for support whenever they feel the need for support. Second, for this to happen, the resources available to crisis victims may need to be increased. There is substantial evidence that a minimum number of referrals are made to mental health agencies, despite feelings by many victims that they could use such services. Under such conditions, it is necessary to discover why such blockages occur and how a better referral system can be established.

Third, since advocates at rape crisis centers tend to focus on helping victims through legal proceedings to prosecute assailants, which is an important global aim, it is crucial that other means are found to link victims to social services that meet more disparate needs, such as helping victims repair their network of intimate social relationships that was disrupted immediately after the rape. Even though many of the women interviewed in the study seemed to have mended old relationships or established new ones, the evident fragility and vulnerability of such networks needs considerable attention and further study. It is apparent, for example, that insufficient work is being done with men to enable them to be more supportive of women who have been raped. It is also significant, according to the study findings, that victims were afraid to talk about the rape with their fathers, although when the fathers were told of their daughters' experience, usually by an intermediary, they became a solid source of support. Accordingly, social workers need to reexamine these complexities in the light of crisis theory and the practice implications of the study findings and to pay special attention to the continuing needs of victims and their socialization. They must also pay attention to the social supports available to the victims in coping with the devastating trauma and how potential social support systems can be better mobilized to help victims to a more comfortable adjustment in the aftermath of rape.

REFERENCES

1. Robert Hirschowitz, "Crisis Theory: A Formulation," *Psychiatric Annals*, 3 (December 1973), pp. 48–61.

2. Sandra Sutherland Fox and Donald J. Scherl, MD, "Crisis Intervention with Victims of Rape," *Social Work*, 17 (January 1972), pp. 37–42.

3. Howard J. Parad, *Crisis Intervention: Selected Readings* (New York: Family Service Association of America, 1965).

4. *See* Morton Bard and Katherine Ellison, "Crisis Intervention and Investigation of Forcible Rape," *Police Chief*, 41 (May 1974), pp. 68–74; Fox and Scherl, op. cit.; Lynda L. Holstrom and Ann W. Burgess, *The Victim of Rape: Institutional Reactions* (New York: John Wiley & Sons, 1978); and Malkah Notman and Carol Nadelson, "The Rape Victim: Psychodynamic Considerations," *American Journal of Psychiatry*, 133 (April 1976), pp. 408–413.

5. Donna D. Schram, "Rape," in Jane R. Chapman and Margaret Gates, eds., *The Victimization of Women* (Beverly Hills, Calif.: Sage Publishing Co., 1978), pp. 53–80; and Martin Symonds, "The Rape Victim: Psychological Patterns of Response," *American Journal of Psychoanalysis*, 36 (Spring 1976), pp. 27–34.

6. Dean G. Kilpatrick, Lois J. Veronen, and Patricia A. Resick, "The Aftermath of Rape: Recent Empirical Findings," *American Journal of Orthopsychiatry*, 49 (October 1979), pp. 658–669.

7. *See* Menachem Amir, "Forcible Rape," *Sexual Behavior*, 1 (November 1971), pp. 25–36; Amir, *Patterns in Forcible Rape* (Chicago: University of Chicago Press, 1971); Lorenne Clark and Debra Lewis, *Rape: The Price of Coercive Sexuality* (Toronto, Ont., Canada: Women's Press, 1977); Carolyn J. Hursch, *The Trouble with Rape: A Psychologist's Report on the Legal, Medical, Social, and Psychological Problems* (Chicago: Nelson-Hall, 1977); Holmstrom and Burgess, op. cit.; Schram, op. cit.

8. Kilpatrick, Veronen, and Resick, op. cit.

OLDER WOMEN AS VICTIMS OF VIOLENCE

Stephanie FallCreek
Nancy Hooyman

In our society, violence is usually inflicted on persons in a lower status group by those in a superior status group. Older women—particularly those who are chronically ill, handicapped, poor, or members of a minority group—are generally of low status, are powerless, and tend to be emotionally, physically, or financially dependent. Hence, the likelihood is great that they will be victims of violence.[1] With the population of women aged 65 or over rapidly growing in this country, violent abuse of older women is a critical issue for service providers and policymakers.

This article presents what is known about violence against older women and discusses the implications of this knowledge for service providers. It focuses on two types of violence: abuse inflicted by familial caretakers and sexual assault by nonfamily members. Although older men may be subject to violent assault, older women more often are victims of these types of violence, hence, the focus on older women.

FAMILIAL ABUSE

Research at the Universities of Michigan, Maryland, and Washington, at Case Western Reserve University, and through Massachusetts Legal Research Services for the Elderly has attempted to determine the incidence and characteristics of abusive situations among the elderly in general, rather than among elderly women. Three types of abuse have been identified: physical, emotional, and financial. Physical abuse has been identified either as intentional physical neglect (withholding medication, food, or exercise) or as the infliction of bodily harm (hitting, bruising, sexual molestation, cutting, burning, or physical restraint). Psychological or

49

emotional abuse includes verbal assaults, threats, infantilization, or requests for unrealistic performance. Financial abuse involves removal of money, real estate, or other assets and diversion of assets by relatives for their own use. Violation of rights includes the forced change of environment.[2]

In most cases, a continuum of abuse has been investigated. Adherence to a unidimensional scale of severity is difficult because some forms of verbal or emotional abuse or neglect may be as damaging as physical abuse, and the physiology of older women may make them susceptible even to mild forms of physical violence. Rathbone-McCuan and Voyles suggest that abuse includes any action or failure to act that is life endangering to an elderly person.[3]

Extent and Types of Familial Abuse

Knowledge of the incidence and types of abuse comes primarily from surveys of service providers or reviews of case records, rather than from interviews with victims or their families. For example, a 1978 study determined that 9.6 percent of the clients seen in one year by the Chronic Illness Center in Cleveland, Ohio, had been abused.[4] Almost 75 percent of the cases involved physical abuse and over half involved psychological abuse. Most victims had experienced three forms of abuse. In a 1979 Massachusetts survey, 55 percent of the professional respondents reported seeing cases of abuse of the elderly within the past eighteen months; of these cases, 41 percent were of physical abuse. Incidents of abuse tended to be recurring events.[5]

Of the professionals who responded to a 1979 University of Maryland study, 13.4 percent reported cases of abuse, although the other respondents were aware of abuse even if they did not have any cases of abuse. Psychological abuse, especially verbal assault and isolation, was cited most frequently. Of the service providers who responded to a University of Washington study, 47 percent had encountered at least one instance of abuse in a one-year period. In 61 percent of the cases, the victims had been physically beaten or struck; necessary personal care had been withheld for 33 percent. In contrast to other studies, respondents in a 1979 Michigan study generally considered the physical and emotional needs of the elderly to be adequately met by caretakers. At the same time, they recognized that neglect and abuse are not uncommon.[6]

Who Are Abused?

Older women who are dependent on their caregivers are the primary victims of abuse. Of the thirty-nine abused clients in the Cleveland study reported by Lau and Kosberg, thirty (76 percent) were women, most of whom had at least one major physical or mental impairment. In the Massachusetts survey, women were the victims in 80 percent of the citings of abuse and were more likely to be abused than men, regardless of age. Of the cases cited by both groups of respondents in the University of Maryland study, 81 percent were low- or middle-income women over 75 years of age; most had some physical impairment. All ten cases described in Rathbone-McCuan's 1978 St. Louis study were women who were dependent on a caregiver. In the University of Washington study, 72 percent of the victims were women, primarily low-income whites.[7]

Who Are the Abusers?

In the Cleveland study, 27 percent of the abusers were daughters; the husband was the abuser in approximately 10 percent of the cases. In the Massachusetts survey, sons, husbands, and daughters were the largest categories of abusing relatives, accounting for 24 percent, 20 percent, and 15 percent, respectively, of all abusers. Adult children were the primary abusers in the University of Maryland study and the study reported by Renvoize. Eight of the ten cases described by Rathbone-McCuan were abused by adult children. Spouse battering was slightly higher in the University of Washington sample, in which 30.4 percent of the abusers were husbands, 21.7 percent were adult daughters, and 17.4 percent were adult sons.[8] From these preliminary data, it seems that older women are more likely to be abused by adult children, in many cases by daughters who have been the traditional caregivers, than by spouses. It is tragic that for many of these women who are widows, abuse by children may have replaced years of abuse by the former spouse.

Problems in Detection

The foregoing studies illustrate the difficulties of obtaining accurate data on abuse. Abuse may be suspected but never reported for a variety of professional or legal reasons. Definitions and interpretations differ, so often abuse is not diagnosed. State statutes vary widely regarding standards for the reporting and confirmation of cases of abuse. An older woman who reports abuse may be discounted by service providers or third parties as confused, "senile," or "crazy."

Another reason for the limited knowledge about violence against older women is the inability or unwillingness of older women to report abuse. Many older women may have no alternative caretakers other than the abuser on whom they are physically or financially dependent; therefore, they may fear reprisals and more abuse if they report they were abused. Handicapped or chronically ill older women confined to the home may not be in contact with anyone to whom they could report the abuse. Other older women may be ashamed to admit the abuse, may be resigned to its occurrence, or may hope that it will stop.

Aware of society's negative attitudes toward them and feeling powerless, older women may view abuse as deserved and unavoidable. For many older women, the fear may be that no matter how bad it is now, "I could be alone, then things would be worse." As Gelles indicated in his study of battered wives, fear of the unknown may be worse than the battering itself. Other factors that may inhibit reporting of abuse are the older woman's confusion on entering treatment and overmedication. Furthermore, although reporting by third parties may be high, there are undoubtedly many cases that friends, neighbors, or other relatives are unaware of or never disclose because of fear of reprisals against the abused person, and eyewitnesses may be unable or unwilling to cooperate with police or other professionals in reporting abuse.[9]

Responses of Service Providers

A wide variety of service providers, including visiting nurses, home health staff, emergency room personnel, police, primary-care physicians, ministers, adult protective service workers, and staff of family service agencies, undoubtedly encounter abuse. In many cases, providers simply may not be looking for signs of abuse or asking questions that would elicit information about it. A 1978 British study found that when physicians and nurses specifically looked for signs of abuse, they found more cases.[10]

Barriers between service providers and other agencies and professionals, especially lawyers and the police, hamper the provision of effective services to victims and their families. For example, professionals from various disciplines may not understand each other's language and perspective or know how to work collaboratively. Gaps may exist between service providers who identify domestic violence as a problem of young women and members of the aging network—those who are involved in the delivery of direct and organizational services to older persons.

Legal barriers are numerous: the lack of legal protection for workers who intervene, the absence of formalized statutes to protect old people from manipulation and exploitation, the requirements that an abused individual must file a formal complaint before the police can act, and the difficulty of locating appropriate guardians. To remedy the abuses of civil commitment, guardianship, and eviction or to obtain a restraining order, the elderly victim must initiate the complaint or be willing to testify. Thus the victim must bear the strain of the criminal or civil proceedings.

Limited service options for victims are another major barrier. Even if the victim of abuse is willing and able to file a complaint and to leave the abusive situation, the only alternative may be institutionalization. Although emergency shelters have met some needs of younger battered women, their structure and philosophy of service may not be compatible with the needs of older women. Therefore, service providers may avoid intervening because they recognize the limited options.

Explanations of Familial Abuse

Explanations of familial abuse may be grouped as (1) developmental and historical, (2) individual pathological behavior, and (3) situational or environmental. The developmental and historical perspective recognizes that families exist in which violence is the norm and individuals cannot sustain personal relationships; parents and children abuse each other throughout their lifetimes. The abused child may become the abuser, often acting out hostility incurred by earlier abuse.

A second cluster of explanations focuses on the abusers' pathological or deviant behavior. "Nonnormal" caregivers may be schizophrenic, retarded, alcoholic, or drug-addicted relatives, incapable of appropriate judgments and actions. Almost three-quarters of the abusers in the Massachusetts survey were experiencing some form of stress, including alcoholism or drug addiction. In the University of Washington study, 33 percent of the abusers suffered from alcohol or drug abuse and 17 percent were perceived as mentally ill by service providers.[11]

The third category of explanations interprets abuse as a situational or environmental phenomenon; that is, abuse is a negative outcome of certain environmental conditions or conflict. In this context, caring for an older person can create major shifts in the functioning of a family and thereby may strain intergenerational relationships. Many familial caregivers may be isolated from support systems to help them handle their emotions and control their destructive impulses as well as perform daily tasks. In the University of Washington study, 20 percent of the abusers were perceived as lacking support from family, friends, and neighbors and 20 percent had financial burdens.[12]

As the distribution of power and resources shifts, the caretaker may be unable to cope with the dependence of an aged relative who is culturally defined as roleless and noncontributing. Hickey suggests that when adult children are unwilling or unable to accept their parents' dependence, they are more likely to define them as vulnerable.[13] The period of dependence of old age may extend too long without relief from recovery or death. Dependence then becomes neither permissible nor easily tolerated by others.

Garbarino maintained, in relation to child abuse, that given the interaction between the stress experienced by the caregiver and the lack of training or skill in performing such a role, no one is immune from becoming an abuser if the stress becomes great enough.[14] In our society, the stress of caring for an aged relative is exacerbated by inadequate preparation and insufficient support for the caretaker's role. Caregivers may feel isolated if they are ignorant of community resources. This isolation and burden may be particularly great for middle-aged women, who face demands from both the older and younger generations.

SEXUAL ASSAULT

Previous research and professional discussion have focused largely on crimes against older persons as a group and on crime in general.[15] Only a handful of reports have examined either violent crime against the elderly or older women as victims.[16] This section will focus on sexual assault, primarily rape, although most of the issues and interventions apply to other forms of violent assault by strangers.

Incidence of Sexual Assault

Although available data vary, women over age 50 report rape at a rate of about two per thousand nationwide, according to several studies.[17] For example, of the 289 cases in 1979, reported to the Rape Crisis Network or to the police and the Rape Crisis Network in Spokane, Washington, only 3 included victims over age 60.[18]

The reported low incidence rates may be deceptive or misleading for at least three reasons. First, they mask the severity of the problem in specific geographic areas, particularly in urban areas where actual reporting rates may be much higher. Second, they fail to take into account the extent of underreporting. Rape, of women of any age, is an underreported crime. Rape and other forms of sexual assault of older women are probably reported even less frequently than for younger women.

In addition to more universal reasons for underreporting, reduced rates of reporting by older women may be aggravated by any or all of the following: (1) feelings of powerlessness in this youth-oriented society, (2) the lack of familiarity and experience with the law enforcement and criminal justice systems, (3) the belief that nothing will be done about the crime, and (4) the lack of language and terminology to report the nature of the crime. Other equally important deterrents to reporting rape include (1) the older woman's socialization to the idea that women are at fault for being raped and the consequent reluctance publicly to acknowledge the assault, (2) the perception by service providers that older women are senile or disoriented and thus their dismissal of older women's complaints, (3) the likelihood that the woman's physician, who may be her initial contact after the crime, is elderly and faces the same barriers to reporting that she faces, (4) the lack of access, for the dependent or institutionalized older woman, to means of reporting assault, and (5) the fear of reprisal, since more older women than younger women are repeated victims of assault.

Third, statistics collected largely during the first half of the 1970s did not adequately portray the increasing violence of this society, particularly that against and among older persons. Available evidence suggests that violence may be increasing, especially in urban low-income neighborhoods, where many older women live. Moreover, according to Groth, when rapists choose victims who are significantly older than themselves, the assaults are likely to be more brutal than those against younger women. Groth's study also corroborated the hypothesized underreporting of sexual assault. For example, of all offenders referred to the Center for Diagnosis and Treatment of Sexually Dangerous Persons during a one-year period, Groth found that 18 percent had chosen victims at least twice their age and that more than half the female victims were over 60 years old. Hahn concluded that the elderly are increasingly subject to a set of violent crimes.[19]

Vulnerability

Many older women appear to potential attackers to be especially vulnerable to violent assault for many reasons. Older women are concentrated in low-income, high-crime urban neighborhoods in deteriorated buildings that are easier to penetrate and more difficult to fortify. They usually live alone and have routinized and highly visible daily behaviors. Furthermore, they are perceived as having or have physical weaknesses and sensory decrements. Moreover, society's devaluation of the elderly may heighten the attacker's confidence that he can get away with the crime.

Despite the society's general devaluation of the elderly, the individual older woman may symbolize female authority and thus be a logical object of a young man's hostility and frustration. Older women, remaining in urban low-income neighborhoods that are in economic and racial transition, may be perceived as remnants of oppression. That is, they may highlight racial, social, economic, and cultural differences with their often routine, genteel, and circumscribed behaviors.[20]

Impact of Assault

The very circumstances that render older women particularly vulnerable to would-be attackers may increase the severity of the damages these women experience when attacked. Physiological changes that accompany aging (such as brittle bones and thinner, less resilient tissues) may result in more severe physical damage and a slower and less complete recovery. Furthermore, the financial losses resulting from violent assault (even modest medical bills and a short stay in the hospital) may threaten the independence of elderly women, especially those on fixed incomes that are barely enough to cover their basic living costs. Since sexual assault of older women is frequently the partner to robbery, loss or damage to possessions is psychologically and economically traumatic, since these women often are unable to replace or repair what they have lost.

The potential psychological effects of violent attack are also multiple. For an older woman, sexual violation, with its attendant embarrassment and humiliation, may come after an extended period of sexual inactivity.

The older woman is also more likely to accept an implied societal message that the assault was sexual in nature rather than an act of violence. Her early socialization has left her vulnerable to the notion that she is responsible for the sexual assault.

The older woman may be experiencing loss of autonomy in many areas of her life. The loss of control over her own body may well represent a crushing psychological blow to her sense of independence. Thus, coping with and accepting her own mortality may be a major task. The closeness to and fear of death often experienced in the violent assault may seriously jeopardize her ability to deal in a healthy way with her own mortality and the normal aging process.

Frequently, it is difficult for the older woman to provide the evidence needed for prosecuting her assailant. In addition to the stresses of the experience, which may limit her ability to recall details and circumstances, perceptual decrements may weaken or destroy the credibility of her testimony. For the older woman who attempts to act as a witness, these frustrations may be devastating and reinforce her overall sense of helplessness.

Beyond the immediate physiological and psychological impact, however, lies perhaps the most severe danger to the older woman's well-being. Fear of violent attack encroaches on the essence of her life-style, leading her to curtail activities and become more vulnerable to loneliness, depression, and social isolation. This pervasive fear is not confined to victims, although it may be more severe for them. Extreme manifestations of this fear may result in the older woman's confining herself to her home. However, unless she acts to fortify her residence and takes other preventive measures, available data suggest that her home is by far the most likely scene of violent sexual assault.[21] The scarcity of research and information about older victims prohibits definitive statements about the extent and duration of damages they are likely to suffer, but the likely multiple consequences seem clear.

IMPLICATIONS FOR SERVICE PROVIDERS

The overall preventive goal of service providers should be to reduce the vulnerability of older women to both familial violence and sexual assault. This may be accomplished by strategies to (1) empower older women, (2) to reduce their accessibility to abuse, and (3) to reduce the desirability of victimizing them.

Empowerment

Reducing the older woman's vulnerability to victimization suggests first an overall strategy of empowerment. Older women need to acquire or strengthen a positive and powerful self-image. Negative self-conceptions, which coincide with the general society's devaluation of older persons, encourage acceptance of violent victimization as understandable, unavoidable, or even deserved.

In relation to familial abuse, intervention should be directed toward empowering the older victim either in the family setting or when she chooses and is able to leave the abusive situation. Service providers must be advocates for older women, informing them of their rights. Renvoize suggested that education in preventive health care is one means to reduce the dependence of older women on familial caregivers. Others have suggested that the best empowerment strategy is to give older women more resources. Women leaving an abusive situation need multiple supports for their decisions: individual therapy, group support, mechanisms to build their self-esteem and sense of control, and the support of other relatives. In one case described by Hooyman in the University of Washington study, seven years of individual and group therapy were necessary before a 60-year-old woman could leave an abusive situation.[22]

Some shelters for battered women have found cross-generational support groups to be effective; younger and older women have mutually benefited from sharing experiences.[23] Furthermore, older women can be trained to be advocates for each other to prevent and report abuse. Telephone checkups and "buddy" systems for older people have been instituted in a variety of settings. Such networks could be set up to detect abuse and provide support to victims of abuse and sexual assault. Building support systems for older women is one mechanism to reduce their social isolation and to empower them.

There are a number of ways that an older woman can reduce her vulnerability to sexual assault. First, the image of vulnerability must be minimized. Maximal physical fitness at any age contributes to the appearance of strength, and the appearance of strength may be particularly important for the older woman who is being checked out by a rapist as a potentially weak victim. Assertiveness training can help the older woman acquire behavior that suggests strength, confidence, and the overall appearance of being in control of her situation. The public image that the older woman presents may well be the attacker's only basis for choosing his victim.

In addition, the older woman's ability to assert herself in a potentially violent situation may be critical. The assertive, self-confident older woman can communicate with a would-be attacker in a manner that suggests "Don't mess with me!" Moreover, she is likely to have the presence of mind to deal constructively with a threatening situation. The most critical empowerment technique, however, may be to educate the older woman about the possibilities and characteristics of sexual assault. Such knowledge can help replace unreasonable fear and possible immobilization with realistic concerns and preventive and protective activities. Providing the older woman with the information she needs to reduce the risk of being the victim of violent assault is empowerment of the most basic sort.

Reducing Accessibility to Assault

The second approach—reducing the accessibility of older women to abusive family situations—requires that practitioners develop skills in the detection and diagnosis of abuse and of older women who are at risk. This is a first step to the removal of the older woman from the home and to working with the family. There are no professional or legal guidelines for determining what information is sufficient for the accurate assessment of potentially violent family situations or cases of abuse of the elderly. However, since professionals have developed considerable expertise in identifying child abuse and violence-prone families, the identification of abuse of the elderly should be possible as well.

Renvoize maintains that although older people bruise easily, a hematological examination to determine if a specific older person bruises easily can be administered, and previous injuries may be revealed by ultraviolet light. Examinations carried out on corpses of abused older people have often found that they had been hospitalized several months prior to the final accident, perhaps with a stroke and heavy bruising after having "fallen down the stairs." Such findings highlight the need for frontline professionals, such as the police, nurses, aides, and physicians in emergency rooms, to be trained to be aware of signs of abuse so they will ask the necessary questions or perform the appropriate tests. Rathbone-McCuan and Voyles have suggested a number of physical, interactional, and environmental signs of abusive family situations.[24] Agencies need to address the extent to which their policies and practices obstruct or facilitate the diagnosis of abuse or of at-risk situations so the situation can be modified before abuse occurs.

Reducing the accessibility of older women to sexual assault requires the cooperation of service providers and older women. The first line of defense is the woman's residence, since the majority of sexual assaults take place in the older person's home. Available strategies, of course, depend on the residential situation. A deteriorating single-family home in a transitional neighborhood requires different fortification techniques from an age-segregated high-rise apartment house in the inner city, although both types of residences may call for the addition of locks, lights, and communication plans.

The older woman who is part of a solid social network has different options from the socially isolated woman who does not know neighbors or have friends and relatives nearby. For those who have a strong social network, one intervention is the education of network members about the importance of joint activities, daily phone checks, and so on. For those without local social supports, network-building is an appropriate intervention; for example, neighbors, storekeepers, bank personnel, and such personnel as mail carriers or public utilities workers can be asked to check on isolated older people. This strategy may lessen the possibility of robbery, since most criminals "case" the situation before they attempt to enter a residence.

Moreover, because robbery of older women can escalate into violence, it is not enough to deter sexual assault. Rather, all types of criminal contact must be prevented if the older woman is to be protected. Fortunately, strategies that reduce risk of assault largely apply to both sexual assault and robbery. Other interventions to reduce accessibility focus on specific behavioral changes, such as direct deposit of checks, locking doors and windows, having keys ready at the door, and listing more than one name on the mailbox. Since many sexual assaults occur after the older woman admits the rapist to her home, education and support for behavior change may prevent such crimes.[25]

Relocating older people to age-segregated or other types of housing may be another way to reduce their accessibility to violent assault. Concentrating them in apartment complexes has several advantages. For example, in such settings, neighbors and friends may be deterrents to victimization and resources in times of crisis. Also, it is easier to establish group surveillance and security measures.

The disadvantages of relocation however, may outweigh the possible advantages. For instance, age-segregated housing may be undesirable to the older woman who values contact with people of all ages. Relocation to any new residence may threaten her sense of independence, which may be symbolized by her ability to maintain her long-time home or apartment. Despite apparently dwindling social and neighborhood resources, the older woman may rely on nearby friends or acquaintances for contact. The stress of learning to manage a new living situation may be so great that it effectively precludes consideration of relocation for many older women. Thus, in any individual situation, these trade-offs must be examined.

Similarly, in considering the issue of visible and predictable behaviors, the particular woman's circumstances must be examined before preventive or protective strategies are suggested. If, in the course of the day, the older woman has habitual contact with people (shopkeepers, traffic guards, or restaurant employees) who are aware of her, count on her to appear, and are concerned with her well-being, she may be better off to engage in her daily routine in this protective network that acts to buffer contact with would-be attackers. If, however, she walks the same path to deposit her check, do her shopping, and go to the cafeteria at the same time every day and yet is not integrated into a conscious social support system, she may appear to be an easy prey to an attacker. Again, the individual context must be examined.

The importance of providing the older woman with information about the possibility and circumstances of victimization cannot be overstated. Information or any recommendation for intervention in her lifestyle must be presented so it creates an atmosphere of concern and constructive action rather than an aura of fear. The older woman has information to share with service providers as well. Accurate knowledge about the multiple dimensions of the older woman's life-style is central to developing an effective intervention plan that maximizes protection and personal independence.

Reducing the Desirability of Abuse

The last strategy—reducing the desirability of abusing older women— raises many legal and policy issues. The need for stiffer penalties for sexual assault is clearcut. What is less clear and more controversial is whether there should be mandatory reporting of abuse cases and whether adult protective service agencies should have statutory authorization to take legal action when appropriate. Eleven states require professionals to report cases of abuse of older people to legal authorities. The 1979 studies conducted at the University of Maryland and University of Michigan recommended that states adopt mandatory reporting. In the 1980 congressional hearings on abuse, it was suggested that the Domestic Violence Prevention and Treatment Act of 1979 be amended to include the elderly.[26] More research is needed to determine how well such legal changes are working and what impact they have on long-term family relationships and on the older woman's ability to make choices freely. When reporting of such cases is mandatory and is accompanied by the legal right to intervene in and forcefully remove a client from an abusive situation, professionals need to be trained to utilize such laws in a humane way.

TREATMENT CONSIDERATIONS

In addition to legal changes, effective interventions with familial caregivers need to be developed to prevent and treat familial abuse. Behavioral intervention may offer an effective alternative for helping the abuser to change behavior toward the older person. The task-centered approach can be a short-term, goal-setting, empirically based method of working with the aged victim and the family to provide necessary social services. For example, a family service agency in Ann Arbor, Michigan, has an intergenerational treatment model that seems appropriate for use with abusive families, and training programs provide the police with interpersonal skills necessary to effect constructive outcomes in deteriorating family situations.[27]

The case of the older woman who chooses to leave an abusive family situation illustrates the importance of considering the individual context. If an older woman decides to leave an abusive situation, service providers face the dilemma of limited alternative living arrangements. For some older women, the only option may be institutionalization, which can be a negative experience and certainly not one that empowers an older woman. More community alternatives are needed, such as share-a-home programs, cross-generational households, emergency housing, and senior companion programs. Practitioners need to be certain that physical, economic, and cultural resources are available to fit the needs of the older victim.

In addition, more community resources need to be developed to support families as effective caregivers or to be alternatives to the family. In the June 1980 congressional hearings on the abuse of the elderly, it was recommended that tax credits be given to families who care for persons over age 65 and that legislation be passed to expand home health care under Medicare.[28]

Recent research on the effects of social supports on reducing health and mental health problems points to the importance of deliberately building supports to mitigate stresses on families and thereby reduce the likelihood of abuse.[29] Effective network-building efforts, such as intergenerational family groups, mother-daughter groups, and support groups for families caring for a chronically ill person, could be implemented with high-risk families. Practitioners need to be sensitive to existing informal natural helping networks and to identify strategies for building on these networks as a means of reducing stress in caregivers.

Another way to reduce the risk of familial abuse is to educate families on how to be effective caregivers. Although the media and numerous handbooks advise parents about what to expect in caring for children, no such information is provided to adult children caring for elderly parents. Children's attitudes toward aging and their parents' health appear to be the most significant factors in determining the affective quality of their relationships.[30] Adult children's negative attitudes may be derived, in part, from their limited knowledge of the "normal" dependences of aging. Families need to be educated about the older person's coping abilities to prevent misunderstanding of behavior or conflicts in the relationship. Information on aging and adult development could be provided as a component of family life education; such information could be dealt with as a preventive strategy and as a means of intervention.

Most families have no opportunity to "rehearse" the caregiver role; they may hold unrealistic expectations for themselves and their parent and therefore increase the stresses they experience. They need information about community support services—where to turn when they reach the "tipping point"—and how to handle the stresses created by an older person's dependence on them. Training programs especially need to convey to families that they are not alone or forgotten in their caregiving efforts. Perhaps an organization comparable to "Parents Anonymous" is needed, where adult children can receive the message that they are doing the best they can with what they have.

When strategies to prevent sexual violence to an older woman fail and she becomes a victim, service providers need to be aware of the special problems she may experience. Since research is limited, the suggestions outlined are not intended to be definitive, but to serve as a minimal checklist or trigger to the sensitivity of service providers. A critical problem facing the older victim lies in the lack of communication between providers of services delivered through the aging network, the law enforcement and criminal justice systems, and the rape prevention and crisis intervention systems. Service providers in these systems are not accustomed to working with older victims of sexual assault, in part because of underreporting and the relatively low incidence of sexual assault of older women.

The initial problem may be the lack of access to service providers. The older victim may lack experience and information about how to enter the service delivery system. Although the police are likely to be more accessible than other service providers because they are familiar to most people, law enforcement may be the most threatening system for the older woman to enter. Despite concern by some law enforcement agencies and individuals, the predominately male and necessarily formal law enforcement agency presents both logistical and psychological barriers to the older victim, as well as to the younger victim. Some of the reasons identified earlier for possible underreporting address these issues directly.

Lack of information about available services and the perceived formality of the service systems also pertain to other service providers. In fact, barriers to access affect many older people in need of any kind of service: the lack of transportation, physical barriers, and different cultural and social values from the predominately younger service providers and clientele of the relevant systems. This last issue may be especially significant for social workers who staff rape crisis and victim assistance programs.

The older victim of sexual violence may experience considerable difficulty in the feminist and youth-oriented environment of many rape crisis programs. Service providers in these programs need to be particularly sensitive to the possibility that the older woman's first exposure to a different political and sociocultural perspective may come shortly after her physical and psychological devastation and thus may be even more threatening and alien than would otherwise be the case. As noted earlier, the older victim's primary socialization occurred when women were blamed for becoming the target of rape or other types of sexual assault. Helping the older victim to identify feelings of guilt or responsibility and to begin to recognize sexual assault as a crime of violence for which the victim is not to be blamed may be a critical early issue for the counselor.

It is also important to recognize, as was stated earlier, that sexual assault in older women may come after an extended period of involuntary sexual inactivity. Service providers must be sensitive to society's devaluation of the sexuality of older women, which renders sexual assault an even more difficult issue. The same stereotype that underlies a service provider's response of "Who would rape an old woman?" and the less obvious discounting of her sexuality often results in the failure of service providers to recognize the complexity of the sexual as well as physical trauma older victims are experiencing.

The older woman may be unfamiliar and uncomfortable with the language used to describe the behavior of the attacker. Even more than the language, the embarrassment and humiliation of participating, however unwillingly, in sexual activities she considers taboo make it difficult to talk about the attack. This discomfort hampers her physiological and psychological treatment and may influence her decision not to seek prosecution because she may feel publicly humiliated when giving testimony. These issues represent some of the long-term challenges to service providers assisting the older woman to repair her psychological damage.

Service providers should also become involved in various immediate practical concerns for elderly victims of assault. The first concern is to obtain adequate medical care. In addition to undergoing the physical examinations that are essential for her health and well-being, the victim needs to maintain the options of developing a good case, should she decide to prosecute. In some situations, the service provider must be prepared to overcome the resistance of the victim's physician, especially the elderly physician who may actively discourage the older client from seeking outside assistance. The second concern is the replacement, repair, and reporting of lost or stolen goods. For many older women on low fixed incomes, the loss of even a small portion of their funds or a temporary absence from their residence could easily result in losing their apartment (or less often, their home). Arrangements with the landlord, family, or neighbors need to be made to ensure that the older woman maintains her option of staying in or returning to her residence. The third concern is to obtain help with routine personal care and housekeeping tasks for those older women who are already physically debilitated yet have managed to live independently. Care of pets and plants may seem insignificant under the circumstances, but pets or plants may be a source of affection and provide a feeling of security, especially if a stay in the hospital or a shelter is necessary. The fourth concern is to get emergency funds, if necessary, to tide the victim over. For example, if a social security check was stolen during the crime, the victim will need a strong advocate to negotiate the system to get the speediest possible response.

CONCLUSION

A critical task for the service provider who is working with an elderly victim is to establish links between the available systems to obtain necessary services. Various types of assistance exist throughout the aging network of which the rape crisis worker or family counselor may be unaware; similarly, service providers in the aging network may be unfamiliar with services of the crisis intervention, law enforcement, and criminal justice systems. A mutual educational effort among these providers would enhance the quantity and quality of services provided to older victims of violence.

Finally, the general community needs to be made more aware that violence against older women is more than a rare isolated occurrence. An aware public may be more able to detect and report abuse and assault and be more sensitive to providing support to family caregivers and informal social networks. Any community education efforts should be directed toward the elimination of underlying ageist attitudes that may perpetuate violence against older women.

REFERENCES

1. Richard J. Gelles, *Family Violence* (Beverly Hills, Calif.: Sage Publications, 1979); and Suzanne K. Steinmetz and Murray A. Straus, eds., *Violence in the Family* (New York: Harper & Row, 1974).

2. *See* Marilyn R. Block and Jan D. Sinnott, eds., *The Battered Elderly Syndrome* (College Park, Md.: Center on Aging, University of Maryland, 1979); Elizabeth Lau and Jordan Kosberg, "Abuse of the Elderly by Informal Care Providers: Practice and Research Issues," paper presented at the Thirty-first Annual Meeting, Gerontological Society, Dallas, Texas, 1979; and Eloise Rathbone-McCuan and Barbara Voyles, "Case Detection Issues for Abused Elderly Parents," paper presented at the Central States Regional Conference, American Public Welfare Association, St. Louis, Mo., April 15–18, 1980.

3. Rathbone-McCuan and Voyles, op. cit.

4. Lau and Kosberg, op. cit.

5. *Elder Abuse in Massachusetts: A Survey of Professionals and Paraprofessionals* (Boston: Massachusetts Legal Research Services for the Elderly, 1979).

6. *See* Block and Sinnott, op. cit.; Nancy Hooyman, "Familial Abuse of the Elderly in Seattle," unpublished manuscript, University of Washington, 1980; Richard Douglas, "A Study of Neglect and Abuse of the Elderly in Michigan," paper presented at the Thirty-second Annual Meeting, Gerontological Society, Washington, D.C., November 1979; and Douglas, Tom Hickey, and C. Noel, *A Study of Maltreatment of the Elderly and Other Vulnerable Adults* (Ann Arbor: Institute on Gerontology, University of Michigan, 1979).

7. Lau and Kosberg, op. cit.; *Elder Abuse in Massachusetts*; Block and Sinnott, op. cit.; Eloise Rathbone-McCuan, "Intergenerational Family Violence and Neglect," paper presented at the Nineteenth International Congress of Gerontology, Tokyo, Japan, August 1978; and Hooyman, op. cit.

8. Lau and Kosberg, op. cit.; *Elder Abuse in Massachusetts*; Block and Sinnott, op. cit.; Jean Renvoize, *Web of Violence: A Study of Family Violence* (London, England: Routledge & Kegan Paul, 1978); Rathbone-McCuan, op. cit.; and Hooyman, op. cit.

9. Richard J. Gelles, "Why Do They Stay?" *Journal of Marriage and the Family*, 38 (November 1976), pp. 659–668; Renvoize, op. cit.; and *Elder Abuse in Massachusetts.*

10. Renvoize, op. cit.

11. *Elder Abuse in Massachusetts;* and Hooyman, op. cit.

12. Hooyman, op. cit. *See also* Tom Hickey, "Neglect and Abuse of the Elderly: Implications of a Development Model for Research and Intervention. Paper presented at the Thirty-second Annual Meeting, Gerontological Society, Washington, D.C., November 1979.

13. Hickey, op. cit.

14. James Garbarino, "The Human Ecology of Child Maltreatment," *Journal of Marriage and the Family*, 39 (November 1977), pp. 721–735.

15. *See*, for example, George Antunes, "Patterns of Personal Crime Against the Elderly: Findings from a National Survey," *Gerontologist*, 19 (August 1977), pp. 321–327; Jack Goldsmith and Sharon Goldsmith, eds., *Crime and the Elderly: Challenge and Response* (Lexington, Mass.: D. C. Heath, 1976); and R. J. Smith, *Crime against the Elderly: Implications for Policymakers and Practitioners* (Washington, D.C.: International Federation on Aging, 1979).

16. *See* Linda Davis and Elaine Brody, *Rape and Older Women: A Guide to Prevention and Protection* (Washington, D.C.: U.S. Department of Health, Education & Welfare, 1979); Norma Feinberg, "The Researcher as a Volunteer Advocate: Crisis Counseling for Elderly Victims of Violent Crimes," *Volunteer Administration*, 12 (Summer 1979), pp. 21–27; Feinberg, "The Emotional and Behavioral Consequences of Violent Crime on Elderly Victims," *Dissertation Abstracts International*, 38 (June 1978), p. 7562; Patricia Fletcher, "Criminal Victimization of Elderly Women: A Look at Sexual Assault" (Syracuse, N.Y.: Rape Crisis Center of Syracuse, 1977) (mimeographed); and A. Nicholas Groth, "The Older Rape Victim and Her Assailant," *Journal of Geriatric Psychiatry*, 11 (Fall 1978), pp. 203–215.

17. *See* Law Enforcement Assistance Administration, *Criminal Victimization Surveys in Thirteen American Cities* (Washington, D.C.: U.S. Government Printing Office, 1975); and Fletcher, op. cit.

18. Personal communication from Chelanne Brown, Spokane Rape Crisis Network, Spokane, Washington, 1980.

19. *See* David Shichor, "Criminal Behavior among the Elderly," *Gerontologist*, 18 (April 1978), pp. 213–218; U.S. House of Representatives, Select Committee on Aging, *In Search of Security: A National Perspective on Elderly Criminal Victimization* and *Crime Against the Elderly*, hearings before the Subcommittee on Federal, State, and Community Services, 94th Cong., 2d Sess., and *Elderly Crime Victimization (Crime Prevention Program)*, hearings before the Subcommittee on Housing and Consumer Interests, 94th Cong., 2d Sess. (Washington, D.C.: U.S. Government Printing Office, 1977, 1977, and 1976, respectively); Groth, op. cit.; and Paul Hahn, *Crimes against the Elderly: A Study in Victimology* (Santa Cruz, Calif.: Davis Publishing Co., 1976).

20. Smith, op. cit.

21. Davis and Brody, op. cit.; Groth, op. cit.

22. Renvoize, op. cit.; Hooyman, op. cit.

23. Hooyman, op. cit.

24. Rathbone-McCuan and Voyles, op. cit.

25. Davis and Brody, op. cit.

26. *See* Block and Sinnott, op. cit.; Douglas, op. cit.; and House of Representatives, Select Committee on Aging, *Domestic Violence Against the Elderly*, hearings before the Subcommittee on Human Services, 96th Cong., April 21, 1980 (Washington, D.C.: U.S. Government Printing Office, 1980), p. 66.

27. Alida G. Silverman, Beatrice H. Kahn, and Gary Anderson, "A Model for Working with Multigenerational Families," *Social Casework*, 58 (March 1977), pp. 131–135; and Morton Bard and Joseph Zacker, "The Prevention of Family Violence: Dilemmas of Community Intervention," *Journal of Marriage and the Family*, 33 (November 1971), pp. 677–682.

28. *See* House of Representatives, Select Committee on Aging, *Domestic Violence Against the Elderly*, p. 67.

29. Marc Pilisuk and Meredith Minkler, "Supportive Networks: Life Ties for the Elderly." Unpublished manuscript, University of California at Davis, undated.

30. Elizabeth Johnson and Barbara Bursk, "Relationships between the Elderly and Their Adult Children," *Gerontologist*, 17 (February 1977), p. 28.

2
Dual Oppression and Power

BLACK WOMEN: THE RESILIENT VICTIMS

Barbara W. White

The black woman has been the least understood person in the history of this country. In spite of her many visible roles—as mother, wife, daughter, maid, co-worker, friend, client, supervisor, lover, or companion—her true identity and plight often have been obscured or ignored. The black woman is referred to alternately as the stabilizer and collective oppressor of her race. One recurring attributed quality is her resilience, her braving of seemingly insurmountable odds to survive. This accomplishment is not to be disparaged, particularly in light of the tremendous obstacles she has had to overcome.

But what is often overlooked in this depiction is this: What has been the cost of her survival? And is mere survival enough in this land of proved opportunities? Oppression through racism and sexism continues to create paradoxes in coping and liberating factors in the lives of black women.

The social work profession has an obligation to assist in struggles against racism, sexism, and oppression. Therefore, any attempt to provide help to victimized individuals, groups, or communities should be preceded by the elimination of ethnocentric attitudes and a willingness to accept a broader sociopsychological understanding of the multiple social realities. If one agrees with Gilbert that social work is an oppressive profession, then a framework for practice with already oppressed people will have to be sought if social work intervention is to have the maximum impact.[1]

Black women cannot be treated as an undifferentiated mass. Much diversity exists in their economic status, family structures, occupational pursuits, life-styles, and politics. Yet a binding tie exists: a relatively cohesive structure that developed in response to oppression, racism, and patterned repression.

The purpose of this article is to explore some of the racial and cultural influences that shape the black woman in an attempt to understand her complexities and priorities. Social workers must avoid being tempted by the attitudes that either the issues related to blacks are no longer newsworthy or that sufficient opportunities for amelioration already have been provided. Until the last vestiges of oppression have been removed, there can be no avoidance of this still-unresolved American problem. As Dreyfuss put it:

> The greatest irony is that for all the economic and political progress we have made, we are ignored and held in greater disdain than ever before. . . . The renewed efforts to degrade us, to write us out of our own history, to pretend that we are just like everyone else, serve as perverse indicators of the progress we have made. . . . As we progress, we can expect more, not less, resistance.[2]

EFFECTS OF SLAVERY

The once-unrevealed horrors of black women's experiences during slavery have now been amply documented.[3] Most writers on the subject agree that, during slavery, black women's lives were characterized by pain, exploitation, and separation. They disagree, though, about the effects of slavery on family life and the mutual support systems of blacks.[4] However, it is generally accepted that slavery created—for the black family and especially for the black woman— the need to adapt to the social structure for survival. Wallace stated that the plight of the black woman was more severe than that of the black man because the black woman accepted the traditional female role in addition to daily "slave labors."[5]

Moreover, because, during slavery, black men were more often sold away from their families than were black women, black women had to become the mainstay of their family if the black family was to survive. As Ladner pointed out in her provocative study, today, many black women cope in the same way as their slave ancestors by maintaining a strong attachment to their children and strong ties to their extended family. In addition, since emancipation, black women have been forced to assume the primary economic support of their family as a result of barriers preventing the economic mobility of black men. Thus, the current situation has the same etiology as slavery, namely, estrangement from society as a result of racism.[6]

The myths perpetuated by these activities for survival produced, if nothing else, many opportunities for writers to repudiate or expand on the idea that the black woman either was the "rock of Gibraltar" or a "black castrating bitch." Such exercises in defining who black women are have persisted since Reconstruction, and the debate continues today. Either way, the black woman lost. Society would not allow her to behave like her white sister in the prescribed female role, nor could she continue to do what was necessary to protect her family without feeling guilty because of the indictment of her efforts.

The situation of the enigmatic black woman was most perceptible during the era of the civil rights movement. If denigration of black women was a deliberate ideological weapon intended to reduce resistance from a "disruptive force" (which many considered the black movement to be), then for a period it produced the desired outcome. The proliferation and acceptance of the myths of a detrimental black matriarchy took hold, and the notion of male supremacy was emphasized. One of the greatest strengths of the black movement—the black woman—receded into the shadows.

A symptom of this phenomenon occurred a few years ago when a group of educated middle-income black women met to organize a chapter of a national organization of black women. The goal of the organization was to support political communication and involvement in the black community. Several women objected to the proposal that the organization should advocate placement of black women in top-level jobs; they thought that the purpose should be to push black men, who need this kind of help more than do black women. Not one woman in the group disagreed. It was as if they would have been resurrecting the myth of the black matriarchy had they said "but that's not necessarily true." Thus the effects of this issue on the lives of upwardly mobile black women were not discussed, and the constraints against discussion demonstrated the sensitive nature of the topic.

Since emancipation, black women have continued to struggle for economic survival, for the overcoming of powerlessness, for gaining control over their lives. As Sizemore noted, black women are on the lowest scale of the achievement ladder (using the indicators of income levels, employment opportunities, and career mobility) consistent with their placement on society's ascription continuum. That is, with no resources, they have no power or authority that has been legitimated and hence lack control or the ability to rule.[7] For all black women, the choice is not between being strong or weak. It is between being one's own person or allowing others to define and denigrate one.

CURRENT PROBLEMS

Although the black woman has suffered personal and historical indignities, nothing intrinsic in her character requires her to suffer. Her perceptions of the world come from being black and female. It is from this dualism that she attempts to deal with her existence.

Recent literature has begun to examine some of the issues that affect the black woman as a consequence of racism and sexism. In providing services to black women, it is important to be aware that the nature of black women's problems may differ, depending on their socioeconomic status, family structure, age, and marital or relationship status. Because of the dearth of literature on middle-income blacks, it may be erroneous to apply monolithic generalizations to a particular black woman.

Helms noted an apparent lack of interest by counseling-related services in black women and suggested as a possible cause the practitioners' unconscious attempts to protect themselves from the women's despair and anger and their own fears of failure.[8] And black women themselves have not as yet expressed concern for their psychological well-being, as have other women in this country. Rather than seeking an identity for themselves as individuals, some black women feel that their responsibility is to black people in total more than to any individual entity such as themselves, their men, their children, or their families. Further, since the only workable solutions for black women must come from themselves, it is to themselves that they must look for answers.

Whichever direction they choose to follow, black women—the resilient victims—cry out for relief. Survival cannot continue to be the impetus for psychological liberation and sociological growth. Laws and Stricklin stated that black women's preoccupation with survival as an adjustment mechanism rather than as a liberating force has created a fear syndrome that paralyzes them and perpetuates the condition of external social control as opposed to internal or self-control.[9] However, Hall noted that internal control and self-determination are among the social patterns of black people.[10] In his delineation of the strengths of black families, Hill reversed some of the negativism associated with survival strategies and emphasized the possible results of a collective existence, such as strong kinship bonds; work, achievement, and religious orientations; and flexible family roles.

Myers suggested that black women have learned to cope with oppression and maintain self-esteem through social interaction with other black women whose views are similar and by discarding the reference group that society assumes for them (white women).[11] The primary role model for black women is the black mother, who transmits knowledge, skills, and information from generation to generation. This process, which is necessary for enhancing self-esteem and setting goals, is different from and more crucial than the socialization responsibilities of white mothers. It is essential because black mothers, in addition to performing the traditional parenting functions, must also prepare their children for life in a racist society.

One result of external control may be the increase in suicide by black women. In the past twenty years, the suicide rate among black women has increased more than 80 percent—an increase that is higher than that of white men, white women, and black men. Although researchers disagree about the specific causes of the increase in suicides, they agree that anger, hopelessness, and isolation play an underlying role.[12]

Poor black women are especially concerned about problems such as mental illness, drug addiction, and other maladies that affect those who are deprived of the quality of life that comes with economic independence. Women who turn to antisocial behaviors are too often incarcerated for survival-related "crimes," such as writing bad checks or prostitution. The women's movement has had little impact on the problems of this group because most of the movement's concerns have been geared to the interests of middle-class women.[13]

WOMEN'S MOVEMENT

The role of black women in the women's movement has provoked a great deal of debate in the last decade and continues to be a controversial social issue among blacks. A recent study conducted among blacks reflected the ambiguity of this issue.[14] In the survey, 60.5 percent of the two thousand respondents thought that the women's movement was not significant for black women. In response to the question "Should Black women participate in the Movement?" 54.9 percent said yes. Slightly more men (55.9 percent) than women (53.0 percent) held this view. These results indicate the ambivalence among blacks about the women's movement, with black women showing even more diversity in their views than black men.[15] The contradictory results may also reflect the views of some black women that the women's movement, although not significant for them now, may become so through their involvement.

When asked about racial issues, 71.8 percent of the respondents thought that racism is still as prevalent as it was a decade ago. The researchers saw a correlation between skepticism about the women's movement and the belief that racial discrimination is a more critical obstacle to the progress of black people than is sex discrimination. The respondents viewed racism as widespread and practiced without regard to income, age, sex, or location.

In spite of the recognition that sexism is a problem for black women, the prevailing view of black women is that the liberation of black women can wait. Because black women think that the women's movement is antimale, it is not surprising that they are reluctant to obtain their rights by participating in a movement they perceive to be detrimental to black men and thus would aggravate the male-female antagonisms that already exist as a result of a multiplicity of forces.[16]

Furthermore, because they consider the movement to be dominated by white middle-class women, black women are understandably skeptical about calling themselves "sisters" of those whose problems seem miniscule in comparison and who bore the offspring of the oppressors of black men, women, and children. Beckett gave an example of the different views of black women and white women. She noted that although both black women and white women may express anger about discrimination in the labor market, there is a difference in whom they view as the oppressor. White women see the white man as their oppressor, while black women perceive the white race as the oppressor.[17]

Yet the fact remains that black women are not exempt from social and material exploitation and domination and that both black women and white women are struggling to change their social, political, and economic status. Research shows that black women have a strong commitment to work regardless of their career aspirations, but nearly two-thirds of black women workers are in the lowest paid service occupations, usually domestic service. Black women suffer the grossest wage and job discrimination of any group in society. And more black women than white women are listed as single heads of households.[18] When black women compare their situation to the overall standard of living of whites, they find abundant evidence of the oppression of black women. If white women are experiencing rocky waters, black women have already been shipwrecked!

The fear that only white women's gains have been or will be recorded as a result of the women's movement is shared by a number of black women and has prevented any large-scale coalition between black and white women. Thus if any political coalescence of black and white women is to occur, then changes must take place in both groups. Black women must be allowed the right and must fight to assert their identity and establish their priorities in the struggle to eradicate sexism. And if they are middle class, they must come to recognize that in spite of their social mobility, the victimization of all black women will not end until poor black women are rescued. Perhaps this period of self-examination and revitalization will bring about the "emotional rescue" that is needed to remove the distortions of history.

White women must recognize the similarities and differences between black women and themselves and appreciate that the courage of black women may have inspired and aroused them to seek freedom from the sexist restrictions on their lives. They must be willing to reject the myths and stereotypes of black women and work with diligence and commitment against the racism endemic in our society. White women should not attempt to speak for black women, but should listen to what black women have to say about their unique status in this country. This does not imply that white women should not continue to fight for their own needs, but they must take note that their attitudes, behaviors, and actions in relation to the struggle of black women will determine whether an alliance can be maintained. If they fight vehemently against sexism because of self-interest but continue to share the racial prejudices of white men, then they defeat their own goal to end discrimination.

ROLE OF SOCIAL WORK

A black female social work student expressed the following sentiments during a conference in which racism in the human services was a topic:

> To pass on to the white power structure that information and knowledge [about blacks] once again decimates our own attempt to get our own people to have more status. It seems as if we share too much, they always win. They come with credentials and they absorb all that you give them and they say, "I am ready for you."[19]

Part of the mistrust underlying that statement emanates from past experiences of black social workers who assumed that education and logic would make a difference in erasing racist attitudes, behaviors, and politics and found that they did not.

The National Association of Social Workers, having emphasized its humanitarian regard for those who are oppressed on the basis of race and sex, is committed to work for the elimination of discrimination. At the 1979 Delegate Assembly, at which a revised policy statement on racism was presented, some social workers did not accept the emphasis being given to "special" categories of people. Although the policy statement was accepted with no obvious dissent, the point was made, at least in this author's opinion, that some professionals still rejected the validity and priority of this issue. As Pettit reported, the attitude of individual social workers in regard to blacks has too often been to maintain that there are no differences (outside of a few biological and cultural factors) and that an insistence on differences implies racism, while other social workers exhibit "tender condescension."[20]

Many of the experiences blacks and other minorities have had with white social workers have led them to conclude that the social work profession cannot meet the challenges.[21] This conclusion is also based on the view that methods other than those of social work are more appropriate to the cause of black people.

As efforts are made to make social work more responsible to the needs of minority groups, the dissemination of new and modified models of practice will offer practitioners valuable frameworks for the design and provision of services. But how much information is adequate support for those whites in the profession who either refuse to or cannot confront their biases and covert acceptance of racist attitudes? Their guilt must be tremendous, especially when they are members of a profession in which any display of these tendencies is taboo. How does one counteract the mounting trend in the profession toward focusing only on the psychopathology of human problems when the situation of minority persons requires additional strategies to overcome powerlessness?[22]

Models that have been introduced for social work practice with black clients take into account the significance of the black experience.[23] To apply these models to meet the specific needs of black women, social workers will need to pay attention to the existing strengths and positive mental health adaptations of black women. These adaptations serve to maintain self-esteem despite oppression and negative valuations by society. As Galper noted:

> The realities of lack of confidence in oneself, depression, anger, underdeveloped capacities, and isolated lives, and the need for these issues to be confronted in the lives of each woman who experiences them are not denied. At the same time, the larger structure of women in the United States . . . is becoming clear.[24]

Galper went on to discuss what he referred to as "radical casework," which promotes an understanding not only of the individual's psychological self, but of the individual's relationship to the fundamental historical and political processes. The relevance of this approach to the factors discussed in this article is obvious. However, because Galper used the term "radical," some social workers will reject the idea, despite its potent justification. The author does not mean that the idea should be imposed on unwilling social workers, but if the goal of social workers is to help black women to the maximum extent possible, then social workers must strive for mutual perceptions of problem-solving strategies that take into the account the needs of black women.

The process has already begun to reshape the understanding of basic social work principles and values. We social workers know that the history and politics of being black and female in contemporary society must be recognized and appreciated if social workers are to understand and provide effective services to black women. The tendency to undervalue these factors must be corrected along with the tendency to overemphasize ethnic factors to the exclusion of individual problems and solutions.

We social workers are learning that if we are to provide services from a cultural perspective, modifications have to be made in the various theories that support our practice. The efficacy of the various approaches will depend on the ability of social workers to adapt and be flexible. Finally, we are discovering that, as social workers, we need to rededicate ourselves to some basic principles of our profession: open communication, empathy, nonjudgmental attitudes, and the ability to identify with the goals of the oppressed. Armed with these principles, our knowledge, and our skills, we should be able to help each other gain the dignity not only to endure—but to prevail.

REFERENCES

1. Gwendolyn C. Gilbert, "The Role of Social Work in Black Liberation," *Black Scholar*, 6 (December 1974), pp. 16-23. The "oppressive" description is applied based on the perceptions by groups of people who view social workers as advocates of the status quo and welfare colonialism and agents of control.

2. Joel Dreyfuss, "A Self Portrait," *Black Enterprise*, 11 (August 1980), p. 49.

3. *See* Angela Davis, "Reflections on the Black Woman's Role in the Community of Slaves," *Black Scholar*, 3 (December 1971), pp. 2-15; Michele Wallace, *Black Macho and the Myth of the Superwoman* (New York: Dial Press, 1979); Herbert Gutman, *The Black Family in Slavery and Freedom* (New York: Random House, 1977).

4. Stanley Elkins, "Slavery and Personality," in *Slavery: A Problem in American Institutional and Intellectual Life* (Chicago: University of Chicago Press, 1959), pp. 81-139. Elkins posits that the effects of slavery were so pervasive as to disintegrate black family life, while Gutman, op. cit., maintains that the value of family life prevailed and was one of the few refuges available to black women and men.

5. Wallace, op. cit., p. 140.

6. Joyce Ladner, *Tomorrow's Tomorrow: The Black Woman* (New York: Doubleday Anchor Books, 1972), pp. 36–37.

7. Barbara A. Sizemore, "Sexism and the Black Male," *Black Scholar*, 1 (March-April, 1973), p. 6.

8. Janet E. Helms, "Principles for Counseling Specific Subgroups of Women," *Counseling Psychologist*, 8 (1979), pp. 40–41.

9. Janice Laws and Joyce Striklin, "Black Mothers and Daughters," *Black Books Bulletin* (Summer 1979), pp. 26–33.

10. Robert Hill, *The Strengths of the Black Family* (New York: Emerson Hall Publishers, 1971).

11. Lena Wright Myers, "Black Women: Selectivity Among Roles and Reference Groups in the Maintenance of Self Esteem," *Journal of Social and Behavioral Sciences*, 21 (Winter 1975), pp. 39–46.

12. Jack Slater, "Suicide: A Growing Menace to Black Women," *Ebony* (September 1973), pp. 152–160.

13. Joyce Ladner, "Black Women in Poverty," *Journal of Social and Behavioral Sciences*, 20 (Spring 1974), pp. 41–50.

14. "Black Americans Speak Out on Leadership, Economics, Race," *Black Enterprise*, 11 (August 1980), pp. 86–88.

15. Ibid., p. 86.

16. Wallace, op. cit.

17. Joyce O. Beckett, "Working Wives: A Racial Comparison," *Social Work*, 21 (November 1976), pp. 463–471.

18. U.S. Bureau of the Census, "Social and Economic Status of the Black Population of the United States: An Historical View, 1790–1978," *Current Population Reports*, Series P-23, No. 80 (Washington, D.C.: U.S. Government Printing Office, 1979).

19. Spoken by Kay Stawder, MSW student, State University of New York at Stony Brook, and a member of the Task Force on "Social Forces and Cultural Factors in Community Mental Health Training." Proceedings of the Community Mental Health Conference are reported in Israel Zwerling, MD, et al., eds., *Racism, Elitism, Professionalism: Barriers to Community Mental Health* (New York: Jason Aronson, 1976), p. 55.

20. Lois Pettit, "Some Observations on the Negro Culture in the United States," in James A. Goodman, ed., *Dynamics of Racism in Social Work Practice* (Washington, D.C.: National Association of Social Workers, 1973), p. 5. "Tender condescension" is most often characterized by giving exaggerated praise or reacting to blacks in a patronizing or paternalistic manner.

21. Gilbert, op. cit., pp. 22–23.

22. Carol H. Meyer, "Social Work Purpose: Status by Choice or Coercion?" *Social Work*, 26 (January 1981), pp. 69–75.

23. Darielle L. Jones, "African-American Clients: Clinical Practice Issues," *Social Work*, 24 (March 1979), pp. 112–118. *See also* Harriet P. Trader, "Survival Strategies for Oppressed Minorities," *Social Work*, 22 (January 1977), pp. 10–13; and Gilbert, op. cit.

24. Jeffrey H. Galper, *The Politics of Social Services* (Englewood Cliffs, N.J.: Prentice-Hall, 1975), p. 210.

ASIAN-AMERICAN WOMEN: A HISTORICAL AND CULTURAL PERSPECTIVE

Angela Shen Ryan

With the influx into this country of hundreds of thousands of refugees from Indochina and the growing immigration of Asians from other countries, the social work profession is and increasingly will be faced with social issues related to Asian Americans. In particular, programs of outreach and service delivery must be developed for Asian-American women, whose needs and concerns have been neglected and dismissed for too long.

It has generally been assumed that Asian Americans have few social problems. Stereotypes depict Asian Americans as hard-working solid citizens, members of close-knit families that provide sufficient resources, and persons highly successful in education, occupation, and economic and social mobility. Asian-American women are seen either as "sexpots" who cater to men or as passive, docile, and accommodating women who are efficient and hard-working secretaries, domestics, or housekeepers.

A review of the literature discloses little about Asian-American women; in fact, data are virtually nonexistent. This lack of materials seems to confirm the stereotype that Asian Americans have no problems. However, this author's experience in finding adoptive homes for Chinese and Korean children and the survey of the social service and mental health needs of Asian Americans in New York City suggest that Asian-American women are not free of difficulties; rather, their problems have not been adequately studied and documented.[1]

The rate of utilization of public and private social services and health and mental health facilities by Asian Americans is generally lower than that of other populations. Studies suggest that Asian-American men and women are unresponsive to conventional social service programs.[2] Among the barriers are the lack of bilingual and bicultural personnel, the stigmatizing of problems, cultural barriers, and a distrust of formal institutions.

This article describes the experiences of Asian-American women, their cultural background, and their social and psychological needs. It also proposes preventive and interventive strategies to improve the quality of life of Asian-American women.

HISTORICAL PERSPECTIVE

Asian Americans come from many different ethnic and cultural groups. They are Chinese, Japanese, Koreans, Filipinos, Cambodians, Thais, Vietnamese, Hawaiians, and Samoans. They may come from urban or rural areas and may be displaced refugees or immigrants. Each ethnic group has its own problems and needs. Each group has its distinct culture, way of life, and values and attitudes. And each has its own social norms for the role of women. The differences must be recognized, but there are, nevertheless, certain salient points in common.

The first Asian women in the United States were Chinese, who came in the 1850s as part of the large influx of Chinese laborers to the West Coast. However, with the Chinese Exclusion Act of 1882 and the Immigration Law of 1924, laborers and their wives were denied entrance to this country. Chinese women were not again permitted to enter this country legally until 1943, when the act was repealed. The "war brides" act of 1947 also helped promote family unity and equalize the sex ratio in the Chinese-American population. The quota was so small, however, that few Chinese women were able to immigrate as permanent residents. Thus, the elderly generations have more men than women. The majority of Chinese women in this country today are refugees from Hong Kong and Taiwan who immigrated since the Immigration Act of 1965.

The immigration history of Japanese women is similar to that of Chinese women; men came first and in greater numbers than women. Starting in the early 1900s, Japanese women were able to enter the country because male immigrants were allowed to bring their wives. Because Japanese women were able to accompany their husbands and thus form family units, there are more females in the elderly Japanese population than in the Chinese population. According to census figures, there were 985 females out of a total Japanese population of 24,326 in 1900 and 22,193 women out of a total Japanese population of 111,010 in 1920.[3]

Other women of Asian ancestry have had a similar immigration history. Men immigrated first and in greater numbers than women. Therefore, today Asian-American women are mostly new immigrants. In some ethnic groups—the Chinese, Koreans, and refugees from Indochina—most of the women are non-English speaking.

The Chinese and Japanese women who immigrated to the United States in the nineteenth century did not lead an easy life. They were faced with the economic struggle for survival in a strange, hostile country. Aside from a few Chinese women entering this country to work in the mining areas during the early years of the Gold Rush, Chinese-American women were employed chiefly as prostitutes because of the highly disproportionate number of Chinese men to Chinese women and because women of other races were inaccessible to Chinese men. The women were often obtained through devious methods. Many were lured to this country by false promises of marriage to a Chinese sojourner, some were sold into slavery in China, and others were kidnapped from their homes in China.

Later, with hard work, some Chinese men were able to accumulate enough money to establish small businesses. Some went back to China to bring their wives to California. Some prostitutes, able to make good money at the time, used their ingenuity and initiative to become madams or to operate small businesses.

Also during the 1800s, a number of Chinese girls were sold into slavery in China to work as domestics for white families on the West Coast. There is no evidence of a similar trade in boys, primarily because girls were sacrificed for the survival of the family more often than boys. Moreover, the owner (white or Chinese) of a girl domestic could sell the girl when she came of age; thus the owner could benefit not only from her wages as a servant but also from her sale as a commodity. In general, the Chinese-American woman's social and economic life during the nineteenth century was characterized by racial antagonism, sexual oppression, and class exploitation.[4]

CULTURAL VALUES

Then as now, the traditional values of the Asian cultures were based primarily on the Buddhist, Taoist, and Confucian systems of ethics. These ethics, while providing the society with a social structure and a strong set of moral values, fostered great injustices against women.[5] Guided by patrilineal, patrilocal, and patriarchal principles, Asian society delegated women to a lower status throughout life. For example, the ancient virtue of Chinese womanhood was the "three obediences": When a woman was young and living at home, she had to obey her father; while she was married, she had to obey her husband; and when she was old and widowed, she had to obey her son.[6]

Women were considered of no value or little value. Their lives were more difficult than the men's in many ways, and sexual discrimination was rampant.[7] Women seldom received a formal education and Asian wives were expected to cater to the demands of all family members and to attend to the menial household responsibilities. This heritage continues to affect the lives of Asian immigrant women.

In the United States Asians often settle in ghettos, such as Chinatown in San Francisco, New York, and Boston or Japantown in San Francisco. The clustering typical of first-generation immigrants continues among Asians, partly because their social world is built on kinship and an extended family structure.[8]

The kinship system meets the needs of its members, particularly the women, who have a definite traditional role in it. It also performs socioeconomic, religious, and psychological functions for the members. The lives of Asian-American women continue to be patterned on Confucian teachings. Cultural values of submission, loyalty, modesty, and passivity are passed on to first-, second-, and third-generation native-born Asian-American women. Thus Asian-American women face sex-role stereotyping and racial discrimination not only in the society at large, but also in the culture of their particular ethnic group.

The socialization process prepares Asian-American women to perceive their role as inferior to that of men. Traditional values clearly dictate the role of the Asian-American woman, and her individuality is defined narrowly in terms of her role in the family. However, the older generations are more committed to the traditional values than are the younger generations, who are more influenced by values of the contemporary American culture. Thus, Asian-American women are now making the adaptation from one culture to another and are defining more appropriate roles for themselves.[9] Some have become outstanding writers, scientists, artists, and scholars.

UNIQUE PROBLEMS

The needs of Asian-American women are influenced by the historical events of their experiences in this country and the cultural values, attitudes, and practices brought by Asian immigrants, who are now the second largest group of immigrants to the United States.[10] Asian-American women are faced with the problems noted below.

Employment

In the late 1800s, owing to increased industrialization, a small number of Chinese women were able to work as seamstresses, tailors, and dressmakers. They kept house in the traditional fashion and did sewing either at home or in a factory. At that time, Chinese men outnumbered Chinese women in the sewing trade; in the twentieth century, Chinese women have taken this occupation over from men. Many writers have discussed the low wages these women receive and their exploitation by employers.[11] Today many recent immigrants from Asia are entering the sewing trade, since employment opportunities for them are limited by their lack of education, language barriers, and racial discrimination.

The 1970 Census revealed that although the labor-force-participation rate of Chinese women increased between 1960 and 1970, Chinese women still tended to be found in low-status white-collar or blue-collar jobs. The median wages for Asian-American women in 1970 were as follows: Filipino women, $3,513; Japanese women, $3,236; Hawaiian women, $2,931; Korean women, $2,741; and Chinese women, $2,686.[12] Preliminary data from the 1980 Census indicate that Asian- and Pacific-American women earn 44 cents for every dollar earned by the average white American man and that nearly half these women are semiskilled laborers.[13]

The lack of adequate education, job training, and counseling, combined with discrimination, permits these women to work only as factory workers, domestics, and seamstresses in sweatshops. Many immigrants are living at the poverty level, making great sacrifices for themselves and their children. The chances of their upward mobility seem low. Even if resources were available to these women, they could not take advantage of them because they do not speak English. Moreover, although many of these women are eligible for public assistance, they either do not know about such resources or are afraid of the red tape involved in applying for assistance, so they do not bother to apply.

When both spouses are working and the wife earns more than the husband, this creates a serious conflict in cultural values and confusion as to which role each spouse should play. As a result, marital problems have surfaced in the Asian community.

Health and Mental Health Problems

Asian Americans tend to be too embarrassed to discuss their physical and emotional problems, especially with people of another ethnic group. The old value system of "shame" and "pride" may prompt a coverup of conflicts and individual problems. Thus, cases of mental illness are apt to remain untreated until bizarre behavior is manifested. The concepts of preventive medicine and self-care have not been emphasized. When they go to a doctor, Asian Americans want to be cured rather than to be told what they can do to help themselves.

Many Asian-American women are subject to more stress than Asian-American men. In addition to being working women, they are expected to fulfill the traditional roles of women but receive little emotional support and have few emotional outlets. Therefore, in many Chinese women the stress caused by the pressures of day-to-day living, poor living conditions, and long working hours is manifested by such psychosomatic complaints as abdominal cramps, insomnia, loss of appetite, and depression.

One factor that seems to be unique to the current generation of Asian immigrants is the arrival of women married to older men whom they know barely if at all. Other women have been separated from their husbands for years because of the political upheavals in Asia.

Many immigrant women came to the United States hoping for better opportunities. What they find is poverty and congested and dilapidated housing. Many immigrant families with five to six children are living in two- or three-room apartments. In New York's Chinatown, for example, many of the houses were built at the turn of the century and may still not have indoor plumbing or heat.

Both men and women find their expectations met with frustration. Thus, one community mental health center in Los Angeles found that the cause of most emotional problems and complaints of its Chinese-American patients was their sparse hope for a better economic future, complicated by experiences of cultural isolation and alienation that they were neither prepared for nor willing to accept. The same center found that Chinese women sought outpatient services to alleviate their emotional distress more readily than did Chinese men.[14]

The study undertaken by Weisman and Shen Ryan of the health and mental health needs of Asian Americans in New York City found that mental health problems included depression, suicidal attempts, psychoses, and lesser emotional distress such as the stress of adaptation.[15] It reported a lack of available services and the underutilization of existing services.

Acculturation

Immigration itself creates stress for individuals and families. A woman coming from Asia to contemporary America undergoes both cognitive and emotional upheaval. For example, the Asian culture taught women to be humble and passive and to obey the man, but, in this country, the emphasis is on self-assertion and individualism. Faced with these changing cultural values in a society that is itself changing, Asian-American women have developed ambivalent feelings that may increase their sense of powerlessness. Their familiar role has been threatened. They feel their misery, but cannot express it in words. They are frustrated and angry because there are so few opportunities for them. The identity crisis common to all American women has created particularly severe problems for Asian-American women, since their socialization has never allowed them to be self-sufficient. They see achievement as the province of white and Asian men. Thus, "in response to this environmental influence, Asian women are psychologically conditioned to invest their energies in familial or interpersonal affairs."[16]

Many Asian-American women have left their families of origin and friends to come to this country and thus have few, if any, relatives in this country. Because of their long working hours and family responsibilities, many women have few opportunities to socialize with other women; social activities usually involve only the immediate family. They are isolated and do not know how to reach out, outside their home. Because they find it difficult to achieve a sense of communication with other women, their needs are not heard or met. Because of strong family ties and the fear of discrimination, many Asian-American women do not know how to cooperate with each other, take responsibility, or carry out plans. Despite the fact that many risked their lives to come to this country, these women need help in applying their courage to end their alienation and take advantage of opportunities to expand their social awareness and the boundary of their identity.

Needs of Special Groups

Teenage girls. In the Asian culture there is no word that corresponds to "teenager" or "adolescent." Historically, no developmental stage between childhood and adulthood was demarcated. Once the family arranged a marriage for a girl, she became an adult. In Asia, it is still common to find women marrying at a much earlier age than in this country.

Asian-American teenagers, like other American teenagers, are struggling to achieve autonomy and independence. However, the gap between generations is greater for Asian-American teenagers. Thus, Asian-American adolescent girls have to reconcile what they want for themselves and what others, such as their family, want for them. The conflict is between the inferior status accorded to women by the Asian culture and the current movement in this country toward social and economic equality of men and women.

Asian-American teenage girls are under pressure from their parents to achieve in school. Furthermore, they may never have been taught about sex. Thus, when they experience developmental problems, they find it difficult to talk to their mothers and often withdraw into themselves. Once they rebel against their parents, the parents find it difficult to understand their needs and often become bewildered.

War brides. During World War II and the Korean and Vietnam conflicts, a number of Asian women married American servicemen and came to this country with their husbands. These women, called "war brides," have special needs.[17] Often these women married only because of the economic and social conditions in their war-torn countries, and both their parents and their in-laws may have been against the marriage. They may be stigmatized by the common belief that war brides are prostitutes.

Many war brides have experienced sexual and physical abuse, and many have been deserted by their husbands. Once deserted, they have few resources because they are usually isolated from their own communities. Because they have not adapted to the American culture and their education has been limited, they find themselves restricted to menial jobs or forced to apply for public assistance to survive. The public's attitude toward them increases their feelings of stigmatization and decreases their self-esteem. Emotional depression, insecurity, feelings of isolation, and suicidal tendencies are common symptoms.

Aged women. Since the enactment of the Immigration Act of 1965, many Asian Americans are bringing their aged parents to this country. Thus the number of women over age 65 is increasing in the Asian community. Aged Asian women face the same problems as other aged people in this country: poverty, poor health, social isolation, and the imminence of death. Yet they must also adjust to changing values, a new life-style, and the challenges of established practices.[18] Because of changes in the family structure and the value system owing to assimilation and acculturation, older Asian women do not receive the respect and support they expect from their children. Many are left to live alone with feelings of disappointment and abandonment. Culturally congruent social services to meet their nutritional, housing, communication, health, and mental health needs are essential.

IMPLEMENTATION OF SERVICES

Stereotypes of sex roles in general and of Asian-American women in particular are often the major stumbling blocks to meeting the needs of Asian-American women. Social workers are not free from these cultural and sexual biases. They should put aside their personal preferences and become sensitized to the needs of Asian-American women as well as knowledgeable about their cultural backgrounds and other factors that influence their position as women. For example, an Asian-American woman may prefer the traditional sex role and be unable to understand the more liberal approaches to feminism that the social worker may espouse.

One difference between Asian-American women and women of the majority culture is that Asian-American women are in transition not only from the traditional sex role but also from their ethnic and cultural sex identity. Helping Asian-American women to define personal values based on new value systems is a complicated process that requires an appreciation of interpersonal differences. However, changes in value will have to be accompanied by both educational and economic changes. Women living at the poverty level cannot indulge in the luxury of seeking self-fulfillment as women. Their lives revolve around day-to-day problems; they have neither the time nor the energy to explore alternatives that could improve their lives. It is important for social workers to help these women enhance their quality of life by using existing governmental programs so they have better access to social and health services. Outreach programs should be developed, especially for first-generation immigrants who have little knowledge of their entitlements.

Networks of services, such as telephone hotlines and comprehensive community-based multiservice agencies, are essential. These hotlines and agencies can provide services to Asian-American women who may need help initially in the areas of day care, financial assistance, health care, vocational training, and education. Preventive services should be offered at workplaces, churches, and schools that have Asian-American students. Primary prevention programs can lower the risk among those who appear to be in greater danger of becoming dysfunctional. They can also permit effective identification and referral of women suffering from culture shock, abuse, identity crisis, and related problems. Furthermore, they can help remove the stigma attached to utilization of existing treatment-oriented services, a stigma repeatedly documented in studies of Asian Americans. Certainly, the training of bilingual workers to provide services to Asian-American women is essential because Asian Americans will go to people who know their needs and they can respond to workers who can relate on a common cultural basis. It has been demonstrated that culturally oriented bilingual workers can provide relevant services and retain Asian Americans in programs.[19]

Immigration involves not only a change in geography, but also changes in life-style, friends, customs, beliefs, and value systems. In the United States, Asian women, whose status and role were more structured in their own culture, find a culture that emphasizes individualism and freedom of choice. Unable to cope with the stress of adjusting to a new culture, they may become anxious and bewildered.

These women rarely have the opportunity to feel sad about or grieve for what they left behind because of the excitement, challenge, and expectation of their new, "prosperous" environment. However, after the excitement wears off, instead of feeling happy and satisfied, they feel ambivalent, angry, and confused. Support groups for immigrant women will help them to share common feelings and make new friends, as well as understand their new life-style and cultural values. In Asia, when someone dies, people mourn as a group. Using the same principle, support groups could help Asian-American women express their sense of loss not only of people, place, and activity, but also of ethnic identity.

Although Asian-American women have not been included in the current social service delivery system, self-help groups are beginning to spring up primarily among educated middle-class Asian-American women. Some of these women are participating in the social welfare and women's rights movements and are dedicated to the realization of social changes that are of particular concern to women. In August 1980, the first National Asian/Pacific American Women's Conference was held in Washington, D.C. As a result, plans are under way to build a country-wide network of social, educational, and political organizations, including self-help groups, to work for equity in employment and education.[20] There is a need to link self-help groups with community agencies and community leaders, which can lead to a better flow of information for Asian-American women. Members of these self-help groups, because they have pride in themselves as Asian Americans and as women, can be role models for their Asian sisters, young and old, who are struggling to overcome the inferior status ascribed to them by their cultural heritage.

Asian-American women have shown they have the ability to endure and overcome their traditional problems. With the help of the social service delivery system, perhaps the problems they still face can be made more manageable, and their capacity to achieve a dignified life in this society can be enhanced.

REFERENCES

1. Irving Weisman and Angela Shen Ryan, *New York City's Asian-Americans: Their Distribution Needs and Patterns of Service Utilization* (Chicago, Ill.: Pacific/Asian Mental Health Research Center, 1981).

2. Bok-Lim C. Kim, "An Appraisal of Korean Immigrant Service Needs," *Social Casework*, 57 (March 1976), pp. 139–148; Frederick P. Li et al., "Health Care for the Chinese Community in Boston," *American Journal of Public Health*, 62 (April 1972), p. 537; and Amy Iwasaki Mass, "Asians as Individuals: the Japanese Community," *Social Casework*, 57 (March 1976), pp. 160–164.

3. Emma Gee, "Issel: The First Women," *Civil Rights Digest*, 6 (Spring 1974), pp. 48–53.

4. Lucie Cheng Hirata, "Chinese Immigrant Women in 19th Century California," in Carol Berkin and Mary Norton, eds., *Women of America—A History* (Boston: Houghton Mifflin Co., 1979), pp. 223–244.

5. Irene Fujitomi and Diane Wong, "The New Asian-American Women," in Sue Stanley and Nathaniel Wagner, eds., *Asian Americans: Psychological Perspectives* (Ben Lomond, Calif.: Science and Behavior Books, 1973), pp. 252–263.

6. Lai Chu Tsui Christy, "Culture and Control Orientation: A Study of Internal-External Locus of Control in Chinese and American-Chinese Women," p. 21. Unpublished doctoral dissertation, University of California at Berkeley, 1977.

7. A. W. Loomis, "Chinese Women in California," *Overland Monthly*, 2 (April 1979), pp. 343–351.

8. Gloria L. Kumagai, "The Asian Woman in America," *Bridge*, 6 (Winter 1978), pp. 17–20.

9. *See*, for example, Ann Umemoto, "Crisis in the Japanese-American Family," *Asian Women* (Berkeley: University of California Press, 1971), pp. 31–34; Editorial Staff of Rodan, "Asian Women as Leaders," in Amy Tachiki et al., eds., *Roots: An Asian American Reader* (Los Angeles: Continental Graphics, 1971), p. 297; and Connie Young Yu, "Notes from an Extra in the American Moving Picture Show," in Sara Ruddick and Pamela Daniels, eds., *Working It Out* (New York: Pantheon Books, 1977), pp. 180–195.

10. Robert Pear, "Immigration Anarchy: Huddled Masses May Compel Change in Law," *New York Times*, May 25, 1980, p. E3.

11. Rocky Chin, "New York Chinatown Today: Community in Crisis," in Amy Tachiki et al., eds., *Roots: An Asian American Reader* (Los Angeles: Continental Graphics, 1971), pp. 282–295; and Anthony Tam, "The Return of the Sweat Shop," *Neighborhood*, 1 (December 1978), pp. 35–38.

12. Kumagai, op. cit.

13. "Asian-American Women: A Bid for Visibility," *New York Times*, August 18, 1980, p. B9.

14. Timothy R. Brown et al., "Mental Illness and the Role of Mental Health Facilities in Chinatown," in Sue Stanley and Nathaniel Wagner, eds., *Asian Americans: Psychological Perspectives* (Ben Lomond, Calif.: Science and Behavior Books, 1973), pp. 212–231.

15. Weisman and Shen Ryan, op. cit.

16. Yuriko Payton-Miyazaki, "Three Steps Behind and Three Steps Ahead," in *Asian Women* (Berkeley: University of California, 1971), p. 117.

17. Bok-Lim C. Kim, "Casework with Japanese and Korean Wives of Americans," *Social Casework*, 53 (May 1972), pp. 273–279.

18. Sharon M. Fujii, "Elderly Asian Americans and Use of Public Services," *Social Casework*, 57 (March 1976), pp. 202–207.

19. Tom C. Owan, "Improving Productivity in the Public Sector through Bilingual-Bicultural Staff," *Social Work Research and Abstracts*, 14 (Spring 1978), pp. 10–18.

20. *Asian/Pacific Women on the Move, First National Conference, August 15–18, 1980* (Washington D.C.: Office of Education, Women's Educational Equity Act Program, 1980).

THE CHICANA IN TRANSITION

Martha Molina Fimbres

The struggle of Chicanas for greater equality is a dual one. It is a struggle not only for personal and vocational choices in the dominant society but also for choices in the Mexican-American culture.[1] This article deals with various facets of that dual struggle and their implications for social work practice. First, the traditional ascribed roles in the Mexican-American culture are described. Next, an example is presented that illustrates shifts and changes in these roles in a multigenerational family. Then, the implications of involvement in the Chicana movement and the dynamic meaning of a Chicana's identity are examined. Finally, the implications for social work practice are discussed.

The reader will note that the terms *Mexican American* and *Chicana* are used interchangeably throughout this article to refer to American women of Mexican descent. The term *Mejicana* usually refers to a woman born in Mexico but may also be used by a Chicana. The term *Chicana* connotes a woman who is involved in a social movement and who believes in self-determination for and improving the status of Mexican-American women.

ASCRIBED ROLES

Until recently, the Chicana passively accepted the roles of daughter, mother, wife, and homemaker and the relationships these roles dictate with the men in her life, whether they be father, brother, husband, or son. The older Chicana may still find herself in such roles, but the young Chicana has been affected by the dominant culture, which is in the midst of a sex-role revolution. Although at a different pace from her Anglo counterpart, the Chicana is also changing her traditional sex roles. Since culture is dynamic, this change is inevitable.[2]

The attitudes and values of Chicanas range from traditional to feminist. In the traditional Mexican-American family, male and female roles are clearly defined. Children are socialized into the roles they will fulfill as adults. Differences in patterns of behavior between boys and girls are taught implicitly and explicitly from infancy. The boy will grow up to be a husband and father and the autocratic head of the household. He tends to be aloof and independent from the rest of the family. He is free to come and go as he pleases without explanation.[3]

The girl will be a wife and mother, completely devoted to her husband and children. Her role is that of nurturer—to serve the needs of her husband, support his actions and decisions, and take care of the home and children.[4] She is loved and respected, but her needs are considered to be secondary to those of her family.

Boys are encouaged to be free and independent at an early age. They are directed to look after and protect their sisters even after they are married and live outside the home. Girls are conditioned to remain close to the home, to be protected and guarded in their contacts with others beyond the family so their femininity and innocence will be preserved.[5] It is obvious, then, that there is a double standard for men and women in the Mexican-American culture. Thus, change in the rigidly prescribed roles of women toward greater equality and less submissiveness can spur conflict.

WOMEN IN A MULTIGENERATIONAL FAMILY

Navar states that to speak of the Chicana is to speak of a multitude of experiences, histories, and realities.[6] She speaks of the Chicana's image of strength and endurance. The different experiences of the Chicana are illustrated in the following description of four women—one from each of four generations of the Ramirez family. The women described are Maria, the 80-year-old great grandmother; Susana, the 60-year-old grandmother; Norma, the 39-year-old mother; and Sylvia, the 22-year-old daughter.

Maria came to the United States from Mexico in her early teens during the Mexican Revolution and married at age 18 to a Mexican-American man. Although she attended elementary school in Mexico, she did not continue her education in the United States. Maria lived in the *barrio* all her life, never learned English, and depended on her husband and children to translate for her when necessary. She retained not only her language, but her culture and religion. Catholicism was an important part of her life and her family. She believes that being a good wife and mother is the primary function of a woman, and sacrificed herself for the sake of her children. Maria thinks of herself as a *Mejicana*, rather than as a Chicana or Mexican

American, and finds the modern concepts of her grandchildren difficult to understand.

Susana was born and educated in the United States. After two years of high school, she had to leave school and find a job to help support her family. She is bilingual and identifies herself as Mexican-American but not Chicana. She has continued to be employed outside the home occasionally after her marriage to a Mexican-American man.

Susana experienced discrimination in school whenever she spoke Spanish and was punished for speaking her native language. She was determined that her three children (two boys and one girl) would never be embarrassed or rejected because of their language. The children were bilingual at an early age and were encouraged to be successful academically and to pursue a higher education. Thus, Susana and her husband were disappointed when Norma married at age 17 after graduating from high school. The sons went to college and are now professionals; one is a teacher and the other is a lawyer.

Norma married a college-educated Mexican-American man and had three girls. She devoted the first ten years of her marriage to being a wife and mother. When her third child entered kindergarten, Norma decided to go to college and obtained a teaching degree in four years. Her parents, husband, and children supported her efforts, but her in-laws expressed their displeasure at a married woman with children returning to school and supposedly neglecting her duties as wife and mother. Norma says that while she attended college, she became aware of who she was as a woman and a Chicana.

Sylvia, 22 years old, is in medical school and does not plan to marry until she completes her education. She has always been bilingual and has been encouraged by her parents to retain the Mexican culture while adjusting to and accepting some facets of the dominant culture. Sylvia is involved in the Chicano movement and has no doubts about her identity.

There is little research to prove the point, but the author believes that the Ramirez women are not atypical. Most of the literature refers to Chicanas as submissive, passive, and uneducated. Although the role of women in the Mexican-American culture may make Chicanas seem powerless and weak according to the standards of the larger competitive society, in terms of the Mexican-American culture, the role involves a spirit that Mexican-American mothers and grandmothers reveal in their strength and wisdom.[7] Chicanas are facing opportunities and demands that are challenging the way of life of previous generations. Their sense of identity is in a state of flux. Often there is potential for conflict with traditional values as they struggle for a better opportunity in this nation and for equality as a people and as women.

CHICANA IDENTITY

The older women do not understand what the young women are saying when they identify themselves as Chicanas. They have difficulty understanding why a young single woman wants to establish her independence by moving from her parents' home to her own apartment. Such a move was unthinkable when they were young.

The elderly widowed Chicana also needs to adjust to living alone or to moving in with a married child. As Chicano families become more mobile, elderly parents may find themselves alone and far from their children. This situation is different from when they were young and children and parents lived together.

Another new phenomenon is the displaced Chicana homemaker who finds herself divorced after many years of marriage. The displaced homemaker is usually in her forties or fifties, had married young, did not complete her education, and was a traditional wife and mother. After the divorce, she discovers what it is like to survive—to try to find employment with minimal skills. She feels undeniably alone and lonely among friends who are no longer like her or, if she has returned to school, the only brown face in a college class of students who are fifteen to twenty years younger than herself. The Chicana professional faces a similar situation when she is the only Chicana in a meeting or faculty room surrounded by Anglo men and a few Anglo women. Social change is never easy; it is sometimes threatening and always unfamiliar.

The very existence of Chicana organizations is an indicator of attempts by Chicanas to attract attention to the issues that are of interest to them. In 1975, the League of Mexican American Women held the first Spanish Speaking Conference for Women in Tucson, Arizona. The conference was attended by more than 450 women who came from all parts of Arizona. An overwhelming number of attendees were homemakers and older women who sought to identify their mutual needs and goals with other Chicanas.

Perhaps one of the clearest pronouncements of the complexity of the Chicana identity was uttered by a student at San Jose State University in California who wrote:

A Chicana is someone like myself. Someone who can't be called a Mejicana because my values are different. I am no longer accepted as a Mejicana just like I've never been accepted as an American because of my differences. I'm caught between two cultures and rejected by both. I can't completely fit into either group. So, I call myself a Chicana, a new breed of awareness. Now we are organizing and demanding what is rightfully ours. We are going to school, reaching higher goals in education so we might earn a better living.[8]

IMPLICATIONS FOR PRACTICE

Social workers need to become aware of who the Chicana is. They must come to understand the heterogeneity of Mexican-American women and their culture. Factors to be considered when serving Chicanas are whether they are first-, second-, or third-generation Mexican American, where they live, their socioeconomic status, their educational level, how they identify themselves, and how the dominant culture regards them. For example, first-generation middle-class women may be traditional and identify themselves as *Mejicanas* or Mexican American, rather than as Chicanas.

There continues to be disparity between what the profession states is its mission and what practitioners actually do, especially in working with minority women.[9] Social workers generally agree that the mission of social work is to alleviate suffering and distress, take care of people, eradicate poverty and injustice, and ameliorate social problems.[10] Yet, because the society that sanctions the profession has continued to adhere tenaciously to the myth of the melting pot, it has been difficult for practitioners to recognize, accept, and appreciate other cultures and the differences among them.[11] Social workers continue to practice according to a white middle-class frame of reference that is often irrelevant to Chicanas. Norton states that social workers need to develop a dual perspective to accomplish the mission of the profession. This perspective, she says, requires a "conscious and systemic process of perceiving, understanding and comparing simultaneously the values, attitudes and behaviors of the larger society system with those of the clients."[12]

Social workers need to be prepared to use an eclectic model in practice with Chicanas. That is, they must focus on the Chicana client as an individual with unique problems and avoid generalizations and stereotypes of women or of Mexican Americans. It is also necessary for social workers to be bilingual if they are to communicate with and understand their Chicana clients. When a Chicana is talking about stressful events in her life, she often speaks Spanish to describe her feelings even though she may have been speaking English throughout the session. She does so because some words in Spanish that describe emotions are not translatable into English. Thus, bilingual social workers, who know the meaning of the words in Spanish, can more easily relate to the client. Furthermore, if they are alert to the nuances of the language, they can make clarifications when there seems to be a lack of communication.

Social workers—especially Anglo women social workers working with Chicanas—must be aware of their biases and prejudices. For example, it is difficult for Anglos to understand why a Chicana may remain in a "bad" marriage or allow herself to be dependent unless they know how culture and religion influence the behavior of Chicanas. Since Chicanas are

Catholics, divorce may not be acceptable, and their families may exert strong pressure on them to remain in the marriage.[13]

Furthermore, social workers must be aware of the stresses that transition brings to the Chicana in the form of value conflicts and the cultural dilemmas that change creates. Thus, they must be careful not to impose their own values but, rather, to recommend only those alternatives that are viable from the client's cultural frame of reference and to emphasize the Chicana's many strengths and values that may help her deal with the changes in her life. The Chicana needs to feel that her values are positive, not negative. Recently, there has been a resurgence of those very values that social workers have sought to question.

Moreover, Chicanas are not as unacculturated as the stereotype leads one to believe. Most Chicanas have always lived in two cultures—the Anglo culture and the Mexican-American culture—have been educated in the dominant society's school system, and are bilingual and bicultural. Acculturation and assimilation create many conflicts in Chicanas because they want to retain their culture and language but also want to let go of those traits, such as the double standard between the Chicano and Chicana, that contribute to their oppression. Thus, although Chicanas aspire toward the American Dream, they are unwilling to pay the price of total acculturation and assimilation. Anglo social workers must learn to accept and respect the pace at which Chicanas are changing socially, economically, and psychologically.

Schools of social work need to include the Chicana and her culture and not just the Chicano in their courses on minorities. Few graduate schools inform students of the social and economic facts of the Hispanic population, which will be the largest minority group by the end of this century.

Social agencies need to obtain facts on this population to serve better their needs and to provide in-service training to practitioners working with Chicanas. In-service training must be done by Chicana professionals who are not only knowledgeable of the culture but have lived through it. Seminars conducted by non-Chicanas who have only book knowledge of the Mexican-American culture are not acceptable.

CONCLUSION

Female Anglo social workers have a special mission. They must acknowledge the problems of the Chicana and assist her in her search for solutions. As women, we social workers share such common problems as oppression and suppression. As women, we share the lack of economic, social, and political opportunities. But, the Chicana may be doubly oppressed, since she is caught in the double bind of being both a woman and an ethnic minority and thus experiences racism and sexism. Thus, Anglo social workers must join with Chicanas to ensure that, in the future, Chicanas and Anglo women will face a world of equal opportunity and equal competition in all areas, regardless of sex or color.

REFERENCES

1. Nathan Murillo, "The Mexican American Family," in Nathaniel N. Wagner and Marsha J. Haug, eds., *Chicanos: Social and Psychological Perspectives* (St. Louis, Mo.: C. V. Mosby Co., 1972), p. 24.

2. Maria Nieto Senour, "Psychology of the Chicana," in Joe L. Martinez, Jr., ed., *Chicano Psychology* (New York: Academic Press, 1977), p. 332.

3. Murillo, op. cit.

4. Ibid.

5. Ibid.

6. Isabelle Navar, "Como Chicana Mi Madre" [I am Chicana like my mother] in *Chicana Feminist Journal, Encuentro Femenil*, 1 (February 1975), p. 8.

7. Ibid.

8. Sylvia Alicia Gonzales, "The Chicana Perspective: A Design for Self-Awareness," in Arnulfo D. Trejo, ed., *The Chicanos: As We See Ourselves* (Tucson: University of Arizona Press, 1979), p. 95.

9. Armando Morales, "Beyond Traditional Conceptual Frameworks," *Social Work*, 22 (September 1977), pp. 387–393.

10. Ibid.

11. Guadalupe Gibson, "Mexican American Children and Their Families." Unpublished paper presented at the Sixth NASW Professional Symposium, Worden School of Social Service, Our Lady of the Lake University, San Antonio, Texas, 1979. (Photocopy.)

12. Dolores G. Norton, *The Dual Perspective: Inclusion of Ethnic Minority Content in the Social Work Curriculum* (New York: Council on Social Work Education, 1978), p. 3.

13. Gibson, op. cit.

OBSERVATIONS ON SOCIAL WORK WITH AMERICAN INDIAN WOMEN

Evelyn Lance Blanchard

The social work literature on American Indians is sparse. Most of the available articles deal mainly with "Indian style" characteristics, such as "noninterference," "Indian time," and other descriptors. Many of these articles propose what social workers should not do, while others have been concerned with alcoholism, family and children's services, and the problems inherent in the delivery of specific services. The literature retains an introductory quality; greater distance is required to develop knowledge based on broadened perspectives.

At issue is a general lack of knowledge of other cultures—and that of the American Indian in particular. The acceptance of a "culture of poverty" and the thrust of the "Great Society" caused a certain blindness in social workers, a narrowing of vision. Decisions about appropriate interventions were not always made with full consideration of the dynamics involved in the worker-client relationship. The efforts of social workers to be aware of and sensitive to the needs of clients led to an atmosphere of "no trespass."

The activities of many social workers were based on a superficial quality of understanding. The perceptions of these workers were, in the main, based on noninvolvement. It became common practice to allow confusion to determine the parameters of self-determination. In the case of American Indians, the common belief was that any approach by an outsider might be interpreted as "interference," which could be translated as "coercion," and, therefore, would be unacceptable. As Good Tracks noted: "In native Indian society . . . no interference or meddling of any kind is allowed or tolerated, even when it is to keep the other person from doing something foolish or dangerous."[1] Good Tracks went on to say:

Coercion appears to be a fundamental element in the peoples of Western Europe and their colonial descendents. All the governments and institutions of these societies use a variety of coercive methods to ensure cooperative action. Traditional Indian societies, on the other hand, were organized on the principle of voluntary cooperation. They refrained from using force to coerce.[2]

The end result is that American Indians in general are not receiving the high-quality services that social workers can deliver.

American Indians have strong feelings that they are being coerced. They do not, in the main, have strong feelings that they are respected. American Indian women in particular do not receive much encouragement to better themselves and their positions from the workers who provide services to them. Perhaps they are not encouraged because the workers think of them as being poor, undereducated, isolationist, and resistant to help from outsiders. This could, perhaps, be interpreted as a sexist response; however, American Indian women most often view the behavior of social workers as racist.

To social workers, the American Indian woman is invisible because her characteristics and problems are not distinguishable from those of the American Indian man. Thus, American Indian people are seen as a composite. Issues pertaining to them are discussed, but the individuals involved are not yet known.

PROBLEMS IN PRACTICE

Child Welfare Services

Social workers work with American Indian women primarily in the areas of child welfare and child protective services. Unfortunately, the workers most often directly involved are those with the least amount of experience and training. Many American Indian workers and clients recognize that it is difficult for most states and counties to employ persons with the requisite skills for the delicate responsibility of child welfare work with a client from another culture.

Although the majority of child welfare workers are women, information about American Indian women as individuals is not emerging, as was just noted. Attitudes, perceptions, and stimuli are general, not specific. The attitudes that American Indian women have about their place in their family and society and toward their men are not being uncovered, primarily because the relationships between social workers and their American Indian clients are not based on the trust necessary for the revelation of such personal information.

The relationships that child welfare workers develop with American Indian women are mainly contractual. That is, if the woman will enter counseling, get a job, and move to a better place or live away from her boyfriend or husband, usually her children will be released from foster care and returned to her. Follow-up efforts have a watchdog quality. The character and quality of these services contribute to the contention by American Indians that non-Indian people cannot work effectively with American Indians.[3] Furthermore, American Indian women continue to be confused about what the social worker is. Is she a person who must be feared and who represents restrictions because she comes with only one solution, and that from some higher authority, or is she someone who comes with contractual "bargains" that may be difficult to resist yet are culturally unacceptable?

One can ponder the reasons for this situation. It could be charged that the situation is sexist in that it represents the female social worker's failure to support the important ingredients of the American Indian woman's life. However, it is often not possible to do so because these ingredients are not yet known.

The author believes that one of the major reasons for the difficulty lies in the reality of social work education. There are some schools in which the students' only exposure to racial and cultural differences among people and their responses is one brief course of study. There may not be sufficient stimulation from this to produce enough trained individuals who have the abilities and knowledge to find and support the sustaining values of racially and culturally different people. These circumstances make it difficult to provide adequate staff for certain positions. Thus, from the perspective of the American Indian client, the worker with the requisite skills for such a delicate responsibility is the exception and not the rule.

Practitioners in this area of work are fully convinced that social work practice with American Indian women must be an integrated learning situation for both the worker and client. Knowledge from one side only cannot be permitted; information must come from both sides. That is, the worker must learn the attitudes and behaviors that are considered good by the American Indian woman and what she believes she can do well. Armed with sufficient knowledge of the client, the worker can then, in turn, support the most beneficial and productive aspects of the client's self-identity and encourage her to avail herself of opportunities for self-determination. This is a clear responsibility of social work practitioners.

Wife Abuse

Many American Indian men take out the frustrations they feel about being discriminated against, poorly prepared and trained, and unemployed on their women, primarily because the women are available, rather than because the men are sexist. That is, American Indian women are victims by default. Often social workers approach such cases of wife abuse from the position of the rights of women. Many times, the beneficial efforts by the social worker on behalf of a woman who has been assaulted turn sour because neither the worker nor the client knows the ingredients of womanhood as perceived by the other.

CULTURAL PERSPECTIVES

The Family

From what is known about American Indian life, the family is the primary unit, not the individual. Difficult situations arise out of difficult relationships in the family; thus, the family—not just the woman—must be helped to correct these difficult relationships. American Indian people are interrelated and have expressed a desire to remain so. American Indian thought requires that the individual and community have the same ends—that one gains freedom within the confines of a philosophical tradition as opposed to propelling oneself away from it. For these reasons, the woman alone cannot accomplish what is needed without a sense of direction from and connection with the rest of her family.

The lack of understanding of the family unit and its place in American Indian life has been the cause of some well-meaning but ineffective activities in social work practice, such as the provision of parenting classes. Most parenting classes that American Indian women attend are centered on the tenets of parent effectiveness training which assume that specific modes of interaction and communication are beneficial to all.[4] This approach, although repeatedly used, has not been thought through with the American Indian woman and her family. Thus, it can be catastrophic that attendance at these courses is often required to ensure the return of a child.

The great diversity among American Indians, tribally and experientially, complicates the problem of social work intervention, since it is difficult to determine entry points. It has been generally proposed that the work requires a thorough knowledge of tribally specific cultures and traditions. In all honesty, this is too much to ask of any one social worker, but all sense an absence of direction and reference. And crash courses in cultural awareness do not always provide the needed distinction.

Tribal Life

Tribal society is concerned with the group and the individual in the group. The group exerts considerable pressure on its members to behave in ways that do not threaten the existence of the group, including the family group.

The pressure that is applied does not cause the individual to become a pawn without the right of choice. It does require that the individual meet his or her own share of the responsibility for keeping the group intact. There is a broad range of activities and circumstances in which these requirements can be met.

An American Indian woman can be a mother, but is not required to be one. She is often employed. The socioreligious relational ties these women possess often place them in major decision-making positions that have a direct impact on all members of the community. It is expected that out of the American Indian woman's activities and circumstances, some contribution will be forthcoming that provides for the cohesiveness and integrity of the group with the initial focus on the family.

Greater understanding between peoples is required to develop the knowledge necessary to place method and technique in the appropriate space or time. Involvement is a necessary ingredient for the development of knowledge in this context. Openness invites the kind of knowledge that social workers can use to help women obtain what is their right. The decision to obtain one's right requires that women use their best intentions, which are their greatest strengths. The natural dynamism of the worker-client relationship allows people to walk side by side without threat. Confidence has been developed. The opportunity for coercive acts is diminished.

Young American Indian women are taught to look at various situations and determine what they need to do to sustain integrity of the community. This often requires the acquisition and development of additional interactional skills. The modes of verbal communication, for example, have been vastly expanded in our lifetime. The acquisition and development of skills do not easily change or obliterate fundamental beliefs. Current relationships between women of different racial and philosophical groups are anachronistic, yet few question the meaning of "Indian time" from various perspectives.

A common myth is that the American Indian woman is an uncomely subordinate squaw. Few social workers are aware that American Indian women maintain positions of the highest rank in tribal government and society. Leadership is not foreign to American Indian women. Among some tribes, women have traditionally held public leadership roles, while in others, leadership is a contemporary experience. Whatever their duration, the models are present. In light of this fact, it is curious that a predominant focus in social work with American Indian women is the development of appropriate role models. Do social workers assume that American Indian women do not have adequate sex-role models? If so, their sexist approach is developed out of ignorance.

Social Control

Many social workers do not appreciate the social control and therapeutic mechanisms of tribal society that are traditional to American Indian people. They do not understand that control is not coercion.[5] Misunderstanding the meaning of these mechanisms can result in descriptions of certain behaviors or practices such as sweatbaths (or "sweats") as superstitious and primitive. "Sweats" are cleansing, ceremonial activities that have both physical and spiritual meaning; the important components of group support and control experienced by the individual may well go unnoticed by those who are unfamiliar with the significance of the activity.

The ceremonial aspects of these activities involve a commitment by the individual to live a life that is of benefit to the group. They are spiritual experiences that are not separated from the practical aspects of rehabilitation. They are not magic or even necessarily secret. It is not always easy to describe the therapeutic qualities of these experiences, and even some American Indians are confused about the role of the spiritual experience in therapy. Gains in the individual's feelings of self-worth and sense of accomplishment can be the gauge by which they are evaluated.

American Indian thought provides a different perspective on the person from birth onward. At birth, the infant is not seen as possessing certain characteristics that require correction and remedy, as is the case of those who believe in baptism to remove original sin. American Indian thought does not assume that people have deep-seated drives or impulses that can be released in harmful ways. The presence of such drives and impulses underlies many of the approaches used in social work. Introspection is encouraged in social work so the individual can develop a greater knowledge and understanding of the self. Popular therapies, such as transactional analysis, teach the individual that he or she is, after all, really "ok" or assist a person to find his or her "center." Whatever the perspective, these approaches help one to overcome the fear of looking at oneself and being oneself. Transformation of a person or of a person's self-perception is required for healing to occur. The individual must choose to be transformed and to assume the responsibility for the remedy.

American Indian thought, however, does not view the roots of undesirable behavior as being embedded in the person. Rather, it pays greater attention to outside influences that have an impact on the person. To bring about change, then, adjustments are required in individual behavior or group action that will remove the person from a position of susceptibility. The person is not required to maintain a level of individual dysfunction; it is possible for one to be perfect within the concept of balance. This approach to behavior and its correction is much more conducive to the preservation of the group than is the notion of deep-seated individual dysfunction or dissatisfaction. Threats from outside can be more clearly identified and dealt with than threats from within.

Perceptions of Behavior

Perceptions of behavior are influenced by the way one is taught to view behavior, including its origins. If one's view is of individual responsibility in difficulty, then the method used for remedy will focus on the individual, often to the exclusion of others. Rewards are experienced and handled in much the same way. If one focuses on patterns of interaction in the group and the individual in the group, rather than the individual interacting with the group, the remedies and rewards will necessarily be different. Thus assessment skills need to be finely honed.

If perceptions of behavior must include its origins, then attention must be paid, at least partially, to the cultural context in which reality is differentially and variously defined. Basic to this pursuit is the question: Whose reality?

It is essential that greater attention be paid to the process by which various realities are codified.[6] Failure to do so ensures that the worker will impose his or her codification of reality on others, perhaps without recognizing that their codifications of reality are different. Interactions like these are fragile and do not often stimulate openness.

Discussions with Ortiz, an anthropologist from San Juan Pueblo, offer further insight into the understanding of codifications of reality.[7] American Indians codify reality in spatial terms rather than lineal terms. Each codification then produces a perspective of reality from the standpoint of either space or time. American Indian people are concerned with rootedness and belonging—direct attachment. In contrast, one of the greatest rewards for non-Indians is to have a place in history, which is a temporal definition of reality to many American Indians.

When American Indian old people get together, they like to talk about how well things are going and that things have not changed. They are expressing the feeling of continued rootedness, of a sense of belonging that, in spite of all, has not been diminished. To some people, their expressions are understood as holding on to something out of the past that has little utility in the contemporary experience. Yet, these rewards can be seen as expressions of relatedness from the perspective of individual acts within each culturally structured situation. Social work is most effectively performed when this level of integration is reached.

The author believes that it is neither the responsibility nor the right of social workers to determine the American Indian woman's identity. However, if some attention is paid to the concerns noted throughout this article, social workers can begin to gauge qualities of relatedness and belonging, to determine their focus, and to assist in strengthening them. These are necessary efforts for the American Indian woman's self-expression.

REFERENCES

1. Jimm Good Tracks, "Native American Noninterference," *Social Work*, 18 (November 1973), p. 31.

2. Ibid., pp. 30–31.

3. William Byler, *Statistical Survey of Out-of-Home Placement of Indian Children* (New York: Association on American Indian Affairs, 1976).

4. Thomas Gordon, *Parent Effectiveness Training: The Tested New Way To Raise Responsible Children* (New York: McKay Publishing Co., 1970).

5. Sylvester M. Morey and Olivia L. Gilliam, eds., *Respect for Life: The Traditional Upbringing of American Indian Children* (Garden City, N.Y.: Waldorf Press, 1974), p. 27.

6. Dorothy Lee, "Codification of Reality: Lineal and Nonlineal," in Lee, *Freedom and Culture* (Englewood Cliffs, N.J.: Prentice-Hall, 1959), p. 118.

7. For further discussion, *see* Alfonso Ortiz, *Tewa World: Space, Time, Being and Becoming in a Pueblo Society* (Chicago: University of Chicago Press, 1969).

HOMOPHOBIA AND SOCIAL WORK PRACTICE WITH LESBIANS

Joan M. Cummerton

The issue of homophobia is important to all social workers irrespective of their gender or sexual preference. Homophobia has been found to be directly related to sexist attitudes and behaviors and inversely related to a positive self-concept of both gays and heterosexuals. This article considers the nature of homophobia and some of the beliefs and myths that serve to maintain it. It identifies different modes of responding to gays, describes prevalent ways in which homophobia undermines social work practice, and suggests how social workers may lessen their homophobic behavior.

NATURE OF HOMOPHOBIA

From a cultural perspective, "homophobia" was defined by Morin and Garfinkle as any belief system that supports negative myths about and stereotypes of gay men and lesbians. More specifically, it includes (1) belief systems which hold that discrimination on the basis of sexual orientation is justifiable, (2) language that is offensive to gay people (such as "queer" or "dyke") and (3) any belief system that does not value homosexual life-styles equally with heterosexual life-styles.[1] The latter generalized belief system has also been called "heterosexism" or "heterosexual bias" because it specifically argues that the heterosexual life-style is superior to the homosexual life-style. As a dynamic of the individual personality, "homophobia" refers to an irrational fear or intolerance of homosexuality or homosexuals—a specific phobic condition, rather than a generalized cultural attitude.[2] In this article, the different dynamics associated with each level of homophobia will be discussed.

NEGATIVE ATTITUDES TOWARD HOMOSEXUALS

At the cultural or societal level, a wide range of beliefs support negative attitudes toward gay men and lesbians. They include beliefs about sexuality, beliefs about sex roles, and beliefs based on myths.

Beliefs about Sexuality

One belief is that the sole purpose of sex is procreation. This belief ignores not only the sexual needs of two persons of the same sex, but also those of women who have had hysterectomies, who have gone through menopause, or who use contraceptive devices. A related irrational belief is that if same-sex relationships are sanctioned, eveyone will immediately choose a partner of the same sex and the human race will disappear. Still another belief is that the insertion of the penis into the vagina is the only appropriate way to express sexuality. This belief condemns masturbation and oral and anal intercourse between partners of the opposite sex as well as partners of the same sex. Then there is the belief that sexual relations between partners of the same sex are unnatural. This belief assumes that everything that is natural is good and everything that is unnatural is bad. If one accepts this premise, then society has no business interfering with the natural order by curing illness or developing technologically and social workers should not intervene in the lives of others.

Beliefs Based on Myths

One myth is that gays are child molesters. However, the data clearly show that the vast majority of child molesters are heterosexual men and that 90 percent of their victims are girls who often are related to them.[3] Another myth is that lesbians, indeed all homosexuals, are pathological because homosexuality is pathological; thus lesbians should be condemned. Yet, research studies over the past two decades have shown that lesbians are as well adjusted as heterosexuals.[4] For example, in Freedman's study, lesbians scored higher than a heterosexual control group on autonomy, spontaneity, orientation toward the present, and sensitivity to one's own needs and feelings.[5]

Beliefs about Sex Roles

One belief is that relationships between the sexes should be complementary and based on the natural biologically related differences between men and women. This belief is related to the myth that women are half-persons, that is, women are born incomplete and can only become whole if they merge with a man. Obviously, to hold such a belief is ridiculous in the face of scientific findings.

MacDonald and Games found that, contrary to popular belief, homophobia is correlated only mildly with attitudes about procreation, promiscuity, or what is sexually appropriate.[6] Instead, they found that homophobia is correlated most strongly with cognitive rigidity, intolerance of ambiguity, and a commitment to traditional sex roles. The more negative the attitudes toward homosexuality, the stronger the negative attitudes toward women in nontraditional sex roles, particularly women who are seen as potent or powerful. In other words, homophobic people fear the breakdown of traditional roles and a blurring of what it means to be a man or a woman.

SOCIALIZATION

Most people grow up knowing practically nothing about lesbian life-styles. According to the Institute for Sex Research, of the 27 percent of the adults who have had any formal sex education, 40 percent heard homosexuality mentioned and only 1.5 percent heard anything positive about gay or lesbian life-styles.[7] Why is homosexuality hushed up? What is to be feared? Infants could not care less who is holding them and being warm to them as long as they like what is happening. A long process of socialization is required to screen out affectional intimacies with persons of the same sex and to teach people to ignore, belittle, or mock relationships between persons of the same sex.

Part of the fear of homosexuality is the fear of sex-role confusion—the uncertainty of what it means to be masculine or feminine in this culture— which stems from a commitment to hierarchical power relationships in this patriarchal society. (Most relationships are hierarchical, such as parent-child, teacher-student, doctor-patient, cleric-laity, boss-worker, and husband-wife.) That is, this society believes that men must be in charge to look after women, who, in turn, care for and support the men. The patriarchy is not geared to flexible, reversible roles or peer relationships.

Much of the fear of lesbians or gay men appears to be a fear of the unknown. Rather than relating to people as people, those who are afraid distance themselves emotionally by feelings of repulsion, pity, tolerance, or token acceptance.

Repulsion. Heterosexuals who are repulsed by gay persons are homophobic. People who respond in this manner clearly see lesbians and gay men as evil or sick and may seek to "cure" them of their "illness."

Pity. "I know you can't help it, some persons are just born that way" characterizes this response. Persons who feel pity for gay persons encourage them to adjust to their second-class life-style.

Tolerance. People who use this mode of distancing themselves assume that everyone goes through a stage when they have same-sex relationships but that most persons mature out of that stage either to exclusive heterosexuality or to bisexuality. This attitude is popular with many mental health professionals.

Token Acceptance. This attitude initially seems supportive rather than distancing. It comes in two forms: "To me you are not a lesbian, you are just a person" or "What you do in bed is your own business." This attitude, which is found among many social work educators and practitioners, is naive. It is also the most dangerous of all the responses in that it ignores the realities of lesbian life. In this society, lesbians do not have equal rights and equal respect. They must continuously live with the pressure of remaining "invisible" ("passing for straight") or, if they admit they are lesbians (come "out of the closet"), of having to deal with others' homophobia. In either case, the pain is great. Lesbians who "pass" pay the price of eventually ceasing to feel good about themselves—of losing their self-respect. Lesbians or gay men are in a unique position among oppressed peoples in that they bring oppression down on themselves if they behave as lesbians or gay men. Almost any lesbian can pass for straight if she just keeps her mouth shut and allows others to assume that she is heterosexual, especially if she is pleasant, charming, attractive, nonassertive, warm, and nurturing.

HOMOPHOBIA AND SOCIAL WORK PRACTICE

What does all this have to do with social work practice? Riddle identified a number of ways in which homophobia or heterosexism can undermine therapeutic work with lesbian clients.[8] Practitioners who are homophobic or heterosexist (1) underestimate the daily stress that lesbians undergo, (2) encourage superhuman expectations, (3) view homosexuality as pathological, (4) are biased toward heterosexual behavior, and (5) ignore problems or issues peculiar to lesbian relationships.

Underestimating Daily Stress

Practitioners do not know or underestimate the kind of pressure with which lesbians live, especially since the stress is cumulative. Every moment of the day, a lesbian must make decisions about being out of the closet in a particular situation. For example, should she go to a small lecture or concert series with her lover? Can she risk inviting guests to her home who may ask questions about her living arrangements? When others start talking about those "homos," should she intervene? How affectionately can she kiss her lover goodbye in public? How should she respond when the male gynecologist asks which birth control method she uses? In conversation, should she refer to her lover as he or she? If her lover is seriously ill and hospitalized, can she pass as a "sister" so she may be permitted to visit?

Because of the potentially high cost in loss of jobs, housing, friends, family, and, especially, children, the safest course is not to take any risks. But that choice results in a feeling of being constrained. The fear of repercussions is constant and realistic, and that fear creates even more stress, which increases the likelihood that the lesbian will "slip up"—a vicious circle.

In general, how one feels about oneself determines how one behaves. Thus, if a lesbian feels there is something about herself that she cannot afford to reveal, then she will be tense and feel she must constantly monitor her emotional responses.

No matter what decision the lesbian makes about being in the closet, stress is involved. If she decides to remain in the closet, then she expends a tremendous amount of energy in the game of "who knows?" Each interaction must be scrutinized for slipups, inadvertent indicators that she is gay. For example, the closeted lesbian must be especially careful with men so she is neither too friendly (and thus does not precipitate being asked out) nor too unfriendly (and thus does not encourage questions about what is wrong with her).

If she has lesbian friends, she places herself in double jeopardy because her identity becomes suspect if the friend becomes known as a lesbian. As a closet lesbian, people will assume she is single and unattached. Depending on her age, this perception may be coupled with pity that she has not yet married or remarried and friendly offers to introduce her to men. She will also have to find a solution to business socializing—always going alone, inviting a willing male friend, or declining and seeming unsociable.

If she decides to be open about her life-style, she will have other stresses to handle. Although she may feel more whole within herself, she runs the risk of people relating to her stereotypically—of dealing with such statements as "I'd rather you didn't stay alone with my children" or "It's too bad you never had a good relationship with a man." Furthermore, she may be treated as a one-dimensional person who is interested only in gay issues. On social agency staffs and university faculties, it is all too easy to become the resident "dyke" to whom others turn with their questions, fears, and hostilities. Obviously, the openly gay person is vulnerable to being hurt by previous friends and family members who reject her for her choice of life-style. She also functions as a kind of "Typhoid Mary," in that any person with whom she is seen who is not obviously in an opposite-sex relationship automatically is suspected of being gay.

Superhuman Expectations

Positive self-esteem or self-respect develops in many ways. One way is to compare oneself with an external image of a good or lovable person. Since widely publicized images are heterosexual, lesbians are constantly made aware that they do not measure up. Thus, many lesbians feel they have to be "extra" good to offset the negative image they project from their choice of life-style.

Another common reinforcer of self-esteem is the idea of "good by association." If one is liked by and seen with persons who are admired, then one must be good herself. A lesbian who accepts this idea tends to narrow her circle of friends primarily to heterosexuals to emphasize her own "normality" or to choose not to associate with other lesbians who might appear to fit a negative stereotype of "bull dyke," "man hater," "alcoholic," or "incompetent."

Work is still another reinforcer of self-esteem. However, a lesbian may continue in a job that no longer challenges her because she does not want to risk questions about her life-style. Few gays who are open about their sexual preferences have the luxury of having a job they want.

Mental health professionals may point out that a person's feelings of self-esteem should be independent of what others think of her and what type of work she does. However, such independence is difficult to achieve, and it is unrealistic to expect lesbian clients to be impervious to what others think of them. It is also unrealistic to think that lesbians will feel no need to share their personal life with heterosexual friends and co-workers or will never resent the limits that secrecy places even on casual conversations.

Suspicions about Pathology

The search continues for the "cause" of homosexuality. One might just as well ask what "causes" heterosexuality. If social workers continue to view homosexuality as abnormal, then they will be tempted to read into lesbian clients' behavior a variety of pathological causes, such as a desire to behave regressively, a hatred or envy of men, or the search for a mother substitute. Unless social workers are open to wondering what makes a lesbian strong enough to go against societal pressures, just asking the question about causation implies that they do not respect the client's life choice. The question also implies that lesbians cannot form mature, committed relationships and that the choice to be a lesbian is made in response to difficulties rather than being a freely chosen positive alternative.

Furthermore, social workers may overlook the actual difficulties that a lesbian client may have in coming out. Coming out is not a linear process.[9] It is a series of personal choices and it happens in bits and pieces throughout a lifetime. One can live as a lesbian for many years without being out to oneself, excusing each same-sex relationship as exceptional. It is still not uncommon to find lesbians trying to go straight because that is what they think is natural. This kind of negative self-judgment is demoralizing. It is hard to be enthusiastic about yourself while feeling that at the core you have some basic fault.

Biases toward Heterosexual Behavior

Often social workers will appear supportive of lesbian clients while subtly pressuring them to go straight. This is usually phrased as wanting the client to be open to the possibility of heterosexual relationships. The problem with this approach is that it contains a double standard; the same therapists seldom, if ever, push heterosexual clients to be open to same-sex relationships. It ignores the fact that the majority of lesbian clients have had both male and female lovers at some time in their lives.[10] Social workers may sincerely feel that their attempts to influence clients are in the clients' best interests. However, research shows that lesbians feel better about themselves when they are comfortable with a clear lesbian identification. Identifying as a lesbian never prohibits a woman from being the lover of a man. However, identification as a heterosexual ignores or makes invisible that part of a lesbian which is open to same-sex relationships.

Ignoring Issues Specific to Lesbians

When a woman chooses to become a lesbian, she must give up fantasies of being taken care of by a man. This involves giving up automatic social support for the relationship she is in. It means stepping outside the system of gaining respect and prestige by virtue of the man with whom she is identified and being willing to be related to on her own merits.

Heterosexual models are not appropriate for same-sex relationships because of the power struggles that are assumed. In heterosexual relationships, the dominance of the man is usually assumed and supported by the institutions of society. In lesbian relationships, there are no prescribed and socially sanctioned ways of relating. Evolving nontraditional interdependent patterns of relating is not easy. It is made much more difficult if it must be done in the closet, squeezed in between the demands of work and family pressures. When children are involved, stress becomes more intense. One is constantly on guard for fear that custody may be challenged and worried about what the children will say. One also worries that the children may be laughed at, ridiculed, or avoided for living in a nontraditional family. Again, there are no easily available role models. Somehow the adults and children must develop a new description of a family constellation.

Then there is the issue of balancing a relationship with a lover and raising children. All single parents face this problem, but lesbian mothers are under a special strain because same-sex relationships are not condoned and natural physical affection may have to be artificially circumscribed. Finding ways in which the family unit can enjoy itself publicly can become a challenge.

In any lesbian relationship that is not acknowledged as such, there is the stress of never having the relationship acknowledged. Much of the jealousy attributed to gay couples comes from the dirth of situations in which they can function as a couple.

LESSENING HOMOPHOBIA

The social work profession has mirrored the prejudices and homophobia of American society. At the organizational level, *Social Work*, a journal of the National Association of Social Workers (NASW), has all but ignored the existence of lesbians and gay men. From its inception in 1956 through March 1981, *Social Work* published only four articles on any aspect of homosexuality or social work practice with gays and one article in which homosexuals were recognized as an oppressed group.[11] After five years of effort, the 1977 Delegate Assembly finally passed the NASW Policy Statement on Gay Issues.[12]

At the individual level, the author has observed a wide range of homophobic behavior. For example, in a recent survey to determine social welfare resources available to lesbian and gay male adolescents, a large number of agency executives claimed they had no lesbian or gay male clientele—this, in San Francisco, where lesbians and gay males are estimated to be 17–21 percent of the population.[13] In another case, a social work supervisor in a Veterans Administration hospital refused to approve a staff member's request to attend the National Conference of Gay Health Workers on the grounds that there were no gays among the hospital's several hundred male patients. Some faculty acquaintances of the author, who teach policy courses, were unaware of the NASW Policy Statement on Gay Issues, while others have indicated they prefer not to serve as faculty advisers to gay students or to serve as field liaisons to agencies serving primarily lesbians and gay men.

Such attitudes and behavior are not limited to heterosexually oriented social work practitioners, administrators, and educators. A closeted lesbian social worker in a mental health setting recently described her practice of joining heterosexual colleagues in derogatory jokes about gay males and in always wearing dresses to work so she may pass as a heterosexual.

If social workers are to be of any use to the 8 percent of the population estimated to be homosexual, they must confront and begin to deal with their own homophobia.[14] Hall posed a number of questions that social workers should ask themselves in examining their attitudes.[15] Morin reported positive results in changing attitudes toward gays through educational programs.[16] Becoming acquainted with the lesbian subculture in the community where one is practicing can also be useful in confronting one's homophobic attitudes and in becoming personally acquainted with a range of resources that may be useful to those lesbians who become clients. Familiarity with research findings of the past decade using nonclinical samples of lesbians can also help to refute some of the myths described earlier.

Although social workers try to eradicate homophobia or heterosexism in themselves, it is still easy to lapse back into it because it is constantly reinforced. The least they can do for a client is to make sure they are not assuming that a client is heterosexual and to connect a gay client with gay professionals or peer advocates so the client may experience pride in his or her identity, support for excessive stress, and validation that one has to be strong to be gay and have survived so long.

REFERENCES

1. Stephen F. Morin and Ellen M. Garfinkle, "Male Homophobia," *Journal of Social Issues*, 54 (March 1978), pp. 29–47.

2. Ibid.

3. *See* Dorothy Riddle, "Homophobia and Psychotherapy," paper presented at the National Conference on Feminist Therapy, University of Colorado, Boulder, January 28–30, 1977; Ellen Weber, "Sexual Abuse Begins at Home," *Ms.*, 5 (April 1977), pp. 64–67; Bernice Goodman, *Confronting Homophobia: Notes on Creating a Lesbian Community* (New York: National Gay Health Coalition, Education Foundation, 1977), p. 8; and Robert L. Geiser, *Hidden Victims: The Sexual Abuse of Children* (Boston: Beacon Press, 1979), pp. 11–67.

4. *See* Mark Freedman, "Homosexuality Among Women and Psychological Adjustment," unpublished doctoral dissertation, Case Western Reserve University, 1967; Alan Bell and Martin Weinberg, *Homosexualities: A Study of Diversity Among Men and Women* (New York: Simon & Schuster, 1978), pp. 207–216; and Marcel Saghin and Eli Robins. *Male and Female Homosexuality: A Comprehensive Investigation* (Baltimore: Williams & Wilkins Co., 1973), pp. 266–294.

5. Mark Freedman, "Homosexuals May Be Healthier Than Straights," *Psychology Today*, 8 (March 1975), p. 30.

6. A. P. MacDonald and Richard Games, "Some Characteristics of Those Who Hold Positive and Negative Attitudes Toward Homosexuals," *Journal of Homosexuality*, 1 (Fall 1974), pp. 9–26; MacDonald et al., "Attitudes Toward Homosexuality: Preservation of Sex Morality or the Double Standard?" *Journal of Consulting and Clinical Psychology*, 40 (February 1973), p. 161.

7. As cited in Riddle, op. cit.

8. Dorothy I. Riddle, "Finding Supportive Therapy," in Ginny Vida, ed., *Our Right to Love: A Lesbian Resource Book* (Englewood Cliffs, N.J.: Prentice-Hall, 1978), pp. 89–90.

9. *See* Dorothy Riddle and S. F. Morin, "Removing the Stigma: A Status Report," *American Psychological Association Monitor*, 11 (1977), p. 16, for a picture of the developmental process of coming out as it has emerged from a recent study of lesbian and gay male psychologists.

10. A. Oberstone and H. Sukoneck, "Psychological Adjustment and Life Style of Single Lesbians and Single Heterosexual Women," *Psychology of Women Quarterly*, 1 (Fall 1976), pp. 172–188.

11. *See* Janet Chafetz et al., "A Study of Homosexual Women," *Social Work*, 19 (November 1974), pp. 714–723; Raymond Berger, "An Advocate Model for Intervention with Homosexuals," *Social Work*, 22 (July 1977), pp. 280–283; Marney Hall, "Lesbian Families: Cultural and Clinical Issues," *Social Work*, 23 (September 1978), pp. 380–385; Karen Lewis, "Children of Lesbians: Their Point of View," *Social Work*, 25 (May 1980), pp. 198–203; and Harvey Gochros, "The Sexually Oppressed," *Social Work*, 17 (March 1972), pp. 16–23.

12. *See* "Gay Issues," in *Compilation of Public Policy Statements* (Washington, D.C.: National Association of Social Workers, September 1980), pp. 12.1–12.4.

13. Personal communication from Carol Migden, executive director, Operation Concern, Pacific Medical Center, San Francisco.

14. Peter Fischer, *The Gay Mystique: The Myth and Reality of Male Homosexuality* (New York: Stein & Day, 1972), p. 254.

15. Hall, op. cit.

16. Steven Morin, "Educational Programs as a Means of Changing Attitudes Toward Gay People," *Homosexual Counseling Journal*, 1 (1974), pp. 160–165.

SOCIAL WORK WITH LESBIAN COUPLES

During the past decade, increased attention has been given to lesbianism as a viable alternative life-style. Articles and books have focused on the variations in lesbian life-styles and on the self-actualizing potentials accompanying the choice to live as a lesbian. The professional literature has provided guidelines for intervention with a gay individual who is experiencing problems and for understanding the dilemmas faced by members of the gay individual's family who are unable to accept the relative's sexual-affectional preference. However, little has been written about social work or counseling with the lesbian couple.

This article addresses strategies for problem solving related to inter-personal conflicts in five basic areas pertinent to intimate relationships. It is based on information provided by two hundred women who contributed data for a research study conducted by the author in 1978–79 in various sections of the United States. Seventy-nine percent of the women (158) were in a committed relationship and slightly more than one-third (83 women) had been involved in counseling since "coming out" (establishing a self-actualizing identity as a lesbian). A stipulated goal of the researcher was to share the results with other helping professionals—an intent enthusiastically endorsed by the participants.

BRIEF REVIEW OF THE LITERATURE

In describing lesbians as a particular group, the literature has moved from a primary emphasis on gay men, which included women only as an afterthought and frequently in stereotypical or male-oriented fashion, to a more equal focus on gay men and lesbians.[1] Furthermore, the prior focus of clinicians on etiological factors is stressed to a lesser degree than it was prior to 1968 when the American Psychiatric Association declassified homosexuality as a mental illness.[2] Since then, researchers have found a significantly high degree of mental health in the lesbian population, and writers in the helping professions have continued to emphasize the positive dimensions of growth and development in lesbianism's diversities of expression.[3]

Concurrently, the gay liberation movement and feminism have stimulated the exploration of such topics as awareness of the deleterious effects of societal oppression, homophobia in the society at large, and homophobia in many gay persons.[4] Such societal forces have been viewed primarily as negative because of the emotional toll that such oppression takes, particularly for those who internalize homophobic stereotypes. However, a number of lesbians have felt increased self-fulfillment after coming out to nongay persons and from entering the battle against homophobia.

The literature on social work practice has emphasized helping therapists to examine their own attitudes and biases and intervening with women who have difficulty in coming out.[5] There also have been articles concerned with the specific problems that lesbians may face (alcoholism, dealing with children, coming out to family members) and with issues that involve nongay significant others, such as the family of origin or children of lesbians.[6]

However, little has been written to enable social workers to develop increased competence in working with lesbian couples. Such an omission in the professional literature may reflect either the myth that lesbian relationships are so short lived that they need not be of concern or the idea that they endure for all time. Another reason for the minimal writing on this topic may be the assumption that what works with heterosexual couples will work just as well with lesbian or gay couples. Such an attitude fails to take into account pertinent social factors and differences in support networks. The following sections of this article focus on the implications of these differences for the problem-solving process.

ASSESSMENT OF PROBLEMS

At intake, presenting problems of lesbian couples may seem similar to those brought by nongay couples, such as lack of communication, nagging, attitudes of one partner's parents toward the couple living together, financial problems, and sexual problems. However, there are some distinctions that must be assessed with the lesbian couple in relation to the effects of homophobia, unclear role expectations, different vocational expectations, coming out and political activism, and sexual functioning.

HOMOPHOBIA

Homophobia—the fear of or revulsion against gays—accounts for many problems that lesbian couples face even though increased publicity about gay liberation and more positive attitudes toward a gay identity may make it easier now for a woman to acknowledge a lesbian identity to herself and to other gays.[7] For example, 51 percent of the two hundred women who were interviewed for the study said they would not acknowledge their life-style to nongays, primarily because they feared thay would be rejected by nongay friends and relatives or would suffer economic reprisals if their lesbian identity was confirmed. Therefore, the social worker may have to assess the degree to which the partners are cut off from their support systems. What may have begun as an idyllic union of "the two of us quietly alone against the world" may have turned into a prison.

A first step toward opening up this closed system would be to assess whether the couple has realistic reasons for preventing others from knowing about each partner's lesbianism or whether the couple's fears are based on myths and negative stereotypes about other lesbians. The worker must be supportive of realistic concerns about oppression, such as the inability to confront a homophobic employer because economic pressures require that each partner keeps her job. "Healthy" paranoia is a necessary coping mechanism of oppressed groups and should not be depreciated. Also there may be instances in which it is irrelevant to the nature of the relationship for the couple to come out. However, it also may be that the partners have avoided social contacts with other lesbians because of their own homophobia. For example, the couple may have accepted the viewpoint reflected in this statement by Janeway:

> Locked out of the larger community of man's world, women and homosexuals develop profoundly ambiguous feelings about any sort of community they may set up for themselves. Both groups are notorious for tight but short lived cliques and personal rivalries. Cattiness and disloyalty are expected and . . . are found, as they are among all those who regard part of themselves as unacceptable.[8]

If anything, this statement implies that being women and living a homosexual life-style, lesbians must surely be a negative group with which to affiliate.

The family of origin is one significant support system that may be homophobic and thus unavailable to the couple. Problems frequently arise because of one or both women's conflicts in loyalty to the family and to the partner or overt harassment by family members of one or both women. Again, the social worker has the responsibility to assess with the couple the practicalities of the situation. Clark and Woodman and Lenna present specific guidelines for this process.[9] Some families either cannot be informed of the specific nature of the relationship or already know and reject it. If the inability to be open about the relationship with the family results in a disruption of the couple's communication and affectional patterns, the worker's first focus should be on the partners' interpersonal support of one another, the meaning of family to each of them, and the availability of alternative support systems.

Unclear Role Expectations

The worker must also explore the degree to which the partners have clarified their role expectations prior to or during the early period of living together. Although researchers have found that there is less compartmentalization in "butch/femme" roles, they still exist even among the 18–25-year-old group.[10] For example, 20 percent of the women interviewed for the study described their relationship as involving a division of tasks according to stereotypical roles. In several cases, one partner considered that such a division of tasks was a cause of friction because she was resistant to being locked into behaviors defined in sexist ways.

The social worker should also assess the more subtle dimensions of heterosexual socialization that are rarely expressed. For example, a partner may have a romantic and idealized picture of what a committed relationship should be. Either one or both partners may expect continuous confirmation of the other's undying love and become confused when "the honeymoon is over." That is, the partners may seek counseling to define and implement new adaptations that are relevant to their day-to-day needs.

Vocational Expectations

Still other problems arise because of a conflict between the fulfillment of partnership needs and the demands of vocational expectations. It is necessary to distinguish between factors related to socialization as a woman, the realities of being a woman in a sexist workforce and being a lesbian. For example, one or both partners may feel the need for "nest building" as a result of socialization, yet encounter exceptional demands on the job to survive in a sexist economic marketplace. Concommitantly, identification as a lesbian may place a woman in double jeopardy (of being a woman and homosexual) and affect her relationship to her partner. Separating such role conflicts from one another and identifying them as distinct problems to be solved are vital preliminary steps.

The social worker also must ascertain that the presenting problems are not rationalizations for the inability to cope with other interpersonal problems that seem overwhelming. For example, one young woman who was interviewed for the study expressed concern about whether her present relationship would last. She stated that she had to work long hours to do a good job and get promoted and that her long working hours upset her partner. Furthermore, she had been offered a job transfer to another state, which would not fit in with her partner's goals. As the interviewer explored other aspects of her support systems with her, the woman revealed that her partner was using drugs and alcohol in combination and was frequently suicidal but would not acknowledge her need for help. Thus, the woman had substituted vocational and geographic issues for her partner's emotional instability as "reasons" for leaving an untenable relationship. The couple may also grow at different paces intellectually and vocationally and not be prepared for such divergence.

Coming Out

Conflicts may arise because one partner wants to come out publicly and one wants to remain in the closet. Some participants in the study reported that problems arose even in regard to discussing the couple's sexual-affectional identity with other lesbians. When the issue was broadened to include political activism, a variety of fears surfaced: fear of exposure to the family, fear of the impact that other activists might have on an established way of life, and fear of losing the partner to new persons and associations. Moreover, those who wanted to come out but felt constrained to remain in the closet considered that their potential for growth was being significantly affected and that they and their partner no longer were communicating in meaningful ways. Again, assessment of the reality of fears is necessary before further intervention can be undertaken.

Sexual Problems

Problems in sexual functioning may occur from a lack of information about how to enjoy sex with one another. However, it also may be that other aspects of the relationship are interfering with the partners' ability to communicate with and express affection for one another. The assessment of such factors obviously is essential before educational or other sexual counseling strategies can be undertaken.

In general, presenting problems can be related to difficulties in dovetailing social, intellectual, vocational, political, and sexual-affectional needs. Achieving a balanced relationship in a sexist and homophobic milieu presents problems for many lesbian couples, but the absence of positive support systems makes it impossible to have a growth-producing relationship.

STRATEGIES FOR INTERVENTION

Many female social workers who work with lesbian couples also are deeply committed to feminist therapy.[11] The dimensions of partnership in the helping process, sharing power and knowledge equally, and dealing with the social realities of dual oppression are particularly relevant. In addition, the social worker should be familiar with local and national resources and be able to help clients use pertinent support systems. When needed supports are absent, it is crucial for the social worker to help develop lesbian-related groups, especially because funding agencies and other community agencies are more likely to provide funds and other resources if a professional is involved.[12]

Coping with Homophobia

Intervention to help the lesbian couple cope with or combat homophobia requires that the couple begin with the social system that is creating the greatest stress. If the couple has been fearful about lesbianism itself and about meeting other lesbians, intervention should involve helping the partners first to reassess the myths and stereotypes they have internalized and then to explore involvement with other couples or a group with which they have common interests. This strategy has the dual purpose of assisting the partners to assess individually and together the attributes they can bring to new relationships and to increase their self-esteem. Growth in self-appraisal can help the partners reassess the validity of their choice of life-style and minimize their perception of lesbianism as "second best to marriage" or as crazy or sinful. Comparing what is true and good about each of them with positive role models can be helpful, as can informing them about books that provide positive images of lesbians.[13]

If the partners feel good about themselves and are able to be open with other gays but have problems in dealing with homophobic family members, the first step is to assess whether it is crucial to the couple's relationship to come out to parents, siblings, or other relatives. For example, approximately 25 percent of the women interviewed for the study continued to have self-actualizing relationships with relatives who the women thought were not aware of the women's lesbianism. Ten percent also indicated that their partner's parents were a support system even though the parents did not openly acknowledge their daughter's living situation. One-third of the women had come out and found family members definitely supportive. Techniques to help a gay individual to come out to the family and significant others may also be used with couples.[14]

In some instances, families are not available as supports either because they know about the lesbian relationship and reject it or because they are overtly hostile to the particular partner. As a result, the couple may need help to ventilate grief reactions related to the loss of those who previously were vital in their lives and to build new kinship networks. Most lesbians replace hostile family members with gay friends as their primary support system. However, unless they accomplish the grief work and accept the advantages to be found in friendship systems, they will not be able to develop new viable support networks. In such instances, it may become necessary to reassess the degree to which the partners can make peace with both families without violating their own integrity. If a compromise between the demands of family and of the love relationship is not possible, the worker may have to help the couple become aware of the dangers to each partner's emotional well-being if one partner leaves and returns to a life that is not true to the self.

In dealing with larger homophobic systems, such as religious institutions or places of employment, the worker should help each partner to consider whether it is relevant to her, individually and as part of a couple, for these systems to be informed of the lesbianism. If the fear that others will "find out" is interfering with the couple's day-to-day functioning or if knowledge by others would enhance self-actualization, then the worker can recommend relevant books and provide supportive counseling as the couple pursues various ways to come out to others. There may be instances when coming out is impossible. However, it should be clear that the reasons are based on reality and that the couple is not operating from global generalizations that "everyone is against us" owing to rejection by parents or antagonism from some friends.

Redefinition of Goals

Some dimensions of behavior are more related to the partners' socialization as females than to their lesbian identity per se. For this reason, it would be helpful for the couple to explore and reevaluate what may never have been expressed by either partner, such as why they entered the relationship. They may express such reasons as these: "I was going to help her to come out and grow up." "If I hadn't brought her out and if we hadn't started to live together, she would have gotten in with the wrong crowd." "We were terribly in love and this was a chance for me to get away from home." Although such statements may reflect good short-term reasons for attraction, they have limited potential for insuring a lasting relationship. Verbalizing these expectations may create anxiety. However, with support, the couple may be able to move from identification and assessment of the past to establishing current short- and long-term goals that are more interpersonal than self-oriented.

Although redefinition of goals is also used in counseling with nongays, additional concerns frequently arise in interviews with lesbian couples. For example, in discussions, it may be found that either or both partners were seeking confirmation of their identity as lesbians from the very act of living together. Coming out may have been fraught with anger, depression, or projection of "badness" onto the partner, but the decision to establish a relationship was seen as a way of proving that the lesbian identity itself was real and that a lesbian life-style had validity. That is, if they could live together as a "permanent couple," then they would "be like everyone else" and their choice of identity would be confirmed as right and good. In such a case, the focus of intervention is to help the couple replace internalized negative ideas about lesbianism with a positive self-image. This may not only enhance self-esteem, but may increase respect for the partner.

Dealing with the expectation that the relationship will provide unconditional love (usually to replace feelings of loss generated by actual or implied rejection from the family of origin) requires reality testing of the implications of loving and being loved. The couple may need to develop skills in communicating with each other so they may be able to send messages of esteem and to express their differences.

Furthermore, one or both partners may not want a long-term exclusive relationship but may be fearful of expressing this feeling. For example, several women who were interviewed for the study wanted to move from a sexually exclusive traditional dyad to a sexually open relationship, yet had never communicated this to their partner. Evaluation of the ramifications of such a choice usually boiled down to concerns about who would be the "primary person" and how time and affection would be shared. If both partners are ready for an open nontraditional relationship, they might find support from other women who have worked out variations in their lifestyles. It is essential that trust in the overall sense of responsibility to a primary union must be solidified for such nonsexually exclusive couples.

If role conflicts exist because of stereotyped dichotomies in the assignment of tasks, the partners may be helped by identifying what needs to be done to maintain their system. Then they can be encouraged to try new tasks that might give them new feelings of accomplishment or help them to develop new knowledge. They can assess who likes to do a particular chore because one partner does it better or because the other partner prefers other tasks. Such problem solving takes the behaviors concerned with household management out of the realm of stereotyped roles into one that affords a new potential for growth. If the couple is closely involved with peers who reenforce sex-role stereotyping, the worker will have to support the partners in expressing their individuality in the group.

Weighing Alternatives

To effect a balance between partnership needs and professional demands, the worker must help the couple to weigh the alternatives. First, the couple can be helped to assess whether they require more time with and attention from each other or whether the quality of the attention is the problem. Next, the partners can evaluate how they may arrive at compromises in balancing the pragmatics of economic survival and the necessities of housekeeping with the non-work time they spend together. The social worker can act as a facilitator to help the couple work out alternative opportunities for meeting vocational, partnership, and educational needs. Furthermore, it may be necessary to discuss openly the degree to which particular functions (economic productivity or household activities) have become value laden and need to be reassessed in a nonsexist fashion.

Political Action

As in other problem situations, a first step in dealing with one partner's need to be politically active is to analyze the actual ramifications of public behavior. If irreparable economic hardship would ensue for one partner who is not willing to accept such a sacrifice, then the other partner must weigh the value of the relationship against her personal commitment to becoming an activist. If the decision is to relinquish ideas of political action, then both partners should explore the ramifications of the decision in relation to the residual guilt and anger they may feel toward each other and toward the homophobic systems that created the dilemma. Conflict may be related to one partner's perceptions of persons involved in the gay liberation movement. For example, one respondent described her view of activists as "strident, separatist, flamboyant, and out to have sex with anyone around." In such cases, two levels of intervention are indicated: dealing with residual homophobia within the individual and stereotypic views of other gays and dealing with issues of trust and mistrust. Such concerns are tied to rebuilding the individual's self-esteem as a lesbian in an established lesbian relationship.

Sexual Functioning

The worker's positive attitude toward the sexual functioning of lesbians is particularly vital because the very nature of the problem involves a major rationale for homophobia—that homosexuality is "deviant sexuality." Unless the worker can convey warmth, acceptance, and the belief that the lesbian life-style is not deviant or evil, clients will be reluctant to express their difficulties. Frequently, lack of knowledge, fear of talking with peers, and absence of references in a community may contribute to the lack of gratification in intimacy. The worker should know about and help the couple obtain pertinent material on the subject.[15] When other issues hamper physical intimacy, then the other issues discussed in this article become pertinent. Techniques for treating orgasmic difficulties are also discussed extensively in the literature and should not be overlooked.[16] Essentially, the primary problem-solving task is to help the partners become more open to expressing their love in ways that will have meaning to each of them.

CONCLUSION

This article briefly discussed five problems that lesbian couples may encounter. The difficulties were selected because they were frequently verbalized by lesbians in committed relationships who were interviewed by this author. Differences between traditional marital counseling with heterosexuals and the specific concerns and resolution of problems related to lesbian life-styles have been stressed. This article is not intended to convey the thought that the majority of lesbian couples require social work help, nor has it covered many presenting problems. For example, coping with major mental illness, death and dying, and bringing children into a relationship have been omitted. It might be anticipated that further attention to the concerns of lesbians will stimulate articles to consider the other needs of lesbian couples.

REFERENCES

1. Betty Berzon and Robert Leighton, eds., *Positively Gay* (Millbrae, Calif.: Celestial Arts, 1979); Don Clark, *Loving Someone Gay* (Millbrae, Calif.: Celestial Arts, 1977); Carmen DeMonteflores and Stephen J. Schultz, "Coming Out: Similarities and Differences for Lesbians and Gay Men," *Journal of Social Issues*, 34 (March 1978), pp. 59–71; and Donna M. Tanner, *The Lesbian Couple* (Lexington, Mass.: D. C. Heath, 1978).

2. *Diagnostic and Statistical Manual of Mental Disorders* (2d ed.; Washington, D.C.: American Psychiatric Association, 1968).

3. Janet S. Chafetz et al., "A Study of Homosexual Women," *Social Work*, 19 (November 1974), pp. 714–723; K. D. Ferguson and Deana C. Finkler, "An Involvement and Overtness Measure for Lesbians: Its Development and Relation to Anxiety and Social Zeitgeist," *Archives of Sexual Behavior*, 7 (May 1978), pp. 211–227; Mark Freedman, "Homosexuals May Be Healthier than Straights," *Blueboy*, 5 (April 1976), p. 28; Margaret A. Kingdon, "Lesbians," *Counseling Psychologist*, 8 (January 1979), pp. 44–45; and Sophie Freud Loewenstein, "Understanding Lesbian Women," *Social Casework*, 61 (January 1980), pp. 29–38.

4. Freedman, op. cit., pp. 24–27.

5. Clark, op. cit.; and Natalie J. Woodman and Harry R. Lenna, *Counseling with Gay Men and Women* (San Francisco: Jossey-Bass, 1980).

6. *See* Stephen Beaton and Naome Guild, "Treatment for Gay Problem Drinkers," *Social Casework*, 57 (May 1976), pp. 302–308; Bernice Goodman, *The Lesbian: A Celebration of Difference* (Brooklyn, N.Y.: Out and Out Books, 1977); Marny Hall, "Lesbian Families: Cultural and Clinical Issues," *Social Work*, 23 (September 1978), pp. 380–385; Clark, op. cit.; Julia P. Stanley and Susan J. Wolfe, eds., *The Coming Out Stories* (Watertown, Mass.: Persephone Press, 1980); Woodman and Lenna, op. cit.; Betty Fairchild and Nancy Hayward, *Now That You Know: What Every Parent Should Know About Homosexuality* (New York: Harcourt Brace Jovanovitch, 1979); Karen Gail Lewis, "Children of Lesbians: Their Point of View," *Social Work*, 25 (May 1980), pp. 198–203; and Scott Wirth, "Coming Out Close to Home: Principles of Psychotherapy with Families of Lesbians and Gay Men," *Catalyst*, 1 (March 1978), pp. 6–22.

7. Loewenstein, op. cit.

8. Elizabeth Janeway, *Man's World, Woman's Place: A Study in Social Mythology* (New York: William Morrow & Co., 1971), p. 111.

9. Clark, op. cit.; and Woodman and Lenna, op. cit.

10. Loewenstein, op. cit.

11. Anne Koedt, "Lesbianism and Feminism," in Koedt and others, eds., *Radical Feminism* (New York: Quadrangle Books, 1973); Susan Amelia Thomas, "Theory and Practice in Feminist Therapy," *Social Work*, 22 (November 1977), pp. 447–454; and Hogie Wyckoff, *Solving Women's Problems* (New York: Grove Press, 1977).

12. Woodman and Lenna, op. cit.

13. Sidney Abbott and Barbara Love, *Sappho Was a Right-On Woman: A Liberated View of Lesbianism* (Briarcliff Manor, N.Y.: Stein & Day Publishers, 1973); Rita M. Brown, *Rubyfruit Jungle* (New York: Bantam Books, 1978); and Isabel Miller, *Patience and Sarah* (New York: Fawcett Books, 1979).

14. Clark, op. cit.; and Woodman and Lenna, op. cit.

15. Del Martin and Phyllis Lyon, *Lesbian Love and Liberation: The Book of Sex* (San Francisco: Multi-Media Resource Center, 1973); Emily Sisley and Bertha Harris, *The Joy of Lesbian Sex* (New York: Simon & Schuster, 1978); and Ginny Vida, ed., *Our Right To Love: A Lesbian Resource Book* (Englewood Cliffs, N.J.: Prentice-Hall, 1978), chap. 4.

16. Lonnie G. Barbach, *For Yourself: Fulfillment of Female Sexuality—A Guide to Orgasmic Response* (New York: Doubleday & Co., 1976); and Nancy Toder, "Sexual Problems of Lesbians," in Ginny Vida, ed., *Our Right to Love: A Lesbian Resource Book* (Englewood Cliffs, N.J.: Prentice-Hall, 1978).

3
Economic Roles and Power

DILEMMAS IN ROLE IDENTIFICATION FOR LOW-INCOME WOMEN

Betsy McAlister Groves
Marie Cassella
Jane Jacobs

Much has been written about the limited choice of roles available to low-income women.[1] In a tight economy, the gap between the middle-class conception of a woman's role and what is actually available to low-income women widens. As Sidel put it: "Society paints a picture of affluence and success but does not help the individual reach that remote level of ease and comfort."[2]

The impact of the women's movement, especially as it is portrayed in the mass media, complicates this issue. The media increasingly are focusing on the image of the "liberated woman"—one who has a career, shares tasks equally with her husband, is assertive, and has a life of her own. However, the lives of low-income women are far removed from this popularized image. Thus, low-income women are in a bind: the mass culture offers them a model of the "liberated woman" but does not give them the financial or economic tools to become liberated.

Much of the existing literature on the formation of the feminine identity and the choice of roles has focused on middle-class women.[3] The authors believe that the particular social and economic features of poverty make identity formation a different process for low-income women. Through an examination of relevant theory and case material, this article presents a different conceptual framework for understanding this process in low-income women and draws implications for relevant treatment.

The article grew out of informal discussions by the authors, who are middle-class social workers, in an attempt to synthesize their understanding of the feminist movement with the realities and experiences of their low-income clients. In examining the discrepancy between society's views of success and the experiences of their low-income clients, the workers shifted from the problems low-income women face to the strengths and distinctive qualities of the low-income culture. Specifically, the article uses what is known about the development of the feminine personality to understand the importance of significant peer and familial reference groups in the identity formation of and role choices for low-income women.

In examining the positive aspects of the low-income experience, it is important to understand some of the factors that contribute to identity formation. For the purpose of this article, two aspects of identity formation will be considered: the role of significant reference groups and the distinctive features of the feminine identity.

IDENTITY FORMATION

Erikson stated that for the adolescent to move from many part identifications to a coherent identity he or she must

> ... find a niche in some section of society ... which is firmly defined and yet seems to be made uniquely for him [or her]. In finding it the young adult gains an assured sense of inner continuity and social sameness which will bridge what he [or she] *was* as a child and what he is *about to become,* and will reconcile his conception of himself and his community's recognition of him. . . .[4]

The need for recognition is relevant to the discussion of the process through which poor women make choices in roles. Because the roles offered by middle-class society often do not help these women validate their inner conception of themselves, low-income women look for this recognition within their culture.

The insularity of low-income cultures has been well documented. For example, Gans wrote of the power of the "peer group society" for low-income people.[5] By this he meant that poor adolescents relate to the value system of peers of the same sex and their extended family to the virtual exclusion of the values espoused by the larger society. This "peer culture" (actually reflecting both peer and family values) defines a broad range of attitudes and behaviors throughout an individual's adult life.

Economic factors often dictate the values of such peer reference groups. Low-income women belong to reference groups that value caretaking skills. In low-income multiproblem families, poverty pervades every aspect of life. The families are typically headed by single parents who work full or part time. Because there is no money for child care or a babysitter, child care responsibilities are left to the older children, usually the oldest daughter. Thus, the oldest daughter assumes the role of parent: running the house, cooking meals, and caring for the younger children.

This "daughter/parent" learns that she is praised and valued for this role—that the survival of the family is contingent on her performance. She incorporates these caretaking attributes into her identity, receiving from her family validation of her competence in assuming the role.

The validation the low-income woman receives for her caretaking skills provides the "recognition" described by Erikson as being crucial to identity formation. She receives this validation from her familial and peer reference groups, rather than from the larger society. The authors contend that extensive use of these reference groups can be a healthy adaptive phenomenon in the low-income culture. To understand this phenomenon, it is important to consider features of personality development that are particular to women.

PERSONALITY DEVELOPMENT

Basic distinctions in the female and male personality influence identity formation and the choice of roles. Despite different terminology, psychologists describe a similar constellation of qualities that differentiate women from men. The most common distinction is the woman's need for affiliation versus the man's need for mastery.

Hoffman discussed the woman's strong need for affiliation (for approval and love) as being a barrier to achievement, since in a competitive situation, the woman's need for affiliation often predominates over her needs for mastery and competence.[6] Bakan described the male personality as "[manifesting] itself in self-protection, self-assertion, self-esteem . . . [and] . . . the urge to master. . . ." He described the female personality as "communal . . . [manifesting] itself in the sense of being at one with other organisms . . . in non-contractual co-operation."[7]

These distinctions have also been noted in relation to career choices and work aspirations of adolescent boys and girls. For example, Davis described a study in which blue-collar adolescents were asked to rank order their career choices and list which qualities or attributes would be most important to them in their job.[8] For girls, the most important features of the job were to have a "chance to help others and to work with nice people." For boys, high pay and job security were among the highest ranked features.

Romer's study—a follow-up of Horner's fear-of-success studies in adult women—discussed adolescent girls' and boys' motives in avoiding success.[9] Romer found that fear of success by adolescent girls usually centers on themes of affiliation, such as success will interfere with personal relationships or will cause a loss of friendship or popularity.

The aforementioned authors stressed that a woman sees herself in terms of relationships with others. She is less individualistic and less concerned with the mastery of tasks than a man, but is more concerned with her self-concept as it is reflected in her significant reference groups. These characteristics make it difficult for a woman to separate from her family. It must be pointed out, however, that psychoanalytic theories that equate independence and autonomy with sound mental health sometimes devalue the greater concern for relatedness than for mastery of tasks. These theories, then, may confuse an interdependent life-style with the inability to differentiate oneself from others.

Such theorists as Chodorow have recently explored the tendency of women to have permeable ego boundaries as an adaptive rather than a pathological mode of functioning. Chodorow also noted that separation from and individuation in the family are more difficult for girls than for boys because mothers tend to identify more with daughters and to help them differentiate less.[10] Because of this close identification and because mothers have far more contact than do fathers with girls early in life, Chodorow suggested that girls develop a personal identification mode which is based on a more intense sense of interpersonal relationship than do boys. In Western cultures, fathers are usually away from home all day. Therefore, a boy is more likely to identify with his perception of what his father does rather than who he is. Chodorow referred to this as a "positional identification" as opposed to the more intense "personal" identification that girls experience with their mothers.

Chodorow went on to say:

> . . . a girl's internalized and external object relations [are] more complex and . . . more defining of her than those of a boy. . . . [Women's] lives always involve other . . . equally deep and primary relationships, especially with their children, and, more importantly, with other women. In these spheres, . . . a girl imposes the . . . object-relations she has internalized in her preoedipal and later relationships to her mother.[11]

Chodorow also suggested that the cultural adaptability of women with fluid ego-boundaries depends largely on the familial and social structures of the society in question. In middle-class Western society, characterized by nuclear households, the intense identification between mothers and daughters may impede the daughter's differentiation because of the mother's social isolation and resulting need for her daughter's presence.

Chodorow contrasted this situation with cultures in which women have established an area of social influence through peer and kin networks. In these cultures, other members of the network can diffuse the intense mother-daughter relationship and offer differential role modeling. The legitimate social functions of the kin network provide important external activities that contribute to the women's self-esteem and further dilute the excessive intensity of interpersonal relationships.

In cultures where such networks exist, women can use their capacity for engaging in more communal activities to their advantage, developing a rich interpersonal network that provides a sense of inner security in the face of poverty and adversity. In these cases, diffuse ego boundaries are not pathological; they allow the formation of a coherent personal identity based on a positive communal experience.

Stack observed this phenomenon in the coping strategies of poor black women.[12] To deal with the demands of ghetto life, the women run multi-generational households. Such an arrangement, in which extended kin assume major responsibility for children and exert authority over the behavior of related adults, has many positive functions in a lower-class environment.

The authors contend that the capacity of low-income women for extensive use of peer and kin networks and the formation of an identity based on communal experiences are indications of good mental health and strong functioning. This leads, then, to a conception of mental health that does not stress separateness of ego boundaries or an individualistic sense of self, but rather assesses a woman's abilities to use the peer and kin networks available to her. In Erikson's terms, this view of mental health focuses on the aspect of identification that stresses the importance of developing a sense of "inner continuity and social sameness" that bridges the gap between the individual and the community.

DILEMMAS OF THERAPY

Considering this concept of mental health, middle-class female social workers are faced with several dilemmas in their work with low-income women. The dilemmas revolve around the impact of the feminist movement on therapy and middle-class culture-bound conceptions of mental health.

The feminist movement accentuates the difference between traditional feminine roles and upwardly mobile middle-class aspirations. In addition, as middle-class women increasingly choose to separate geographically from their nuclear family, postpone childbearing, and invest themselves more in careers, low-income women have fewer grounds on which to identify with them. In the therapeutic relationship, this polarization may cause problems. It is a temptation for middle-class workers to view low-income peer cultures in a negative way, either by seeing them as too limiting or by devaluing the traditional nurturing roles the culture espouses for women.

This polarization of cultural views often places the low-income client in a bind with the social worker. The client feels pulled between loyalty to the worker and to the peer network; however, she chooses the peer network because of its considerable power. A more positive view of the peer and kin networks of low-income women would facilitate a better alliance between client and worker. Careful assessment of these networks also enables the worker to exploit their positive aspects and use them as an integral part of therapy. Through these networks, women share necessary responsibilities they cannot afford to purchase. Depending on the cohesiveness of the networks, the women may be able to internalize the supports as an inner sense of security in a hostile environment. The individualistic psychology practiced by many social workers does not account for these positive functions.

A mediating figure, such as an aunt, cousin, or neighbor, is particularly useful in helping the low-income woman achieve desired goals, especially if her aspirations involve nontraditional roles. She does so by serving as a crucial role model for the client. Because the client may be able to identify more readily with such a figure, she may be able to use this person as a mediator between the low-income culture and the wider society. Although the mediating individual may not necessarily have high status, according to the standards of the larger society, she may have prestige in the neighborhood because of her parenting skills, stability, or some other valued trait. By inviting the active support of such a figure, the social worker may be able to help the client feel she can pursue whatever role she wishes without having to cut crucial ties with her family and neighborhood. In this view, the worker acknowledges the interdependent nature of female identifications as a characteristic, not necessarily as a pathological process, and thus uses a different set of therapeutic interventions.

CASE EXAMPLES

In the following two case examples, the clients were able to negotiate separation and role choice by using significant figures in their peer culture. The social worker's acknowledgment of the importance of these networks was of crucial importance to the success of each case.

Mary M

Mary M, age 16, was referred to the community center by her school counselor because she was depressed and not living up to her academic potential. Mary was the oldest of five children in an intact first-generation Irish Catholic family. Mary's father, a bus driver, was an alcoholic; Mary's mother suffered from disabling high blood pressure. As a result, Mary was placed in a caretaker role, babysitting for the younger children and calming down her mercurial father.

Mary's family devalued her because she had ideas that made her seem alien to them. To everyone's astonishment, Mary loved the public television station, was emotionally effusive, and wanted to become a political scientist or a journalist. Mary felt furious at her family for their criticism, but could not use her anger to fuel separation from them because of her caretaking responsibilities.

Mary was able to ventilate her feelings to the social worker, but was unable to confront her parents with her anger at their failure to assume the appropriate responsibility. Fortunately, Mr. M's employer threatened to fire him if he did not go to Alcoholics Anonymous. Within a few weeks, Mr. M was sober and a more available and responsible parent.

Mary was now freer to think about separating from her family and establishing career goals. Although she discussed them at length with the social worker, she remained deeply affected by her family's and friends' indifference to her aspirations.

A turning point came when Mary's father took her on a long-awaited trip to Ireland to visit his extended family. There Mary met two "wonderful" aunts who heartily supported her plans. Although not professionals, these women were highly regarded in their town as strong, decisive figures. Mary wrote the social worker a long letter from Ireland about her aunts. When she returned home, she was able to ask the worker to help her apply to colleges and to make other plans.

This case illustrates the importance of kinship networks in the development of a coherent identity. The Ms' modest income intensified Mary's isolation and dependence on her family, so their devaluation of her was powerful. By itself, the social worker's support was not sufficient to provide Mary with the validation she needed to separate from her parents and to pursue a nontraditional career. Mary's aunts were crucial in providing the "inner continuity and social sameness" (as Erikson put it) that links the developing self to the values of the community. As in Chodorow's schema, Mary especially needed to feel she was still connected to a community of women in her extended family. This was not indicative of pathology; rather, it was an affiliative mode of identification that enabled her to develop further.

Patricia

Patricia, an 18-year-old woman with a young son, was forced to leave home after she told her parents she was pregnant. At first, her parents were angry, expressing feelings of betrayal and sadness. As the oldest daughter in a family of six children with an alcoholic father and depressed mother, she had functioned as the caretaker and organizer of the family.

Patricia's reason for seeking mental health treatment was that she felt ambivalent about the pregnancy and despondent about her family's reaction to it. Although she stated her belief that becoming pregnant might have been the only way to separate from her family, she was not prepared for their anger or rejection.

With the help of the social worker, Patricia was able to negotiate the welfare system, obtain an apartment, and prepare, emotionally, for the baby's arrival. Once the baby was born, Patricia demonstrated an exceptional ability to assume the role of mother. Both she and her child thrived.

In therapy, she began to look at her mothering skills as a source of pride and self-esteem. She became much less depressed as she recognized that this role was highly valued by the reference groups that were important to her, specifically her family and friends. It was through this skill that Patricia regained status in her family.

Patricia was then able to use the social worker's help to enroll in a nontraditional job-skills training program, where she learned welding and electronics. She arranged for full-time child care with a family friend, and another friend provided transportation. She saw her mother daily. Her family became proud of her ambitions and her ability to manage a child and a career.

Patricia's initial difficulty lay in her inability to separate from her family. Like Mary, she was the oldest daughter in a family that depended heavily on her. Her pregnancy provided a means of exit from the family, although it also brought anger and rejection.

It is significant that Patricia used her skills as a parent and caretaker to regain esteem and position in the family system. Thus the process of separation involved her choice of a role that was self-sustaining, self-gratifying, and valued by significant reference groups. By choosing the role of parent and caretaker and performing competently, she was able to internalize the achievement and the validation she received for it. She was also able to synthesize her image of herself with the image others had of her.

It is also significant that after consolidating these gains internally, Patricia was then able to use her peer and kin networks to make the more autonomous step of pursuing a nontraditional career. Applying Chodorow's theory to Patricia's gains, it may be said that Patricia was able to use her capacity for a more communal experience in negotiating separation and in choosing a role for herself. This ability can be viewed not in terms of diffuse ego boundaries, but as a healthy resolution of the task of identity formation.

CONCLUSION

This article has examined the ways in which distinctive aspects of feminine identity formation facilitate separation and the successful choice of roles by low-income women. In a larger sense, this mode of identity formation suggests a concept of mental health that views women's social interdependence and affiliative needs as potentially positive. The authors contend that an interdependent form of functioning is particularly adaptive for women living in poverty.

The women's movement has spurred a fresh examination of these communal qualities. For example, Miller called for a reconceptualization of psychological maturity. As she put it:

> Women are quite validly seeking something more complete than autonomy as it is defined for men, a fuller not lesser ability to encompass relationships to others, simultaneously with the fullest development of oneself.[13]

Miller stated that such affiliative concerns, through which women have historically subordinated themselves to the success of others, should now be channeled into helping each other with their own development. The social worker also needs to utilize the supports inherent in the social networks of low-income women to help them develop an identity—even a nontraditional one—that incorporates their sense of being connected to their family and friends.

Social work is committed to understanding the social context of human behavior. The interplay between the individual and a hostile or a facilitating environment has been a hallmark of social work theory. For this reason, the role of kinship networks in women's development constitutes a natural area for social workers to explore. Moreover, the social work field can use this orientation to make an important contribution to the reconceptualization of feminine identity formation.

REFERENCES

1. *See,* for example, Catherine S. Chilman, *Adolescent Sexuality in a Changing American Society: Social and Psychological Perspectives* (Washington, D.C.: U.S. Department of Health, Education & Welfare, 1979); H. Dansereau, "Work and the Teen-age Blue-Collarite," in Arthur B. Shostak and William Gomberg, eds., *Blue-Collar World: Studies of the American Worker* (Englewood Cliffs, N.J.: Prentice-Hall, 1964); Lillian B. Rubin, *Worlds of Pain: Life in the Working Class Family* (New York: Basic Books, 1976); and Nancy Seifer, *Nobody Speaks for Me! Self Portraits of American Working Class Women* (New York: Simon & Schuster, 1976).

2. Ruth Sidel, *Urban Survival: The World of Working Class Women* (Boston: Beacon Press, 1978), p. 167.

3. Matina Horner, "Femininity and Successful Achievement: A Basic Inconsistency," in Judith M. Bardwick et al., eds., *Feminine Personality and Conflict* (Belmont, Calif.: Brooks/Cole, 1972); Karen Horney, *Feminine Psychology* (New

136 / GROVES, CASSELLA, AND JACOBS

York: W. W. Norton & Co., 1967); and Jean Baker Miller, *Toward a New Psychology of Women* (Boston: Beacon Press, 1976).

4. Eric Erikson, *Identity and the Life Cycle* (New York: W. W. Norton & Co., 1959), p. 120.

5. Herbert Gans, *Urban Villagers* (New York: Free Press, 1962), pp. 74–103.

6. Lois Hoffman, "Early Childhood Experiences and Women's Achievement Motives," *Journal of Social Issues*, 28 (February 1972), pp. 129–155.

7. David Bakan, *The Duality of Human Existence: Isolation and Communion in Western Man* (Boston: Beacon Press, 1966), p. 15.

8. Ethelyn Davis, "Careers as Concerns of Blue-Collar Girls," in Arthur B. Shostak and William Gomberg, eds., *Blue Collar World: Studies of the American Worker* (Englewood Cliffs, N. J.: Prentice-Hall, 1964), pp. 154–164.

9. Nancy Romer, "The Motive to Avoid Success and Its Effects on Performance in School-Age Males and Females," *Developmental Psychology*, 2 (November 1975), pp. 689–699; and Horner, op. cit.

10. Nancy Chodorow, "Family Structure and the Feminine Personality," in Michael Z. Rosaldo and Louise Lamphere, eds., *Women, Culture and Society* (Stanford, Calif.: Stanford University Press, 1974), pp. 43–66.

11. Ibid., p. 53.

12. Carol Stack, "Sex Roles and Survival Strategies in an Urban Black Community," in Michael Z. Rosaldo and Louise Lamphere, eds., *Women, Culture and Society* (Stanford, Calif.: Stanford University Press, 1974), pp. 113–128.

13. Miller, op. cit., pp. 94–95.

WORK REQUIREMENTS FOR AFDC MOTHERS

Kathleen Spangler Hill

Economic and societal changes have stimulated the increased participation of women in the labor force. As of May 1980, women made up 42.4 percent of the U.S. civilian labor force—a 50 percent increase over twenty years ago. Yet, the median weekly earnings of women were only 62 percent of those of men.[1] The purpose of this article is to examine the special policy implications of these conditions for single mothers in the Aid to Families with Dependent Children (AFDC) program as they seek to reconcile traditional parental responsibilities with mandatory work requirements.

Increased inflation, more single-parent homes, and the women's movement have contributed to the growing number of women in the workforce. The women's movement, in particular, has strengthened the conviction that women can and should work outside the home—that work is a source of self-identification, self-fulfillment, and full citizenship. Feminists see work as the means of gaining access to the rewards of American society. Thus, the role of women has been expanded to include work outside the home as well as the traditional responsibilities of home maintenance and child care.

This changed definition of the role of women has lent support to the increasing emphasis on work requirements in the AFDC program, beginning with the 1967 amendments to the Social Security Act, which created the Work Incentive (WIN) program. Former President Jimmy Carter's welfare reform package included a provision to encourage the employment of welfare recipients through the work test, which demands proof that the recipients are making a minimal effort to find employment, not that they have found a job.

The author acknowledges the help of Marilyn L. Flynn, DSW, and Edmund V. Mech, Ph.D., School of Social Work, University of Illinois, Urbana-Champaign, in developing the ideas presented in this article.

President Ronald Reagan's proposed reform of "workfare" goes one step farther. It would require AFDC mothers to work twenty hours a week at public service jobs to "earn" their grants. An additional twenty hours each week would be required for job-search activities. Mothers with children under age 3 and mothers with children aged 3–6 who are unable to find day care would be exempt. This is a modification of the current requirement that mandates AFDC mothers in good health with children over age 6 to seek employment by registering with WIN or the local office of their state employment service.

ORIGINAL INTENT

Yet, there is an inherent contradiction between the new emphasis on employment and the original intent of the AFDC program. When the program was established in 1935, grants were provided to mothers on the condition that they function as "suitable" parents. As Barth, Carcagno, and Palmer stated: "One avowed purpose of the program was to substitute benefits for the earnings of missing husbands so that mothers could devote their time to raising their children."[2]

That mothers in the AFDC program are increasingly being included in the able-bodied, employable category is a reflection partly of the change in the typical AFDC recipient over time and partly of the increased number of recipients. For instance, in the 1960s, the largest group in the female-headed-family category was widows (35 percent). In the 1970s, the largest group was divorced women (29 percent), followed by separated women (28 percent) and widows (26 percent).[3] Haveman put it this way:

> By the early 1960's the program had clearly become the repository for those welfare cases that involved dependent children whose mothers or fathers or both were neither blind, nor old, nor sick, nor widowed, nor apparently between jobs, and who, therefore, had as far as welfare critics were concerned, no obvious excuse to receive public charity in a work oriented society.[4]

UNCHANGED OPPORTUNITY STRUCTURE

Moreover, although social expectations have changed, the opportunity structure for low-income female entrants in the labor market has not. Research sponsored by the Carnegie Corporation concluded that white men still dominate business, government, the media, education, and health institutions even though 60 percent of all Americans are women or minority members.[5] For example, of the 441 occupations listed in the Census classification report, working women were in the majority in only 20, and 60 percent of all working women were found in the job classifications of clerk, saleswoman, waitress, and hairdresser. The consequences of this complicated and conflicting situation, in which there is an increased emphasis on work requirements without an increase in opportunities derived from work, reduces the likelihood that single mothers in the AFDC program will derive meaningful benefits either from the new impetus to work or from the traditional role of parent.

To demonstrate this more clearly, consider the following three points. First, the economic welfare of a female-headed AFDC family is not apt to improve significantly through employment. The analysis of census data showed that women aged 25–34 can earn enough to keep a family of three children out of poverty in 80 percent of all traditional male occupations, but in only 45 percent of all traditional female occupations.[6] Yet, as noted earlier, 60 percent of the employed women are still located in the traditional twenty female job classifications.

A second related issue is the lack of jobs for single mothers. The economy is suffering from a loose labor market in which many skilled and experienced persons are seeking work. Programs to train and upgrade the disadvantaged have had little success in this kind of market.

A third issue is the growing evidence that the condition of the labor market has a measurable impact on the decision to apply for and receive welfare.[7] The economy is not healthy. For example, the unemployment rate for March 1981 was 7.3 percent nationwide and 9.4 percent in Illinois. Although these percentages are not as high as they were in 1974, they are still above the accepted definition of a healthy economy with an unemployment rate of less than 4 percent.[8]

An important consequence of this low opportunity structure is the cost to the public of work requirements. Welfare mothers move from inadequate AFDC benefits to inadequately paid full-time jobs or to continued welfare benefits that supplement their low wages. Imposing a work requirement does not move welfare mothers off the roles in appreciable numbers. Garfinkel and Orr analyzed the parameters of the welfare program and concluded that the imposition of a work requirement would increase the employment rate of AFDC recipients from 18 percent to a little more than 20 percent.[9] Although this is a relatively large percentage increase in employment, its impact is minor because the percentage change is based on so small an existing employment base. Moreover, if the objective is to get AFDC mothers to work, the imposition of a work test is likely to be ineffective because the decision to work includes so many other variables. And, the work test would entail higher administrative costs and higher benefits to those single mothers now working.

One parameter of the program that has been successfully manipulated is the program guarantee, which is the basic dollar amount allocated to families for food and maintenance. Before 1968, the guarantee was manipulated in twenty-six states in the following way: An amount of X dollars was established as the minimum money needed to maintain a family with proper food and housing. Then a percentage of that amount, perhaps 50 percent, was given to eligible welfare families. Thus, if the guarantee was $200, a family received a monthly allotment of $100. The family would be allowed to keep any earnings between the $100 check and the $200 established guarantee. After the $200 amount was reached, deductions would be made in the family's check. This approach was designed to encourage welfare recipients to work. However, a family that was unable to earn the additional money would be forced to exist on a starvation-level income. Although this approach encourages work behavior and seemed to be a part of the Carter administrations's proposed welfare reform, it is questionable whether an existing benefit could be removed from recipients and whether it is ethical to allow people to starve to encourage them to work.

An equally important observation is that single mothers in the AFDC population are workers and that AFDC is not a permanent way of life for them. For example, in 1976, one-fifth of all the WIN applicants were volunteers and were exempt from mandatory work requirements. Virtually all on the AFDC rolls have had work experience. AFDC seems to act as a buffer when earnings are low or irregular. Also, researchers have found that most recipients stay on the rolls fewer than three years.[10] Work requirements do not, then, motivate a nonworking population to work, and the low employment-opportunity structure does not enhance the well-being of families on AFDC.

SHORTAGE OF TIME

Second, low-income families, especially single mothers who are AFDC recipients, are time poor as well as income poor. They cannot provide the services their families need in the home and earn enough money at a job to raise themselves from poverty. For example, in-kind programs such as Medicaid and Food Stamps characteristically require frequent long periods of waiting in public assistance offices to establish and maintain eligibility. Furthermore, agencies that administer these programs do not maintain hours that are conducive to an employed mother, requiring her to lose essential time from work. Such losses affect her job and her work performance. Programs such as the Food Stamp program are built on the assumption of unlimited time by the user. The food stamp allotments, designed for the purchase of minimum staples needed to provide basic nutrition, require comparison shopping at several stores if the user is to be able to purchase the necessary foods for adequate meals. A mother, employed full time, cannot practice these food economies effectively.

The value of home-produced goods and services takes on added importance in low-income families whose incomes are limited and who lack the time benefits of a two-parent home. For example, home-produced goods and services such as cooking inexpensive cuts of meat, preparing only home-cooked meals, doing simple appliance repairs, and basic automobile maintenance are more economical but more time consuming than purchasing these services. Yet, single mothers on AFDC lack funds to purchase these services and lack the time to do them themselves. Although the importance of these goods and services is frequently mentioned, little has been done to replace the time lost with other services or sources of income or to include the costs in the determination of income needs.

Time shortages have their effect on the children too. For example, research studies have indicated that working mothers provide less adequate supervision for their children than do nonworking mothers.[11] Although one cannot infer that children of low-income mothers are more likely to be delinquent, lack of supervision has been directly linked with increased delinquency. Thus, the absence of the working mother from the home often results in increased contacts with school and legal officials, which further strains the mother's limited time.

AFDC earnings are often taxed over 100 percent when other in-kind program benefits and lost home-production time are added in. Expenses that may be directly attributed to work, such as transportation and purchased meals, are frequently counted as income for housing subsidies and the like, even though they do not add to the family's spending ability. The loss of the mother's time in the home increases the family's income needs if the family is to maintain itself at the level it was prior to the mother's reentry into the labor market. Failure to account for this leads to overestimation and overtaxation of income, which reduce the actual financial rewards of working and deprive AFDC children of adequate income to meet their basic needs. Thus, publicly supported transfer programs unintentionally contribute to the neglect of these children.

Increased income partially compensates for the shortage of time that many employed mothers experience. However, this is not true for AFDC mothers who cannot simultaneously provide the services their children need in the home and earn enough money outside the home for their families to be nonpoor. As Vickery explained:

> A single parent with two or three children has only thirty-eight hours available for household work after working at a full-time job. She is time poor. Indeed, [one] study has estimated that one adult with two or three children required $78 in weekly income [$161 by 1980 standards] and *61 hours of nonmarket work* . . . for the family to be at the poverty threshold (of $4,540) in 1973 [$8,410 in 1980].[12]

As was noted earlier, few welfare mothers can earn this amount of money in traditional female jobs. This underscores the benefits of a two-parent home that are often discounted in social agencies when budgets and criteria for eligibility are established. The result is that AFDC mothers who work tend to invest less of themselves in family life while obtaining fewer essential services.

MULTIPLE ROLES

How can single mothers on AFDC be helped to manage the multiple roles of parent, employee, and adult when faced with poverty and personal crises? Although information about the effects on the child of the parent's employment tend to be contradictory, much research starts from the premise that it is harmful. Similarly, studies have assumed that children growing up in welfare homes are also being harmed, especially since the role model of a nonworking parent promotes nonwork in the child when he or she reaches adulthood.[13] However, several studies have indicated that the employment of the parent is irrelevant to the child's aspirations to work. For example, Kriesberg, in a comparison of female-headed and male-headed homes, determined that adult sons from AFDC families were as likely to have a high occupational status as those from the population at large, which implies that family form is not a significant contributor to occupational achievement.[14] Brandwein, Brown, and Fox speculated that problems in single-parent homes come not from lack of a father but from the lack of a full-time mother because the mother is forced to spread her energies beyond her child-rearing tasks.[15]

Little is known about the resources needed by working mothers on AFDC other than the extensive cost-benefit and related studies on day care.[16] The single parent's management of her multiple roles has been given little consideration, even with the increasing evidence that the redefinition of women's role has meant the addition of responsibilities—not just a change in responsibilities. Women, especially low-income women, are still socialized from an early age to choose limited areas of opportunity. Furthermore, the schools have not helped women widen the range of options open to them so they may choose from the same alternatives available to men. Moreover, the current socialization process will perpetuate the placement of greater value on ascribed statuses (such as physical appearance or mothering) than on achieved statuses (such as a career or offices held). The result is that women will be expected to manage more roles with limited skills and with less knowledge of the resources that might help them.

Owing to the current emphasis on day care benefits and work skills, the focus of public policy has been on the time the mother is at work. The importance of her time at home and her child care responsibilities have been ignored. The working mother must deal with the strain involved in assuming two roles—that of a good parent and that of a good employee. This strain in roles is increased in low-income families because the mother is less likely to work by choice. It is further magnified by large-sized families, less income, and more difficulty in making child care arrangements.

Ignoring the complexities of this situation is a problem for the society as well as for the family. For instance, the parent's attitude toward work has been determined to be the decisive factor in the child's approach to work as an adult. It is not whether the parent works, but whether the parent finds work rewarding and satisfying that has the greatest influence on the child's attitude toward work.[17] If the parent is overburdened and cannot handle any role well, her dissatisfaction with work will be great, her child will not be motivated to work or be attached to the workforce, and thus society will have difficulty in maintaining itself.

Social workers, with their vast experience in helping families deal with role stress, must begin to consider the special problems of single AFDC mothers. Public policy on employment for AFDC mothers must also recognize the importance of the time the working parent spends at home and its effect not only on the parent but on all family relationships.

A CREATIVE APPROACH

The conclusion is not that low-income women should remain at home, but, rather, that more creative policies are needed to assist AFDC mothers to manage their multiple roles. New employment and training programs under the Comprehensive Employment and Training Act and job placement efforts through WIN attack some of the structural problems (such as inadequate training and discrimination in employment) that AFDC mothers face in the labor market. They were designed to change the current market system and to move women's traditional jobs to a parity with men's jobs and to generate the earnings necessary to make women self-supporting and independent. Although the aim of the current policy to alter the system is necessary and admirable, it is not sufficient to bring about the changes needed by women who will be required to seek employment in the next decade.

A more creative approach, which would also be more responsive to the total needs of AFDC women, would (1) eliminate the categorization of AFDC female heads of families as employable based on such arbitrary criteria as a child's age, (2) develop an employment scale based on the individual characteristics of the parent in which the AFDC mother would be ranked from "very employable" to "not employable," and (3) establish a fixed dollar amount to be used each year to help AFDC mothers improve their skills so they could eventually return to work.

The first feature of this approach—eliminating employment categories based only on the age of the child—recognizes that age is not the key variable in the decision to work. When children reach 6 years, no major transformation occurs that suddenly gives them the maturity needed to fend for themselves while their mothers are working. Mothers must be involved in the decision about when their children are ready for more independence and when the home situation is most conducive to the loss of a major portion of the mothers' time.

The second feature has two elements. First, an individualized employment scale would capture the numerous factors outside the workplace that affect employability. It would include not only demographic characteristics such as age, sex, and education, but also the management of home time, child care responsibilities, cost of care, an employer's acceptance of the mother, and the mother's ability to manage multiple roles.

Second, such an employment scale would be based on the recognition that all the individual variables combine to influence the acceptance of a mother in the labor market as well as her willingness to be in the labor market. That is, a person deemed "highly employable" would be more ready to start working and more acceptable to an employer. Furthermore, she would need fewer costly support services than a person scored as "slightly employable." Consequently, the "highly employable" mother would require less expenditure of tax funds to become self-supporting. This ranking of employability would not prevent an individual who wished to find work from doing so, but it would provide a sounder basis on which to decide how funds to promote work efforts should be allocated.

The third part of the option—a predetermined dollar amount to be used to encourage work among AFDC mothers—recognizes that the taxpayers' commitment to the work ethic is in an inverse relationship to the amount of tax dollars needed to encourage work efforts. There is a point at which work expenditures for mothers become too expensive for the taxpayers and for the families involved. The use of a set figure removes the current open-ended system of expenditures and places the burden of thoughtful expenditure on program administrators. It would be essential for administrators who used the proposed employment scale to determine how to obtain the most benefit from the funds available and to provide the most benefit to AFDC mothers covered by the program.

CONCLUSION

This approach to work requirements, which seeks to reconcile the parenting and working roles of AFDC mothers, would continue to support the desirability of work, but at a fixed dollar amount each year. It would establish a program in which administrators could use more cost-effective guidelines to make decisions about programs. Further, it would permit AFDC mothers to decide when they should go to work and provide more support for them in managing their many conflicting roles. It would again recognize that AFDC was established to provide for the care of children.

The quality of family relationships, as much as earnings themselves, will contribute materially to whether the work experience is satisfying for welfare mothers. The negative consequences of work on the family life of the poor will be reduced by increasing the flexibility of administrative provisions, and AFDC mothers will be able to derive the maximum benefits from work for themselves and their families.

REFERENCES

1. U.S. Bureau of the Census, *Statistical Abstract of the United States: 1980* (Washington, D.C.: U.S. Government Printing Office, 1980), pp. 394, 424.

2. Michael C. Barth, George J. Carcagno, and John L. Palmer, *Toward An Effective Income Support System: Problems, Prospects, and Choices* (Madison: Institute for Research on Poverty, University of Wisconsin, 1974), p. 168.

3. Heather L. Ross and Isabel V. Sawhill, *Time of Transition* (Washington, D.C.: Urban Institute, 1975), pp. 50–61.

4. Robert H. Haveman, ed., *A Decade of Federal Antipoverty Programs* (New York: Academic Press, 1971), p. 73.

5. Council on Interracial Books for Children, *Racism and Sexism* (New York: Carnegie Corporation, 1976).

6. Ross and Sawhill, op. cit.

7. David W. Lyon, *The Dynamics of Welfare Dependency, A Survey* (no place listed: Institute of Political Science and Public Affairs, Spring 1977), p. 75.

8. *Employment and Earnings* (Washington, D.C.: U.S. Department of Labor, May 1981), pp. 5, 114.

9. Irwin Garfinkel and Larry L. Orr, *Welfare Policy and the Employment Rate of AFDC Mothers* (Madison: Institute for Research on Poverty, University of Wisconsin, 1975), pp. 282–284.

10. Lyon, op. cit., p. 5.

11. Lois Wladis Hoffman and F. Ivan Nye, *Working Mothers: An Evaluative Review of the Consequences for Wife, Husband, and Child* (San Francisco: Jossey-Bass, 1974), p. 165.

12. Clair Vickery, "Economics and the Single Mother Family," *Public Welfare*, 36 (Winter 1978), p. 19.

13. Jacqueline Macauley, *Is Welfare Bad for Children?* (Madison: University of Wisconsin, December 1975), p. 2.

14. Louis Kriesberg, *Mothers in Poverty: A Study of Fatherless Families* (Chicago: Aldine Publishing Co., 1970).

15. Ruth A. Brandwein, Carol A. Brown, and Elizabeth Moury Fox, "Women and Children Last: The Social Situation of Divorced Mothers and their Families," *Journal of Marriage and the Family*, 36 (August 1974), pp. 498–514.

16. Suzanne H. Woolsey, *Pied Piper Politics and the Child Care Debate* (Washington, D.C.: Urban Institute, October 1976).

17. Hoffman and Nye, op. cit., p. 164.

TOWARD A FEMINIST MODEL OF PLANNING FOR AND WITH WOMEN

Cheryl Ellsworth
Nancy Hooyman
Ruth Ann Ruff
Sue Bailey Stam
Joan Hudyma Tucker

The purpose of this article is to develop a feminist framework for social planning in a sexist society—a framework that will help women plan services for and with other women, either in traditional institutions or in alternative organizations. The article begins by examining the current situation with regard to social planning and women planners and then delineates the characteristics of a feminist value base and planning process. It identifies the ways in which organizations need to be restructured to implement this perspective and discusses the impact of the process on women at the personal level. Throughout the analysis, the authors specify the continuous interplay among the personal, interpersonal, organizational, and institutional levels.

Women are undergoing many changes at the personal and interpersonal levels; accordingly, individual feminists, perhaps as token women planners, may move into the system, but still face the struggle of being effective in sexist organizations and institutions. Thus, it is insufficient merely to increase the number of women in planning positions in the human services. Future efforts must be directed toward changes in the organizational and institutional levels. The ultimate goals are to develop feminist organizations and institutions; to eliminate sexism, racism, and class bias; and thus to transform the way society is structured. The implementation of a feminist planning process is one step toward these goals.

Given the authors' assumption that current institutions are sexist and new structures must be created that emerge from and are determined by feminism, what is meant by "feminist alternatives"? Harstock's view of femi-

The authors' names are listed alphabetically in keeping with the collaborative style described in this article.

nism "as a mode of analysis, a method of approaching life and politics, a way of asking for questions and searching for answers" underlines the authors' model.[1] As a mode of analysis, feminism has clear implications for action, for permitting choices, for acting responsibly to change the existing social order. But a feminist analysis does not present fixed political conclusions or a right or wrong way for all women. Such an approach is consistent with the basic values inherent in social work practice.

In an effort to reconceptualize the planning process, the authors avoided absolutes or polarities and eliminated the dichotomy of powerful-powerless; instead, they substituted the concept of a continuum, of a common ground, that allows for differences and contradictions. In a sense, the way this article developed represents the process the authors advocate. The authors—members of a study group of masters-level social work students and a faculty consultant—have different perspectives and life-styles. Yet they share a struggle to develop alternatives to the traditional planning process. In learning together over a year's time, the author's themselves were empowered by the experience in which individual differences were respected, personal experiences valued, roles diffused, resources shared, conflicts and tensions dealt with, and multidimensional thinking encouraged. Likewise, the model developed is not final, since the authors are still questioning and challenging what exists and still examining alternatives and diversities.

CURRENT SITUATION

Although few studies have documented the number of women in planning in social work, it can be assumed, for a variety of reasons, that women are a disproportionately low percentage of human service planners. Hapgood and Getzels, Leavitt, and McCormack documented the barriers facing women in urban planning.[2] Adams, Chafetz, Chernesky, and Scotch have shown the low percentage of women in administrative and policymaking positions in the human services.[3] Because such positions tend to be perceived as the domain of men, it is likely that similar barriers exclude women from all the administrative, policy formulation, and policy planning positions in which women have not been traditionally employed.

Although the majority of planners are men, their decisions affect women in countless ways. Not only are women the majority of the population, they are also undergoing major changes that planners need to consider. These changes include added economic roles, the increase in the number of low-income women who head families, and a longer life expectancy than men. The poverty of women of all age groups is perhaps the single-most-important factor for planners to consider. It has far-ranging implications for women in the areas of child care, health care, low-income housing, public transportation, and numerous other publicly funded social services.

The traditional planning process often creates an expert-client, we-they dichotomy. The planner is viewed as the expert who has the power to define and solve the client's problems; accordingly, services may be planned on the basis of myths or false assumptions about women rather than in response to their needs, especially the needs of women who are of a different color, class, age, or sexual preference from the assumed middle-class norms.[4] A feminist model aims to demystify the planning process, to eliminate the expert-nonexpert dichotomy; it assumes that all women can and should be involved in the planning process. This concept of women taking care of themselves and their own can be threatening since, in essence, it means that women must seize part of the process and become their own experts.

IMPORTANCE OF POWER

The planning of services for women by women reflects the reemergence of women's leadership in the social work profession. Female social workers struggle to practice in a sexist environment and a society in transition. They are faced with the formidable task of working on the social problems of women in the sexist "here and now," while envisioning a future when they will no longer have to justify their position.

The authors' preference for a feminist analysis of planning immediately raises the issue of power, especially the power of women to define their social reality as women in this culture. As Becker pointed out: "In any system of ranked groups, participants take it as given that members of the highest group have the right to define the way things really are."[5] Women are subject to this external definition by the dominant traditional system. To plan for women, then, feminist planners must counter this external definition with their own analysis. They must become aware of and responsible for the direction and focus of practice.

Yet there are risks in advocating the seizure of the power to define. As Caplan and Nelson stated: "To question established definitions is to challenge important institutions and belief systems that have their origins in those definitions."[6] In the process of developing this article, the authors debated the ramifications of this approach. They recognized the dangers both of being co-opted by an established organization and of turning to the most radical solutions. Given these risks, they chose to offer suggestions for a process, not a solution; for a means, not an end. Thus, the authors advocate the incorporation of feminist analysis and vision into all social work practice so the power to define, intervene, and evaluate will be the responsibility of all female social workers. For too long, women have relinquished their planning responsibility to the male-dominated segment of the profession. To empower others, female social workers must first empower themselves.

STAGES OF PLANNING

The traditional process of planning for the social services has several basic stages: identification of the problem, data collection and analysis, identification of cause and effect, consideration of alternative interventions, selection of criteria of service delivery methods, implementation, and evaluation.

Sexism clearly has an impact on the first stage of the traditional planning process, especially on what is considered to be a social problem in this culture. One definition of a social problem is this: "A pattern of behavior or condition among individuals which is unacceptable to some segment of society."[7] Because of the collective silence of female social workers, some social problems were never defined as such. Women remember when rape was not a recognized social problem, when rape crisis or prevention services did not exist. The burden of responsibility was placed on the victim who, it was said, "unleashed" the sexual nature of man with her provocative behavior. Rape is now recognized as an act of violence toward women because women voiced their collective experiences and rage.

The process of identifying a social problem such as rape is linked not only to definition, but also to identification of cause and effect, consequences, and solutions. Blaming the victim is one of the outcomes of the male-dominated traditional process of planning for the social services.[8] One can cite numerous practice-related examples in which feminist social workers differed with colleagues in definitions of cause and effect. For instance, many female social workers have witnessed the victimization process in the case of incest. How long did they remain silent about the prevalence and devastation of this act and about their knowledge that the cause was not the "seductive" child? Incest is a social problem that affects a large number of girls as well as women who were once victims; it is a challenge that must be met by planners of service delivery programs.

The data collection and analysis stage is of crucial concern to feminist planners. The extent of sexual bias in research is just becoming known. Biases in the questions asked and the methodology used affect both the definition of the problem to be solved and the selection of practice models for intervention.

Much of social work practice is grounded in theories and conceptual frameworks that reflect the bias of the dominant system. The history of intervention in domestic violence is an example of one area in which biases have been evident. The belief that women are inferior and exhibit natural submissive characteristics, as well as the theoretical foundations of this belief (such as Parsons's structural functionalist perspective), have played a part in the neglect of battered women.[9] Battered women were not viewed as deserving special concern; rather, they were considered to be having difficulty "adjusting" to the natural submissive female role. The "domestic squabbles" referred to in police reports were defined as normal responses of men to women's supposedly unacceptable behavior. The choice of family counseling as an intervention recognized the importance of maintaining the family's status quo and did not acknowledge the women's pain.

The results of traditional male-based planning are also evident in the traditional view of poverty. The labeling of the poor, mostly women, the lack of creativity in program planning, and the failure to address the economic basis of poverty on a national level all indicate the inability of the planning establishment to address the centuries-long plight of low-income women and children in this country.

Fortunately, some planners and practitioners are beginning to question the very basis of their practice. This climate of change is a part of the willingness of female social workers to become involved in the fundamental reform that must occur to facilitate the incorporation of the principles of feminist planning.

VALUE BASE OF FEMINIST PLANNING

As feminists begin to assume responsibility for planning services for and with women, it will be necessary to demystify the process by making explicit its value base, which can provide a continuum of choices for planning. The underlying values of feminist planning include egalitarianism and a reduction of the status-power differential between planner and consumer and among staff; cooperation and collaboration, nurturance and support, and sharing of resources; and divergent thinking and articulation of values. They also include a prowoman, proactive stance; self-definition, self-determination, and rejection of labels; responsibility to self and others; process orientation and a focus on relationship, including the use of developmental feedback; and the acknowledgment of various explanatory systems, interdependence and connectedness, inseparability of knower and known, and the emergent dynamic nature of change.[10] These values are different from those on which the traditional planning of services for women has been based.[11] By knowing the values toward which they want to move and by applying planning concepts that intentionally envision creative alternatives, feminist planners can begin to change the traditional planning process.

However, along with the formulation of new values, comes the process of reconceptualization. One example of a new way of thinking involves the valuing of movement toward multidimensional thinking. The valuing of multidimensional thinking, intuitions, and feelings is a viable option to the rational thinking processes of a more traditional planning model. To reconceptualize the logical and rational as no longer supreme or linear thinking as no longer natural can open up a realm of new possibilities in planning. Such a reconceptualization also moves one away from a dichotomous, either-or perspective toward a holistic, synergistic approach.[12]

Another example of the reconceptualization process is the redefinition of power. The patriarchal culture views power as finite and zero-sum; thus, it defines power as control, dominance, and the oppression of others. The feminist view of power is that it is unlimited. This definition of power involves the ability to do or act, to accomplish something; energy; strength; and effective and collective interaction.[13] Central to this redefinition is the concept of the empowerment of others.

The reconceptualization of power also has implications for the movement toward cooperative planning. Cooperative planning would involve coalitions or networks of planning groups rather than independent planning, which is often manifested in the competition for funds and clients. A continuum planning model is shown in Figure 1.

Figure 1.   Continuum Model for Feminist Planning

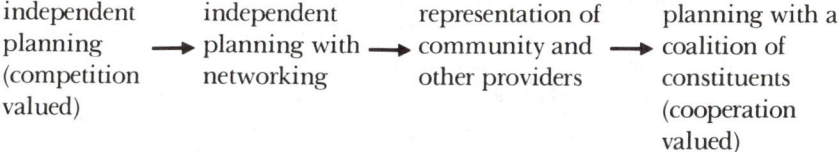

independent planning (competition valued) → independent planning with networking → representation of community and other providers → planning with a coalition of constituents (cooperation valued)

Such a planning model using a coalition of constituents is consistent with a feminist value base. Given the value base that the authors have explicated, criteria for the development of a feminist planning model would include the following: process orientation; divergent thinking; consumer input throughout the process; an open statement of values, biases, and assumptions; the collection of qualitative as well as quantitative data; criteria for service delivery that address the elimination of sexist, racist, and class-biased practices; integration of the principles of empowerment; the use of process and outcome evaluation; and a commitment to the self-determination of all women.

Each social worker might ask herself the following questions based on the criteria just mentioned:

■ In the process of identifying problems, what assumptions are made about women?

■ What theoretical frameworks are planners and practitioners using in the work setting?

■ What methods of data collection and analysis are being used?

■ Who in the planning hierarchy has the power to analyze data?

- What are the ramifications of cause-and-effect determinations?
- By whom and by what criteria are intervention strategies selected?
- If I were partly responsible for the planning process, what would be different in the service delivery system?

If female social workers try to demystify the planning process and if they become empowered and responsible, they can assist other women to frame their own questions, end their silence, and facilitate their own participation in planning.

RESTRUCTURING ORGANIZATIONS

Next, the criteria of a feminist planning model need to be transferred to structural changes. The authors maintain that the hierarchical structure within which most organizations operate is sexist. They have questioned the assumptions, norms, and values of traditional organizations and have identified ways in which organizations need to be restructured to implement a feminist perspective. Restructuring traditional organizations and developing alternatives using the criteria of a feminist framework are essential because women are affected by all social planning processes, both as consumers and as planners. The ultimate goal is a society that empowers its members rather than controls them.

According to Kanter, ". . . organizational reform is not enough; it is important to move beyond the issues of whether or not concrete individuals get their share to questions of how shares are determined in the first place, how labor is divided, and how power is concentrated."[14] In line with Kanter's statement, demystifying the concept of power and leadership is an important foundation for restructuring institutions. One way to demystify the concept is to define leadership as a set of learned behaviors that all members of an organization can learn and share. Such behaviors include the initiation of action or change; creating a statement of agreement, clarification, or summarization; and sharing information and resources. By sharing and rotating the responsibility for leadership in an organization, individual members learn new skills and gain access to more information. This enables them to take an active part in all aspects of the organization. The structure, then, becomes the enabler, which is equivalent to the concept of empowerment discussed by Solomon.[15] Empowerment becomes a formally stated goal of the organization, work group, or unit, rather than power over or dominance by an authority figure.

There are several ways to implement the concept of empowerment, including job sharing, contractual work agreements that encourage the development of a variety of skills in the members, a consensual or open system of decision making, flexitime, and rotation of tasks. These changes are also consistent with the valuing of relationships and moving away from a focus primarily on the self and the product. Members of the organization and consumers of the service become empowered by any or all these work arrangements. They are encouraged to take control of their own work lives, which leads to a greater satisfaction with the job and life in general. Individual needs, skills, and interests are a primary concern throughout the process. Responsibility for setting goals and decision-making is delegated to particular work groups, planning teams, or projects, and each person is accountable to the others in the same project. Thus, coercive power (the power of sanctions and the power of position) is removed from the structure of the organization.[16] Just as the planning process becomes the model for planners-consumers, the organizational structure becomes the model for members-consumers.[17]

In the traditional organization, attempts have been made to involve others in planning, but involvement has been viewed as a task rather than a valuable and valued process on which the organization and planning process are based.[18] Feminist planners, however, think process is as important as task and value it as such.[19] The empowerment strategies that have been identified by feminist planners depend heavily on small groups of people working together. The divergent needs, values, skills, and interests of the individuals interface with the goals and needs of the organization, so the institutionalized norms are not the primary essence of the organization. Consequently, as people change, the structure of the organization changes. The overall effectiveness of the empowerment process is dependent on the conscious effort of the people involved to create a fit or balance among the component parts of the organization.[20] Thus, the structure of the organization can be viewed as always being in process.

The conscious involvement of members-consumers not only empowers them but assures that the planning process will no longer operate on the basis of false assumptions and will actively seek out the real needs of women. How can the problems, issues, and concerns of people be adequately defined, understood, and addressed if the persons affected are not directly involved in the planning process?

IMPLICATIONS FOR PERSONAL CHANGE

Clearly, the basic philosophy of feminists is to define themselves and their purpose instead of adhering to established norms and structures. What are the personal risks and benefits they face in choosing between work in a more traditional organization or implementation of a feminist-based planning model?

Kanter and Zurcher stressed the necessity of developing alternative standards for organizations, such as small size, process, power sharing, and wholeness.[21] In addition, each woman must establish her own standards and conclusions about her effectiveness as an individual. Feminist analysis does not offer a right or wrong way or a politically correct standard. Instead, the emphasis is on personal choice and self-determination; this emphasis enables each woman to formulate her own personal values and goals. In formulating personal standards, each woman needs to ask herself the following questions: Do I need approval from my colleagues? Is it important to me that consumers' needs are met? Am I willing to lessen the power differential between myself and the consumer? Can I work in alternative structures? Will I risk censure on the behalf of women? Will I chance promotion by not following rules set up by the "old boy" network? Is money a primary concern, or am I willing to forgo money for other personal satisfactions?

These questions are not meant to polarize or create absolutes. The authors are not trying to create a dichotomy between prowoman and antiwoman thinking. Feminist planning is based on multidimensional thought and respect for differences. What is being asked of the individual is this: What is your level of comfort? Where are you on the continuum and where would you like to be? What are your personal limits? In relation to the organizational planning structure in which you are currently working, where are its values and assumptions on the continuum? How far are the organization's values from your own? What degree of dissonance would motivate you to act from your own value base?

Each female social worker should give herself permission to question the existing structure and her own values at any time. She should set the limits and the level of comfort in which she can work. Further questions to be asked include these: Are colleagues making tolerable assumptions about women? Is the theoretical framework currently supported by the organization acceptable? Will the agency allow the individual worker to use her own theoretical framework with consumers? Can the organization accept differences and be flexible and open ended when planning services? Does the organization teach consumers how to question?

Each female social worker should evaluate the organization and herself according to the following criteria of feminist planning:

- Is the empowerment of all women a goal?
- Has the planning process been demystified?
- Has the power-status differential been lessened?
- Is process emphasized?
- Is the value base clearly stated and known to all?
- Is the thrust proactive toward the elimination of sexism, racism, and class bias?
- Is the power to question and define power accessible to all?
- Is there a belief in the necessity of structural and institutional change?

The authors are not asking for compliance with their beliefs or acceptance of their model. For them, a feminist planning model meets the consensual perspective and goals, not a standard of perfection. They do not see the planner or practitioner as being the expert, but instead as being one with the consumer. Thus, the authors seek to base services and organizational structures on actual needs rather than on assumptions and control of power.

None of these questions or statements will be answered without conflict. In traditional organizations there is conflict, but often it is not acknowledged, and oppression is dealt with by silence. Silence, however, does not bring growth to the individual or organization. It does not modify the myths or assumptions about women. Consistent with social work ethics, the underlying theme of feminist planning is human dignity. As history has taught, women have been identified by myths and false assumptions, and where there is oppression, there can be no human dignity.[22]

We female social workers are the planning experts by the very fact that we are the consumers of services. To seize the process and power to plan services is a right, not a privilege. We have the services we have today because we trusted ourselves and exercised our right to define our needs. What we accomplish tomorrow will be measured by our definition of social problems, by our creating programs and organizations to meet our needs, and by setting up our own standards for success.

REFERENCES

1. Nancy Harstock, "Feminist Theory and Revolutionary Strategy," in Zillah R. Eisenstein, ed., *Capitalist Patriarchy and the Case for Socialist Feminism* (New York: Monthly Review Press, 1979), p. 71.

2. *See* Karen Hapgood and Judith Getzels, "What Are the Issues?" in Hapgood and Getzels, eds., *Planning, Women, and Change*, Report No. 301 (Chicago: American Society of Planning Officials, Planning Advisory Service, April 1974), pp. 15-21; Jacqueline Leavitt, *Women in Planning: Do the Numbers Really Matter?* (New York: Graduate School of Architecture and Planning, Columbia University, 1978); and Margaret McCormack, "A Feminist Perspective," *Social Policy*, 8 (May 1977), pp. 18-24.

3. Margaret Adams, "The Compassion Trap," in Vivian Gornick and Barbara K. Moran, eds., *Women in a Sexist Society: Studies in Power and Powerlessness* (New York: Basic Books, 1971), pp. 147-159; Janet Saltzman Chafetz, "Women in Social Work," *Social Work*, 17 (September 1972), pp. 12-18; Roslyn Chernesky, "Women Administrators in Social Work," in Elaine Norman and Arlene Mancuso, eds., *Women's Issues and Social Work Practice* (Itaska, Ill.: F. E. Peacock Publishers, 1980), pp. 241-262; and C. Bernard Scotch, "Sex Status in Social Work: Grist for Women's Liberation," *Social Work*, 16 (July 1971), pp. 5-11.

4. *See* Janet Abu-Lughod, "Designing a City for All," pp. 37–43, and Phyllis Kaniss and Barbara Robins, "The Transportation Needs of Women," pp. 63–69, in Karen Hapgood and Judith Getzels, eds., *Planning, Women, and Change*, Report No. 301 (Chicago: American Society of Planning Officials, Planning Advisory Service, April 1974); and Hapgood and Getzels, op. cit.

5. Howard S. Becker, "Whose Side Are We On?" in William J. Filstead, ed., *Qualitative Methodology: Firsthand Involvement with the Social World* (Chicago: Markham Publishing Co., 1970), p. 18.

6. Nathan Caplan and Stephen D. Nelson, "On Being Useful: The Nature and Consequences of Psychological Research on Social Problems," *American Psychologist*, 28 (March 1973), p. 201.

7. Robert R. Mayer, *Social Planning and Social Change* (Englewood Cliffs, N. J.: Prentice-Hall, 1972), p. 113.

8. *See* Edna I. Rawlings and Dianne Carter, "Psychotherapy for Social Change," in Rawlings and Carter, eds., *Psychotherapy for Women: Toward Treatment Equality* (Springfield, Ill.: Charles C. Thomas, 1977), p. 449.

9. Nancy Hooyman and Susan Johnson, "Sociology's Portrayal of Women: Socio-Political Implications," *Soundings: An Interdisciplinary Journal*, 40 (Winter 1978), pp. 449–465.

10. *See* Barbara Solomon, *Black Empowerment* (New York: Columbia University Press, 1976); and Janice Wood Wetzel, "Defining Feminist Pedagogy: A Female Systems Model," paper presented at the Second Annual Women Studies Conference, University of Minnesota, Duluth, April 1979.

11. *See* Leavitt, op. cit.; and Kathleen Barry, *The Fear of Feminism: Report on the West Coast Women's Studies Conference* (Pittsburgh, Pa.: KNOW, 1979).

12. *See* Harstock, op. cit.; and Joan Rothschild, "Taking Our Future Seriously," *Quest: A Feminist Quarterly*, 2 (April 1976), pp. 17–30.

13. Kathryn Girard, *Power and Leadership* (Amherst: National Women's Centers Training Project, University of Massachusetts, 1978).

14. Rosabeth M. Kanter, *Men and Women of the Corporation* (New York: Basic Books, 1977), p. 285.

15. Solomon, op. cit.

16. Paula Johnson, "Women and Power: Toward a Theory of Effectiveness," *Journal of Social Issues*, 32 (September 1976), pp. 99–109.

17. For descriptions of organizations illustrating some of these changes, *see* Barry, op. cit.; Pauline Bart, "Seizing the Means of Reproduction: An Illegal Feminist Abortion Collective—How and Why It Worked," paper presented at the American Sociological Association, Chicago, September 1977; Emilia Bellone, et al., "Building a Feminist Organizational Structure: Criteria and Models," paper presented at the Association of Women in Psychology Conference, Los Angeles, March 1980; Mary Jane Lupton and Anne Thompson, "Living with Conflict on the Journal," Editorial, *Women: A Journal of Liberation*, 6 (1980), pp. 48–50; and "Organizational Process and Structure," unpublished paper (Seattle, Washington: Wallingford Wellness Project, 1980).

18. *See* Warren G. Bennis, "Post-Bureaucratic Leadership," pp. 180–196, and Jack R. Gibbs, "Dynamics of Leadership and Communication," pp. 107–121, in William R. Lassey and Richard R. Fernandez, eds., *Leadership and Social Change* (La Jolla, Calif.: University Associates, 1976).

19. *See*, for example, Ginny Crow, "The Process/Product Split," *Quest: A Feminist Quarterly*, 4 (October 1978), pp. 15–23; Lupton and Thompson, op. cit.; Dorothy Riddle, "Integrating Process and Product," *Quest: A Feminist Quarterly*, 4 (October 1978), pp. 23–32; and Caroline Sparks, "Process/Product Split: A Misnomer," *Quest: A Feminist Quarterly*, 4 (October 1978), pp. 32–36.

20. Joan Sweeney, *Organizational Issues* (Amherst: National Women's Centers Training Project, University of Massachusetts, 1978).

21. Rosabeth M. Kanter and Louis A. Zurcher, "Concluding Statement: Evaluating Alternatives and Alternative Valuing," *Journal of Applied Behavioral Sciences*, 9 (1973), pp. 381–397.

22. Adrienne Rich, *On Lies, Secrets and Silence: Selected Prose* (New York: W. W. Norton & Co., 1979).

TOWARD ANDROGYNY
IN COMMUNITY AND
ORGANIZATIONAL PRACTICE

Ruth A. Brandwein

In the last ten years, social workers have examined the sexist practices of their profession. A key finding has been that men have dominated administration, planning, and community organization in social work—a "women's profession." The differential career patterns of male and female social workers have been well documented in the last decade. Giovannoni and Purvine, for example, maintained that men have controlled the leadership of social work throughout its history except for a limited period and for a few fields of practice.[1] Many explanations have been promulgated for this phenomenon, usually based on assumptions that men and women are socialized for different roles. Women, it is argued, are drawn to or tracked into the nurturing, compassionate, interpersonal side of social work—direct practice with individuals, families, and groups (micro practice)—while men choose the rational, aggressive, directive side of social work—community and organizational (macro) practice.[2]

Recent research findings seem to support these assumptions. However, on closer inspection, the dichotomy proves to be too simplistic. Moreover, if one examines the history of community and organizational practice from its inception with Jane Addams and other nineteenth-century female reformers, one finds that, until recently, women played a more central role in community and organizational practice than generally has been acknowledged.

This article traces the history of women in macro practice and how the role of female social workers has differed from that of male social workers. For the purposes of the article, the author uses the term "community and organizational practice" interchangeably with that of "macro practice." These terms encompass what is generally considered macro practice, such as, locality development, social planning, and social action, as well as what is now called "mezzo practice," that is, administration, program planning and development, and organizational change. The common factor in all these interventions is that the focus of change is on the social structure or institutions, rather than on the individual.

The second part of the article examines the key issues that emerge from the historical analysis and proposes a new, androgynous approach to practice.

HIDDEN HISTORY OF WOMEN

Most readers are familiar with the ongoing schism in social work between community and individual practice. This schism has frequently been conceptualized as the movement from *cause* (social reform and social action) to *function* (professionalization and therapeutic techniques). However, even within community practice there has been a cause/function dichotomy that can be characterized as "radical" versus "conservative."[3]

One branch of community and organizational practice is associated with the growth of community chests and community councils and has focused on the development, coordination, and monitoring of costs and services. Its locus is the formal organization. This is the "conservative," status quo, maintenance branch of community organization. Male social workers have clearly dominated this branch of practice. Yet, as will be demonstrated, women may have played a greater role than is generally recognized.

The other branch grew out of the social reform and social movement efforts of the late nineteenth century. It is associated with the growth of settlement houses and has focused on social legislation, neighborhood organizing, and advocacy for the poor and other oppressed groups. Its locus is the communal organization.[4] It is in this branch of community practice that female social workers have been more in evidence.

Over the entire period of social work's development, these competing branches have struggled for dominance in community and organizational practice. The ebb and flow of social action versus management efficiency and of neighborhood organizing versus program development have followed larger sociohistorical patterns that cannot be fully explored here. Nevertheless, what is significant for this article is the role of women in both these branches of community and organizational practice.

It must not be forgotten that social work itself had its beginnings in the social reform movement of the late nineteenth century. This movement was fueled by middle- and upper-class women who were becoming increasingly discontented with the stifling role of the Victorian lady and who sought to fulfill the values of compassion and altruism women were believed to embody. In addition to their involvement in the abolitionist and suffrage movements, women turned to reform efforts in public health, slum housing, child labor, women's protective legislation, and treatment of the mentally ill. To list but a few of the women in these movements is to list the giants of social work: Jane Addams, Edith and Grace Abbott, Sophonisba Breckinridge, Dorothea Dix, Florence Kelley, and Lillian Wald.

Of the 107 biographies in the 1977 edition of the *Encyclopedia of Social Work*, only 38 were of women.[5] (This low proportion of women may reflect the dominance of men in a women's profession or it may reflect the selection process used by the editors.) Of the 38 famous women listed, 29 (over 75 percent) were community organizers. If community and organizational practice is now dominated by men, it is important to remember that it was not always so. At least the social action component was women's work. Yet in the early days of the profession, the outstandig women who were known as social reformers also were managers, according to Conway.[6] Conway argued that the activist or "prophetess" role was more in keeping with what were perceived as women's roles than that of manager or technocrat. She described women such as Julia Lathrop and Jane Addams as "social engineers" who utilized logic, analysis, and expertise to organize programs, amass data, and shepherd bills through legislatures. This aspect of their roles, however, did not captivate the public imagination, since, even less than social activism, it was not an accepted role for women.

As the profession turned from "cause" to "function" in the 1920s and professionalism of services meant use of the business model for efficiency, men tended to move into more dominant roles in the administration of social work services. Because men tended to be the business leaders in the community and had access to funds for charitable purposes, male social workers were preferred as heads of fund-raising organizations.

Although it has been generally acknowledged that men dominated the administrative leadership roles, what is less generally known is that women continued to play important roles in community and organizational practice until the early 1960s. This differentiation of male and female roles is related both to status and constituency. Administrative positions were of higher status and their constituencies of important community leaders were men. Neighborhood organizing, locality development, working with volunteers, and developing needed services for clients were lower status roles in which the constituents or clients were more often women or men with lower status. These positions were open to and more often filled by women. Those women filling administrative or planning positions tended to be confined to the smaller community councils with low budgets or in planning functions closely related to clinical services.

The major shift in sex-role identification in community and organizational practice did not occur until the early 1960s. Through the 1950s, women were still prominent in the field. For example, in the 1950s, the National Conference of Social Work published several collections of papers on group work and community organization selected from those presented at their annual conferences. In each of the three volumes published in 1953, 1954, and 1955, more women than men were authors (a total of twenty-three women and fifteen men).[7] As late as 1959, when the Council on Social Work Education published its project report on the curriculum of community organizations, women were still well represented.[8] In that volume, fifteen of the forty-nine participants were women, and they wrote six of the fifteen position papers.

However, in the late 1950s, the social work profession was already actively recruiting men to raise the "prestige" of the profession.[9] Throughout the fifties, men were using their veterans' benefits to complete their graduate education, and they were tracked into community organization and administrative positions. Also during the late fifties and early sixties, central planning and the importance of involving community elites in decision making for social welfare were popularized.[10] As in the 1920s, the ethos was efficiency and a businesslike approach, which was associated with the sex-role stereotypes of men rather than women.

Community and organizational practice was perceived to be more compatible with appropriate behavior for men, since it was seen as requiring more "activism and aggression."[11] Administration continued to be a way for men to have higher status and salaries, thus reducing role inconsistency and the conflict in status associated with being in a woman's profession.[12] Also for reasons of status, men discarded the title "social worker" and substituted titles such as "policy analyst," "planner," "community organizer," or "urbanologist."

It is interesting to note that during the same period, such popular authors as Roth and Wylie condemned "momism."[13] Mothers were blamed for all their children's problems and a general antiwoman attitude prevailed. No wonder, then, that men entering a women's profession would want to seek roles and titles that disassociated them from such negativism and low status. The prevailing put-down of casework by community organizers may have been a concealed derogation of women or behavior associated with women.

Although the sixties have generally been viewed as a time of social activism in pursuit of people's liberation, the position of women in social work was deteriorating rather than improving. By 1969, men filled three times as many community organization positions and twice as many administrative positions as women in a profession whose overall ratio of women to men was 2:1.[14] This change in one decade is also reflected in the number of women authors represented in books of readings on community organization that were frequently used in schools of social work. For example, in one book of readings published in 1969, only two of the forty-two authors were women. In another book of readings published in 1974, the breakdown was forty-three male and four female authors. Furthermore, in a national conference on social planning in the same year, none of the thirty-three invited participants was a woman.[15]

With the development of the Community Action Program in the 1960s, neighborhood organizing and community action reemerged as acceptable activities for social workers in community organization. However, at that time, the "facilitator" and "enabler" roles were denigrated as weak, effeminate, and ineffective, just as the caseworker's concern for individuals was seen as oriented to the "status quo." Instead, community practice favored a more active, directive, adversary style that has stereotypically been considered "male." This style created frequent controversies about citizen participation. Although it was promulgated as desirable, the directive, sometimes controlling style of organizers raised questions about the nature of that participation. The literature and practice virtually ignored earlier efforts and writings by such women as Follett, who had promulgated conflict resolution in task-centered groups, and Sieder, who stressed the need for volunteer participation and the social action role of agencies.[16] Thus, even the neighborhood organizing role, which heretofore had been less closed to women than the managerial role, was now being recast as appropriate only for male social workers.

By the start of the 1970s, the pendulum had swung once again from citizen involvement and neighborhood organizing to central control, accountability, and an emphasis on management techniques. As in the 1920s and late 1950s, in the 1970s this kind of community work was identified with men. For example, in Fanshel's study of members of the National Association of Social Workers in 1971–72, twice as many men as women classified themselves primarily as administrators, as planners, and as community organizers.[17] It was not until the late 1970s, when the women's movement forced social work to recognize the extent of sex discrimination in the profession, were there small but perceptible hints of change in community and organization practice. Thus, in a 1978 book of readings in social work administration co-edited by a woman, one-third of the authors were women.[18] However, during this period, women still seemed to be losing ground to men in administrative positions in agencies.[19]

Perhaps the most important finding to emerge from this brief review is that women have played an important and ongoing role in the development of community and organizational practice. Women entering the social work profession are more likely to become macro practitioners if they are acquainted with female role models who were leaders in the field. This awareness is a result of the women's movement, in which women are rediscovering their own history and reclaiming their roles as advocates for the oppressed. But this knowledge of women's roles in community and organizational practice is equally important for men entering the profession. Male social workers need to know that women were and are identified with community organization and administration. As important as this awareness of women's past heritage is, what further implications does it have for practice in the future?

TOWARD ANDROGYNY

A more controversial issue that emerges from this discussion is the very nature of the community organizational and administrative role. It is now fashionable to encourage women to enter professions and occupations previously dominated by men. However, the message given to such women is that to be successful, they must put aside "feminine" attitudes and behaviors and instead act and think like men. Women are urged to become rational, decisive, hard nosed, and aggressive. If they assume such a "take-charge" attitude, perhaps their sex can be forgiven or ignored. A more radical approach is to question the appropriateness of the role itself, rather than the gender of the person filling the role. Are there qualities in the traditional female stereotype that can balance those of the male stereotype of organizer and administrator? What lessons can male administrators and organizers learn from the women's movement?

Androgynous Roles

The women's movement has wrestled with a number of issues that are significant for community and organizational practice. The most pervasive of these is androgyny, a term that combines the Greek *andro* (male) and *gyn* (female).[20] *Psychological androgyny* is the "balance between and the integration of both masculine and feminine characteristics" in an individual.[21] It suggests that both women and men may express the full range of human attitudes and behaviors without being labeled masculine women or effeminate men. That is, women should be freed to be logical, assertive, and direct, and men should be freed to be sensitive, nurturant, and caring. Thus, the implication for macro practice is that both men and women should be taught to be facilitators and enablers as well as advocates and adversaries.

In the 1960s, writers emphasized the use of conflict and contest as strategies and tactics. They urged social workers to be bolder in assuming the roles of advocate and adversary. These roles are indeed necessary in dealing with the target system—the individuals, organizations, or other systems toward which change is directed.

Unfortunately, the literature has not differentiated between the appropriate strategies, tactics, and roles for organizing one's action system and those necessary for changing one's target system.[22] In macro practice, the worker devotes much time to creating a constituency that recognizes and is concerned about the problem to be addressed and then to building an action system beyond the professional worker which will actively work for planned change. Although contest may be the appropriate strategy for dealing with the target system, consensus and collaboration are more appropriate strategies for building one's action system. Accordingly, the enabler and facilitator roles are more appropriate to this task than are the adversary and advocate roles.

Similarly, it has become unfashionable to encourage administrators to be enablers and facilitators with their staff. Yet the organizational staff is the administrator's action system. Coercive tactics may get the job done, but a high price is paid in the staff's resistance, backlash, subversion, and low morale. Individual staff development and group cohesiveness may be slower, but their results, in terms of the effectiveness of organizational functioning, are more long lasting. Thus, by negating process (female) and emphasizing only product (male), administrators lose sight of an essential element. An androgynous approach recognizes the synergistic quality of both product and process, rather than creating a false either/or choice.

Power and Control

For both the administrator and the organizer, decisions about what strategies to use and what roles to assume are directly related to issues of power and control. These issues are difficult in different ways for women and for men.

It is often difficult for women, traditionally socialized, to take and use power. Yet it is often essential for them to do so in leadership positions. In the secondary positions that have been open to women in the home (wife-mother) and work setting (administrative assistant or assistant to the director) the use of power has tended to be covert and manipulative.[23] It is important that women seek top positions and learn to use power more openly and comfortably. This will not be easy because men often respond negatively to women's open use of power.

Men in community organizing, planning, and administrative positions often have the opposite problem; they cannot relinquish control. By learning how to let go, to share power and decision making, and to realize that they as individuals cannot unilaterally determine outcomes, men will enhance their effectiveness in these roles. For example, one area with which administrators have difficulty is the connection between employee relations and the achievement of goals. Theoretically, social workers understand that the use of coercion to achieve goals is least effective in the long run. Yet, of late, social work educators in macro practice have embraced this style of tough, no-nonsense (and by implication no namby-pamby, weak social worker) administration. Their knowledge of human development and group dynamics, however, should inform them that reaching goals consensually, developing an employee's strengths and sense of self-esteem, and sharing power are often more effective approaches to successful community and organizational practice. Moreover, such an approach is more in keeping with the values of the profession.

Women's groups have experimented extensively with collective rather than hierarchical decision making. Social work practitioners and educators would do well to explore these alternative models. This is not to imply one must never engage in confrontation. Rather, honest confrontation is an essential aspect of collective decision making that is often avoided or absent in hierarchical decision making. Confrontation often leads to a more careful examination of options and thus a better decision than is feasible through the unilateral decision making or the false consensus reached in a hierarchical structure.

Nor does collective decision making mean that one must never make difficult, controversial, or unpopular decisions. Most people work in hierarchically structured organizations in which one person has the ultimate responsibility for the decision. Therefore, even if the decision-making structure maximizes the input of all staff members, there are times when administrators, on the basis of their own judgments or because of external circumstances, must make decisions that are contrary to the preference expressed by the collectivity.

Thus, what the author is promulgating is a full range of options for community and organizational practitioners. These options should be used differentially as appropriate to the situation; practitioners should not embrace or reject a particular approach because of stereotyped categorizations.

HOLISTIC PRACTICE

Another issue for community and organizational practice emerges from an understanding of an early credo of the women's movement: the personal is political. This credo meant that one cannot divorce issues of personal change from change in the social structure. It helped women reject victim (self) blaming attitudes by understanding that the institutions of society had oppressed women as a collectivity. Simultaneously, it helped women to deal with political issues without ignoring the importance of the individual or human element in the situation.

The separation and tracking of micro and macro practitioners is analogous to the separation of the personal from the political. The separation or integration of methods in the curriculum has been an underlying concern throughout the history of social work education. Is community organization really social work? Should it be taught separately from clinical services? What is generic social work practice? Does it include macro practice? In the last decade, the movement toward separation and specialization at the graduate level has accelerated. This dichotomization can be considered as a stereotypical "male" analytic approach to practice. In contrast, synthesis, or a holistic approach to practice, is more consistent with what is stereotypically "female."

The concept of a holistic social work practice calls for macro and mezzo practitioners who understand human behavior and the dynamics of small groups and who can utilize interpersonal skills. It also calls for direct-service practitioners who understand the forces in the social structure that affect individual behavior and who can identify and work to rectify social problems on behalf of their clients. Some would call this just good social work. Overspecialization in one or the other track results in the lack of integration of the individual and the societal—the personal and the political. This integration is crucial to social work.

Hardware and Software

This article began with a review of the dichotomy between cause and function in social work. Cause is related to social action and social values while function is related to professionalism, skills, and technology. In Western civilization, a stereotypical male orientation emphasizes machines and techniques. Hence, the concentration on management information systems, computer hardware, cost-benefit analyses, and the like in administration is not surprising. It is important that women, as well as men, become familiar with and adept at using these techniques and tools. However, it is equally necessary for men, as well as women, to acknowledge the importance of heuristic decision making in human service organizations, of the integration of values in community organization and administration, of identification with social causes, and of volunteer, consumer, and employee participation in decision making. All these are part of the social work heritage to which practitioners must do more than pay lip service; they need to become a basic part of each practitioner's daily work.

Salience of Gender

The final issue is the salience of gender of both the worker and the action system, including the unacknowledged sexual tensions frequently underlying community and organizational practice. (The reader should note that this discussion refers to heterosexual interactions. Other dynamics would prevail in gay male or lesbian interactions.) This issue must be addressed by macro practitioners, as it has begun to be discussed by micro practitioners.[24] The sexual games played by male organizers when they were organizing women welfare clients are perhaps the most obvious example. Flirtation, at the least, was a powerful tool in organizing that action system of predominantly single mothers. Obviously a female worker attempting to organize such a constituency would be in a different position. Nor would the situation be parallel for a female organizer with a male action system. Sexual innuendo is perceived differently for men and women. The assumption of male bonding and the discomfort felt by men at the entrance of a woman into a male group make such organizing more difficult for the female worker. In the organizational setting, both male and female workers who are accustomed to working for men may be unwilling to accept the authority of the female administrator.

On the other hand, until the women's movement began to emphasize the importance of sisterhood, the strength of female bonding was not acknowledged. Female organizers may be more sensitive to the kind of issues around which to organize women, such as neighborhood and school conditions and safety for their children, which are powerful rallying cries.[25] A female organizer may have more credibility than a man in relation to such issues as women's health, rape, wife abuse, and the organization of clerical workers. These have been powerful organizing issues in the women's movement in which social work, to date, has not played a prominent part.

Table 1 summarizes some of the distinctions between the "male" and "female" paradigms of community and organizational practice. It must be pointed out, however, that the paradigms are a generalization and that individual men and women will find themselves in either paradigm; furthermore, none of these characteristics is intrinsically male or female.

CONCLUSION

If the social work profession is to go forward in the eighties, it must move beyond the outward sexual stereotypes of the society. The stereotypes have not only dehumanized social workers as individuals but have also limited the effectiveness of social work practice.

As a first step, the skewed male-female ratio in macro practice must be rectified. Not only must women be encouraged to seek positions of authority and power, but organizational structures must be opened to provide women with opportunities beyond those available in subordinate, behind-the-scenes positions or in top positions in small-budget agencies or agencies serving only women and children.

The second step, which will be more difficult because it represents a more radical and far-reaching change, is to alter the very nature of positions of authority and power. To open positions to women is necessary but not

Table 1. Paradigms of Community and Organizational Practice

Characteristic	"Female"	"Male"
Role	Facilitator Enabler Coordinator	Advocate Adversary Technocrat Manager
Orientation	Collaboration Win-win	Contest Win-lose
Decision making	Participatory	Directive
Style	Collective	Hierarchical
Locus	Informal settings: neighborhood, movement, communal organization	Formal settings: agency, department, formal organization
Status	Lower	Higher
Approach to social work	Cause: values	Function: skills and tools
Approach to social work education	Holistic	Analytic

sufficient. If women take on male stereotypical roles and perpetuate existing patterns and practices, they will have won the battle but lost the war. Both women and men in macro practice need to free themselves of stereotypical sex roles and dare to become androgynous practitioners.

REFERENCES

1. Jeanne M. Giovannoni and Margaret E. Purvine, "The Myth of the Social Work Matriarchy," Social Welfare Forum, 1973 (New York: Columbia University Press, 1973). See also Alfred Stamm, "NASW Membership: Characteristics, Deployment, and Salaries," Personnel Information, 12 (May 1969), pp. 34–45; Janet

Saltzman Chafetz, "Women in Social Work," *Social Work*, 17 (September 1972), pp. 12–18; David Fanshel, "Status Differentials: Men and Women in Social Work," *Social Work*, 21 (November 1976), pp. 448–454; Diane Kravetz, "Sexism in a Woman's Profession," *Social Work*, 21 (November 1976), pp. 421–426; Louise Bakke and Jean Edson, "Women in Management: Moving Up?" *Social Work*, 22 (November 1977), pp. 512–514; and Toby Weiner and Sophie Engel, *The Status of Women in Jewish Communal Services* (New York: National Conference of Jewish Communal Services, June 1977).

2. Margaret Adams, "The Compassion Trap," in Vivian Gornick and Barbara K. Moran, eds., *Woman in Sexist Society* (New York: Basic Books, 1971), pp. 555–575; George Brager and John A. Michael, "The Sex Distribution in Social Welfare: Causes and Consequences," *Social Casework*, 50 (December 1969), pp. 595-601; Chafetz, op. cit.; and Alfred Kadushin, "The Prestige of Social Work—Facts and Factors," *Social Work*, 3 (April 1958), p. 40.

3. Martin Rein, "Social Work in Search of a Radical Profession," *Social Work*, 15 (April 1970), pp. 13–28.

4. George A. Hillery, Jr., *Communal Organizations: A Study of Local Societies* (Chicago: University of Chicago Press, 1968).

5. *Encyclopedia of Social Work* (17th issue; Washington, D.C.: National Association of Social Workers, 1977).

6. Jill Conway, "Women Reformers and American Culture, 1879–1930," *Journal of Social History*, 5 (Winter 1971–72), pp. 164–177.

7. *Selected Papers in Group Work and Community Organization* (Chicago: National Conference of Social Work, 1953); *Group Work and Community Organization, 1953–1954* (New York: Columbia University Press, 1954); and *Group Work and Community Organization, 1955* (New York: Columbia University Press, 1955).

8. Harry Lurie, ed., *Community Organization Method in Social Work Education*, Vol. 4 of the "Project Report of the Curriculum Study" (New York: Council on Social Work Education, 1959).

9. Kravetz, op. cit.; and Kadushin, op. cit.

10. Ruth Brandwein, "A Working Framework for Approaching Organizational Change: The Community Chest–Council System, 1946–1971." Unpublished Ph.D. dissertation, Brandeis University, Waltham, Mass., 1977.

11. Brager and Michael, op. cit.

12. Alfred Kadushin, "Men in a Woman's Profession," *Social Work*, 21 (November 1976), pp. 440–447.

13. *See*, for example, Phillip Roth, *Portnoy's Complaint* (New York: Random House, 1967); and Philip Wylie, *Generation of Vipers* (New York: Holt, Rhinehart & Winston, 1955).

14. Stamm, op. cit.

15. *See* Ralph Kramer and Harry Specht, eds., *Readings in Community Organization Practice* (Englewood Cliffs, N.J.: Prentice-Hall, 1969); Fred M. Cox et al., eds., *Strategies of Community Organization* (2d ed.; Itasca, Ill.: F. E. Peacock Publishers, 1974); and Robert Mayer, Robert Moroney, and Robert Morris, eds., *Centrally Planned Change: A Re-examination of Theory and Experience* (Urbana, Ill.: University of Illinois Press, 1974).

16. Mary Follett, *Creative Experience* (New York: Longmans, Green & Co., 1924); and Violet M. Sieder, "Community Organization and the Direct Service

Agency," *Social Welfare Forum, 1962* (New York: Columbia University Press, 1962).

17. Fanshel, op. cit.

18. Rosemary Sarri and Yeheskel Hasenfeld, eds., *The Management of Human Services* (New York: Columbia University Press, 1978).

19. Juliana Szakacs, "Survey Indicates Social Work Women Losing Ground in Leadership," *NASW News*, 22 (April 1977), p. 12. *See also Womanpower* (February 1977), p.1.

20. Alice Rossi, "Equality Between the Sexes: An Immodest Proposal," *Daedalus* (Spring 1964), pp. 607–652.

21. Nancy E. Downing, "Theoretical and Operational Conceptualizations of Psychological Androgyny: Implications for Measurement," *Psychology of Women*, 3 (Spring 1979), p. 284. *See also* Sandra L. Bern, "The Measurement of Psychological Androgyny," *Journal of Consulting and Clinical Psychology*, 42 (1974), pp. 155–162.

22. Harry Specht, "Disruptive Tactics," in Ralph Kramer and Specht, eds., *Community Organization Practice* (Englewood Cliffs, N.J.: Prentice-Hall, 1969), pp. 372–386; Jack Rothman, "Three Models of Community Organization Practice," in Fred Cox et al., eds., *Strategies of Community Organization* (Itasca, Ill.: F. E. Peacock Publishers, 1970), pp. 20–36.

23. Jean Baker Miller, *Toward a New Psychology of Women* (Boston: Beacon Press, 1976).

24. Mary C. Schwartz, "The Importance of the Sex of Worker and Client," *Social Work*, 19 (March 1974), pp. 177–185.

25. "Block by Block: Women in Community Organizing," *Women: A Journal of Liberation*, 6 (1978), pp. 24–28.

4

Social Work
and Power

ISSUES OF POWER IN SOCIAL WORK PRACTICE

The twin topics of power and powerlessness are at the heart of social workers' understanding of what it is to be women in today's society. Throughout the ages, women have been victims of those needing to assert their powers but rarely have they been the ones to enjoy the prerogatives of power. The problem does not arise from a failure to recognize this fact. Rather, it arises from the need to understand more deeply the reasons for its persistence and see more clearly the myriad ways in which this pattern of power perpetuates itself.

The study of all the complex shadings of power is far too ambitious a goal for a single article. However, it is possible to study one area of power in a way that raises some of the critical issues about power wherever it is found. In this article, the author uses professional power as the keyhole through which to view some of the intricacies associated with the exercise of power and to consider how they affect the practice of social work with women.

The entrée to this consideration of professional power is two areas of concern to social workers: (1) the nature of the helping process itself and its requisites for the role of "helper" and (2) how change is related to power and how social workers envision the exercise of power in a framework of change. The way social workers untangle these issues bears directly on how they practice social work with women.

POWER IN SOCIETY

Although the focus of this article is on professional power, it is important to set the discussion in the larger context of societal power. One way to approach this subject is to examine, in a general way, some of the basic elements of power.

The Latin root of the word "power" is *posse*, meaning "to be able." In that rudimentary form, it simply refers to the ability to act. A more sophisticated notion would be the view of power as "the ability to cause or prevent change."[1] But power usually is not thought of or treated as such an innocuous ability. Since the beginning of the industrial age, power has been associated with the need to prove one's worth through self-assertion, an act that frequently rests on one's desire to exert power over others. As Miller wrote, power "has rested almost solely in the hands of people who have lived with a constant need to maintain an irrational dominance; and in their hands, it has acquired overtones of tyranny."[2]

A key element in this dominant pattern of power comes from an individual's access to resources. Kipnis analyzed how power is acquired and how resources are used by a person who holds power. He explained that when an individual possesses resources that are needed by others, he or she immediately exercises some control over the lives of others. As Kipnis put it, "even the most ordinary people can change the course of society if they have access to resources that are needed by others."[3]

The resources outlined by Kipnis are not only tangible ones, although those are clearly significant. They may also come from a person's unique characteristics, such as intelligence, beauty, or cleverness or may be the result of a person's institutional connection, for example, the teacher's authority to give students grades or the social worker's authority to declare someone eligible for services. A crucial dynamic in the relationship between powerholder and recipient is the belief that the needed resource cannot be obtained outside the relationship with the powerholder.

The notion which supports that dynamic is scarcity. Deeply ingrained in the economic and political consciousness of this society is the belief that needed resources are in short supply. Belief in the scarcity of resources engenders competition for access to them. Scarcity allows for the exercise of power because it insures that there will be people willing to comply with the demands of those in power to obtain the resources they want. This dynamic sets up the basic paradigm for all unequal relationships: the powerholder, as Kipnis calls him, needs to have someone over whom to exercise power as much as the powerless person needs to behave in a way that will bring the needed resources. Collusion is always at the base of such relationships; each party needs the other to fulfill certain needs.

PROFESSIONAL POWER

Because the dominant model of power so deeply affects the exercise of professional power, it is important to examine in some detail how professional power is used to constrain and shape the behavior of women who seek social work services. This analysis is based on the assumption that social workers exercise power in their professional work and that the effects of such power, particularly on female clients, are significantly at odds with the professed values of the profession and with its ideas about how meaningful change occurs.

A discussion of the profession's exercise of power is immediately confounded by the political reality in which social workers live. Social workers function both from a base of expert knowledge they gain as individuals and from an expectation of social control shaped by society. Because the demands of each for the exercise of power are different, social workers work under conditions of an uneasy compromise.

From the standpoint of modes of power, expert knowledge can be thought of as being closely associated with the exercise of influence.[4] That is, social workers expect change to occur when they convey their specialized knowledge and skills to clients who see their expertise as legitimate and therefore persuasive. In sharp contrast to this view is social work's role as institutional representative; in this role, the exercise of social control carries with it the threat or existence of coercion.

To see the consequences of professional power, one must only be reminded of the types of resources to which social workers have access and over which they exercise control. At one end of the continuum are the basic resources of life—the arena of income transfers and in-kind services; at the other end are the less tangible but nonetheless important resources called personal social services. Arrayed between them are programs of substitute care such as foster homes and adoption, community programs, and institutional care.

To the extent that social workers function as agents of social control, their individual and collective power is substantial. However, such power is predominantly coercive; it allows social workers to do what they think is best for clients, with little regard for the clients' choices. For example, in mental hospitals, patients are subject to physical isolation, loss of privileges, verbal humiliation, physical restraint, and sedation. Depending on the philosophy and practice of the administrators, these measures can be taken in spite of patients' direct opposition to them.

Although coercive power is not gratifying to many social workers, it flows from the sanctions given to the profession by the larger society. Social work has won a place in the public welfare, mental health, and corrections systems. At the same time, it has placed itself in a position in which its expert knowledge may have to serve certain coercive practices of the systems.

Motivations of 'Helpers'

At issue in these various exercises of power are some fundamental questions: Why do social workers become involved in a profession that purports to facilitate individual and social change? What is their individual and collective motivation for what seems to be, at its most benign, an outpouring of benevolence? Or, more simply put, why do social workers want to change other people's behavior?

On one level, their belief in the efficacy of their expert knowledge leads social workers to a certainty about intervening in other people's lives. In addition, the society mandates specific activities as being within the purview of the profession, which reassures social workers that they have not only the skills but the right to intervene.

The organizations within which practitioners work set additional definitions of the nature and limits of their activity. Given the strength of organizational influence, most social workers accept, to some degree, the way their role is defined and the way service is to be given.

A basic and revealing level of motivation is the individual's need to exercise power, even if that need is defined as an interest in influencing others. As Kipnis suggested, the elements of resources, influence, and behavioral change come together in the following way:

> . . . the possession of appropriate resources raises the powerholder's expectations that he will gain compliance if he exerts influence. . . . the therapist who wants to change his client's behavior will do so by invoking his [the therapist's] specialized knowledge.[5]

Because an individual's motivations for becoming professionally involved in other people's lives are complex and sometimes obscure, the likelihood of unintended consequences is greatly increased. As difficult as it is, social workers must be willing to embrace the duality that underlies the professional role of "helper." As Guggenbühl-Craig, a psychiatrist, cautioned:

> In his consciousness, a social worker feels obliged to regard desire to help as his prime motivation. But in the depths of his soul, the opposite is simultaneously constellated—not the desire for help, but lust for power and joy in depotentiating the "client."[6]

This quotation may seem like a harsh reminder, but it comes from an awareness of the antithetical forces that ultimately stir each social worker. To ignore it is to maintain "innocence without responsibility," which, as May pointed out, is one way to defend oneself against the realities of power.[7]

Effects on Clients

The literature of the past decade has struggled with the fact that women have always lacked significant economic and political power. Complex psychological, economic, and social-cultural explanations have been given for this lack of power.[8] Yet, no theoretical approach has adequately explained the deep resistance to women as powerholders. What have been more adequately documented are the soul-shriveling consequences of women's powerlessness. In the social services, both basic economic support and mental health services, the effects on women have been dismal.

Pervasive sexism results in women being treated in stereotyped, growth-limiting ways. And one tragic result has been the self-destructive ways in which many women respond. As Miller so perceptively noted:

> All forms of oppression encourage people to enlist in their own enslavement. For women, especially, this enslavement inevitably takes psychological forms and often ends in being called neuroses or other such things.[9]

Sarton expressed this thought even more poignantly through her elderly character:

> If helpers are corrupted by having absolute power, what about those they keep? We learn to ingratiate ourselves, to pretend we do not notice the slights and humiliations. Or we close ourselves off into that terrible place of anger, of rage and despair. . . .[10]

The impotence felt by Sarton's character of an elderly nursing home resident reminds one of the shocking waste exacted by misused power. Perhaps it is not surprising that the term "madness" refers both to anger and insanity.

Because women are prohibited from acting independently and from being self-assertive and because they are socialized to remain demure and self-effacing, their expressions of power often are covert. The two stereotypes of women as "temptress" and the "power behind the throne" epitomize the subterranean ways in which women must express their power. These roles cause women to disassociate their view of themselves as rightfully powerful and, instead, reinforce an appearance of weakness.

Reinforcement of Powerlessness

The interaction between women's socially conditioned role of powerlessness and a profession's desire to maintain control through expert knowledge sets up a dynamic that can be lethal for women. Understanding some of the ways this dynamic is played out can serve as a basis for a sharper vision about what social work practice can contribute to the well-being of female clients.

How do social workers exercise power over female clients? One fundamental way is by reinforcing the "one-up" position. Miller's delineation of temporary and permanent inequality offers some insight into this process.[11] As Miller noted, in a situation of temporary inequality, although society defines the "lesser" party as unequal, the basis for the inequality is removed through the interaction between the lesser party and the "superior" party, who imparts knowledge or other abilities. An example of this type of inequality may be seen in parent-child and teacher-student relationships. Such a situation is in sharp contrast to that of permanent inequality in which the lesser person is never expected to overcome the unequal status. Permanent inequality resembles a caste system, as in the relationship of minority to dominant group, servant to master, and, in many respects, women to men.

The social worker-client relationship would ordinarily be considered one of temporary inequality. However, certain professional judgments and behaviors may lock the client into a position of permanent inequality. That is, the social worker's view of the female client in her social role as a woman, a welfare recipient, a mental hospital patient, and the like and the social worker's need to preserve an image of his or her professional role may result in interactions that serve the worker's need for power and professional control.

One consequence for the female client may be devaluation and distancing. In his study, Kipnis found that the reliance of powerholders on strong influence led them to assume they had caused the change in behavior.[12] Because of this, the powerholder tended to devalue the other's worth. Kipnis also found that having control over another's behavior resulted in a desire to increase social and psychological distance from that person. Johnson reinforced this finding with his observation that the power relationship between practitioner and client may increase social distance if the practitioner engages in a process of "mystification." He went on to say that "uncertainty is not . . . entirely cognitive in origin but may be deliberately increased to serve manipulative or managerial ends."[13]

Mystification is a particularly easy technique for professionals. Because specialized knowledge confers power, it is possible to withhold information to maintain control. If knowledge is treated as a scarce and valuable resource, it can be kept in the professional's bailiwick, leaving the client a continual supplicant. The client will then have to rely on the social worker not only in a particular instance but for all future instances. In the process, her feelings of vulnerability and ignorance will be reinforced.

The power to diagnosis is another troublesome although prized way for professionals to exercise power. At one level, diagnosis is a knowledge-based skill that is thought to facilitate treatment or the resolution of problems. But at another level, it is a powerful tool for defining a person's situation and, through that definition, for deciding what resources will be available. In effect, it removes a person's power to define her own reality and replaces it with an interpretation that will bring consequences she has not chosen and may not wish. Through such definitions as "unfit mother," "promiscuous," and "manic-depressive," processes are begun which may insure that the woman will lose control over the direcion of her life.

This effect of diagnosis is exacerbated by the attitude that many women bring to a professional encounter. Because most women are socialized to feel powerless, they often seek help in a way that seems to require the social worker to exercise power. As May put it, the powerless think that "some other force must have the power to change things since obviously [they] don't . . . [thus they] frequently rely on the practice of magic rites."[14] For many, professional help is a magical rite. It seems to provide access to all the secret knowledge that will solve their problems. Given these expectations, it is well to attend to Wheelis's caution:

> Many patients go to psychiatrists as if to surgeons, and many psychiatrists regard themselves as psychic surgeons. When such a patient comes to such a therapist, a relationship of considerable length may result, but little else. For the job can be done, if at all, only by the patient.[15]

Although Wheelis was referring to psychiatrists, his point is important for the study of professional power. Social workers too must be aware of their motivations for exercising power, as well as recognize that many clients wish to attribute power to them. Because female clients are more likely than male clients to locate the source of power outside themselves, they are particularly susceptible to a professional person's willingness to assume that power. Unless social workers are clear about the nature of their professional power and of how people change, they may intervene in a way that reinforces the very powerlessness that prompted the client to request help.

THREE PROBLEMS

Recognizing the many power traps that limit or prevent effective work with women is the important first stage in an assessment of professional practice. Certainly, what social workers and clients bring to the interchange has the potential for undermining some basic principles of good social work practice. In moving beyond these traps, social workers must come to grips with three major problems. First, they must confront the notion of power and whether power is necessarily a negative force. Second, they must reassess the principles that are purported to guide their practice so they may understand more clearly their professional role. Third, they must consider the basic elements of change.

New Definition of Power

Power is most often exercised, in society at large or in professions, under the guise of exploitation, manipulation, or competition.[16] That is, a person uses power to exploit others through the use of force, to manipulate others by preying on their vulnerabilities, or to compete with others so they will have or be less than oneself. As Miller pointed out: "Power has generally meant the ability to advance oneself and, simultaneously, to control, limit, and, if possible, destroy the power of others."[17] Because such exercises of power are usually destructive, it is tempting to abhor power as a force and choose to eradicate it. However, is such a solution necessary or even desirable?

One may begin to answer this question by quoting from May: "Power is essential for all living things. . . . [It] is the birthright of every human being. It is the source of his self-esteem and the root of his conviction that he is interpersonally significant."[18] According to May, then, power is not a force for controlling others; it is a necessary ingredient for asserting one's individuality and worth as a person.

The task of developing one's unique individuality is a challenge deeply revered by social work. The belief in the inherent worth of each individual is intimately connected to the notion that each individual, if allowed to develop fully, can contribute in a special way to the human condition. This goal of "individuation" is, as Guggenbühl-Craig explained, "a matter of the fulfillment of human life, the flowering of the basic design of an individual existence, the experience of individual meaningfulness."[19] Individuation does not mean, however, that an individual should be engaged in an introspective, narcissistic, ego-centered life mission. The development of self requires a community of others in which one can experience one's significance as a person while respecting the right of others to maintain their self-esteem. Each person needs to be seen as worthy in another's eyes. How can social workers foster a climate in which women can experience their power and yet not deny the existence and effects of professional power?

Reconsideration of Principles

In grappling with the question just asked, perhaps the first principle to be clarified is that of *self-determination*. Although self-determination has always been a fundamental principle of social work practice, as with all radical notions its force has been diminished by the addition of a string of provisos. Social workers often limit its application by saying "but not in this situation." However, for women truly to gain from their interaction with a social worker, the nature of the relationship must be restructured. Miller identified "the first essential new ingredients [as] . . . self-determination and the power to make self-determination a reality."[20]

Self-determination means that a woman has the right to direct the course of her life. By accepting this definition, social workers assume that a woman will choose the course which best suits her at the time from the range of options open to her. The problem is whether social workers think she can make a choice and, in a power dimension, whether they think the choice is wise.

The desire to influence another is a complex one, particularly as it is enacted in a professional setting. Aside from whatever coercive power may be available to the practitioner, the power to move a person in a particular direction by the influence of one's specialized knowledge is considerable. Because a professional relationship is affected by what Miller referred to as "temporary inequality," one must contend with the element of power. But, as Miller cautioned, ". . . power alone will not suffice. Power exists and it has to be taken into account, not denied. The superiors hold all the real power, but power will not accomplish the task."[21]

The task that social work takes for itself is to facilitate change. Because social forces and an individual's patterns create barriers to the realization of her dignity and personal significance, social work can be thought of as providing the encounter by which powerless people can learn to experience their own power. This may happen in an individual encounter or it may happen in a group or community. The critical element is the social worker's perception of her or his role as one of fostering an individual's or group's movement toward greater equality.

Given the power traps that may subvert practice, what principles can social workers use as guides for better practice with women? How can the principle of self-determination be applied so that one's expert knowledge or access to coercive measures does not undermine the development or expression of self-assertion by clients?

Perhaps the first principle to establish is this: "Acting against the will of the client demands conviction. One must be certain that one's ideas are right."[22] Guggenbühl-Craig's pinpointing of certitude as the key to overriding a client's wishes leads to the question of whether the state of social work's professional knowledge and wisdom allows practitioners to act with such certainty. When social workers make a decision that is contrary to the client's, they are saying, in effect, that they can determine the course of her life better than she can. That speaks of an awesome power and responsibility—one which may be beyond the healthy exercise of power. Whether the decision comes through the use of administrative force or through more subtle means of influence, social workers have taken the responsibility for the choice they claim belongs to the client. There may well be situations in which a worker's conviction is sufficiently strong for such a decision, but the dictates of self-determination suggest that these instances are far fewer than is usually practiced.

The second principle has to do with the social worker's use of persuasion or influence. Although it is also a power-related technique, influence differs in an important way from coercive power. Rather than making needed resources contingent on the client's behavior, as is true when a negative consequence is present, "reliance on persuasion alone allows the target person (in this case, the client) a good deal of latitude to decide whether or not to obey."[23] The social worker assumes the role of information-provider by presenting available resources and by stretching the client's view of her personal-social situation. Of course, the worker's biases are present in this interchange, but the important point is that the client's dignity and feeling of worth should not be adversely affected by the decision she makes. The sense of respect that surrounds the encounter should not be disrupted if the client makes a decision contrary to the worker's sense of what is desirable.

The technique of withdrawing approval is potent when working with women. The socialization of women to be "people-pleasers" makes it difficult for them to act when important others disagree with the action. When the encounter between a worker and client develops into a professional relationship, the client comes to value the worker's opinion. This increases the client's vulnerability and the likelihood that she will try to please the worker rather than herself. The worker should be sensitive to this dynamic and vigilant, so the client's power to direct her life is not usurped.

It is difficult for those who hold strong beliefs about the condition of women in society to restrain their use of influence in behalf of women. Although feminism has been an important force in reawakening awareness of the limitations that policies and practice create for women and in voicing the demands for equality and justice, there is a danger in making feminist values a new orthodoxy. The introduction of an ideology that dictates what women should believe or how they should behave is simply a new version of oppression. Social workers are dedicated to helping women develop their potential, but, as Wheelis pointed out, such dedication may be excessive "if that is not what the [person] wants."[24]

The principle that must undergird professional practice is the belief that each woman is the source of her own change. When a social worker believes that his or her power causes change in another person, the worker's sense of power is reinforced at the expense of the client. Such a belief may lead to devaluation of the client and social distancing.

How can professionals safeguard the principle that each woman is the source of her own change? As Guggenbühl-Craig explained, to create a climate conducive to change, the practitioner "must always strive to constellate the healing factor in the patient. Without this, he can accomplish nothing. And he can only truly activate this healing factor if he bears sickness as an existential possibility within himself."[25] In other words, a practitioner must recognize his or her own vulnerability in the ongoing battle to grow and change. May stated that compassion is the essential quality. "Compassion is felt toward another because he doesn't fulfill his potentialities—in other words, he is human, like you or me, forever engaged in the struggle between fulfillment and nonfulfillment."[26] A key, then, to the proper use of power is the knowledge that one shares the condition and struggles of those one may be called on to help. Because each woman's life is a private journey, her gropings and false starts and small successes belong to her. Professionals may be able to create a wider arena within which a client may choose her path. But they must never forget that they also are on a journey.

POSITIVE EXPRESSIONS OF POWER

Power is more complex than has heretofore been recognized. Acceptance of the elements of force, manipulation, and competition as the essential ingredients of power means acceptance of others' definitions of the bases for change. In doing so, one is left with the unpleasant decision of whether to join forces with those who exercise this power or whether to absent oneself from what Dinnerstein called "history-making."[27] However, there is another choice. The meaning of power can be extended to include more positive expressions of power—ones that May identified as "nutrient" and "integrative" power. Nutrient power is "for the other"; integrative power is "with the other. . . ."[28] Both of these positive expressions of power suggest collaboration in a common enterprise in which cooperation becomes a form of power. As Miller stated: "Women need the power to advance their own development, but they do not 'need' the power to limit the development of others."[29]

It is critical for women "to learn to use these different kinds of power in ways adequate to the given situation."[30] Negative expressions of power cannot be dismissed, and the ways these expressions may subvert social workers' relationships with clients cannot be ignored. However, social workers can learn to use more shrewdly the power of institutions on behalf of clients, rather than against them, and to teach clients to use that power as well. They can also recognize the positive expressions of power and learn how to teach these integrating and strengthening forms.

The interest of many women in power does not come from a positive attraction to it but from a fear of power and the "desire to be free from the control of others."[31] Women and other oppressed groups need to experience the power to be—to stretch themselves as individuals and take a larger role in history-making. That power to be will create what Morgan called the "ripple effect"—the momentum that comes from

> . . . each woman gaining self-respect and . . . power over her own body and soul first, then within her family, on her block, in her town, state and so on out from the center, overlapping with similar changes other women are experiencing, the circle rippling more widely and inclusively as they go.[32]

Morgan believed that the rippling effect will occur from the feminist movement. However, that effect also epitomizes the potential for change which social work recognizes in its radical affirmation of every individual's right to experience the power of his or her own worth.

This society does not believe that the development of each individual's special strengths and talents will result in a gain for all. It does not encourage women to recognize their power and often quashes such attempts when they emerge. Social workers have to function within the constraints of this society and within the bureaucratic power model that works against the assertion of individuality by both the worker and client. Thus, there can be no illusion that attempts to create a climate of greater freedom and equality will be supported by the institutions of this society. But, ultimately, such support may not be important. If social workers can invigorate their practice, in whatever arena, with a keen understanding of and commitment to empowerment, such small encounters may set the ripple effect in motion. Social workers do not have to accomplish this alone. In fact, they cannot accomplish this alone. They can only seize the moment as it comes; from the moments of many, the power of change may come.

REFERENCES

1. Rollo May, *Power and Innocence* (New York: Dell Publishing Co., 1972), p. 99.

2. Jean Baker Miller, *Toward a New Psychology of Women* (Boston: Beacon Press, 1976), p. 115.

3. David Kipnis, *The Powerholders* (Chicago: University of Chicago Press, 1976), p. 3.

4. Ibid., pp. 10-11.

5. Ibid., p. 181.

6. Adolf Guggenbühl-Craig, *Power in the Helping Professions* (Zurich, Switzerland: Spring Publications, 1978), p. 10.

7. May, op. cit., p. 63.

8. For two examples, *see* Dorothy Dinnerstein, *The Mermaid and the Minotaur* (New York: Harper & Row, 1976); and Marvin Harris, "Why Men Dominate Women," *New York Times Magazine*, November 13, 1977, pp. 46 and 115-117.

9. Miller, op. cit., p. 94.

10. May Sarton, *As We Are Now* (New York: W. W. Norton & Co., 1973), p. 74.

11. Miller, op. cit., p. 4.

12. Kipnis, op. cit., p. 196.

13. Terence J. Johnson, *Professions and Power* (London, England: Macmillan Press, 1972), p. 43.

14. May, op. cit., p. 94. *See also* Guggenbühl-Craig, op. cit., p. 38.

15. Allen Wheelis, *How People Change* (New York: Harper & Row, 1973), p. 7.

16. May, op. cit., pp. 105-109.

17. Miller, op. cit., p. 116.

18. May, op. cit., pp. 1 and 243.
19. Guggenbühl-Craig, op. cit., p. 138.
20. Miller, op. cit., p. 96.
21. Ibid., p. 5.
22. Guggenbühl-Craig, op. cit., p. 2.
23. Kipnis, op. cit., p. 185.
24. Wheelis, op. cit., p. 19.
25. Guggenbühl-Craig, op. cit., p. 101.
26. May, op. cit., p. 251.
27. Dinnerstein, op. cit., chap. 9.
28. May, op. cit., p. 109.
29. Miller, op. cit., p. 118.
30. May, op. cit., p. 113.
31. Kipnis, op. cit., p. 164.
32. Robin Morgan, *Going Too Far* (New York: Vintage Books, 1978), p. 9.

Beyond Advocacy

Betty Sancier

Advocacy is an integral part of the ethical practice of social work. It involves the responsibility of social workers to assure that consumers of services are afforded dignified and humane treatment by teaching and encouraging them to assert their rights.[1] *Client advocacy* is based on a commitment to the interests of individual clients, and *reform advocacy* focuses on changes in social policies on behalf of an aggrieved class.[2] The activities of social work advocates range from advising individual clients about legal matters, to organizing constituents around important issues in a neighborhood, to lobbying for legislative changes through professional associations.[3] As used in this article, the term *advocacy* may encompass any of these or other activities.

Today, many female social workers are beginning to apply the principles and techniques of advocacy to their work with female clients. They are contributing important new insights that hold promise for the eventual elimination of the sexist bias from social work practice.[4] The gains made through advocacy must be carried forward case by case. However, to transform social work into a truly humanistic profession, these advocates must broaden their base of support to include all people—men as well as women—who share their vision.

ADVOCACY IN THE PAST

In the early days of social work—before social work moved toward the goal of professionalization—the upper-class women who were the leaders of the charity organization movement saw clearly that women and children suffered oppression and grinding poverty through no fault of their own. Some of the women worked as individuals to ameliorate conditions among the poor and oppressed, while others sought legislative and other social reforms by advocating various causes or by persuading influential husbands and relatives to do so. The women who became the founding mothers of the profession marched in picket lines, worked for women's suffrage, lobbied in statehouses, boycotted employers of child labor, petitioned for prison reform, championed birth control, and more, in the cause of social justice.[5]

As social work sought to find its mission, persons committed to differing views of causality flourished in creative competition. Thus, women who believed that individuals should adjust themselves to the demands of society sought to establish services directed to that end. Those who thought society itself was deficient were in the forefront of movements for social reform. And a few, such as Richmond, predicted that a dual approach toward the individual and the environment would be the core of any unique contribution of members of the emerging social work profession.[6]

In 1915, Flexner, addressing the question of professionalization among charity workers, declared that social work could not take its place among the older, established professions because it lacked a base in empiricism and a uniquely defined method.[7] As a response to Flexner's criticism, social workers adopted the new psychoanalytic theories of human behavior as the base of an acceptable professional discipline. Advocacy came to be regarded as "unscientific"; the emerging profession shaped itself according to a medical model. Programs of professional education spread; their curricula stressed treatment of individual pathology. In agencies, services to individuals were emphasized to the neglect of activities directed toward social change.

ADVOCACY REDISCOVERED

Although advocacy was practiced during the Great Depression of the 1930s, it did not regain status as a legitimate, widely applicable approach until the War on Poverty in 1964. Participation of citizens, manipulation of the environment, redistribution of income, and other ideas were reintroduced as ways to promote the betterment of individuals, families, and communities. The consumer movement, which burgeoned later, extended the concepts of advocacy still further. Yet, not all social workers were quick to add advocacy skills to their professional armamentaria. So tenacious was the grip of individual treatment on the profession that in 1969, the NASW Committee on Advocacy was still referring to "the new interest in advocacy among social workers."[8]

As the debate about treatment versus reform continued, a new generation of practitioners, inspired by visions of social justice, became involved in contest, controversy, and conflict. Concepts such as self-help, taking responsibility for one's behavior, self-respect and self-worth, and working with, not for, clients entered the professional consciousness with renewed force. But, with few exceptions, it was the men who stormed the barricades of social injustice, while the women tended the fires of neurosis.[9]

In the 1960s, the only movement of women was the National Welfare Rights Organization (NWRO)—a membership organization of welfare mothers. Some welfare workers—mostly women—acted as advocates for NWRO members. They risked their jobs by smuggling agency manuals and organizational charts to welfare recipients so these women could understand and influence the agencies that controlled allotments. The welfare workers risked arrest and injury by marching, picketing, and sit-ins. They risked disapproval from peers by confronting issues rather than seeking consensus. Yet, no lasting alliances were formed between the advocates and the recipients. Despite common experiences in confronting the political and welfare establishments, including sharing the same jail cell, these women did not identify the oppressive economic system as the enemy of all women.

FEMINIST THERAPY

Some female social workers used what they had learned from the civil rights movement and poverty programs to examine the conditions of women.[10] They spotlighted the needs of battered women, rape victims, and displaced homemakers, among others, whom they came to view as oppressed and disadvantaged, rather than neurotic. Unable to find support for these efforts among traditional agencies, they started alternative services of women for women. Other female practitioners reexamined basic precepts, such as self-determination, from a feminist perspective or turned their attention to social policy and legislation. Still others began to reappraise the role of women in the profession.[11]

Feminist therapy developed from these changed perspectives. Now feminist therapists are analyzing and defining components of their practice that are different from other forms of practice. Although some elements of feminist practice may prove to be unique, other elements may be applied to all nonsexist practice—that is, practice from which psychosocial theories and assumptions based on the inferiority of women have been eliminated.

Several elements of feminist practice are now ready for incorporation into overall practice. For example, it was feminist therapists who first called attention to the negative assumptions about the nature of women contained in the model of behavior based on dynamic psychology. Rape victims, for instance, were commonly treated less for the psychological stress of assault than for their unconscious impulses that allegedly invited assault. Now the ongoing responsibility for building new theory, revamping practice, and monitoring progress falls on all social workers.

Feminist therapists have also led the way toward demystifying the therapeutic process. They describe their techniques and share insights as part of a mutual problem-solving partnership with their clients. The therapist acts as a role model of competent adult behavior, not as a distant, omniscient authority figure. Through these means, women are helped to move toward independence and control of their lives.[12] Extensive reversal of approaches to counseling that reinforced dependence, adaptation, or acceptance of intolerable circumstances is imperative in keeping with the new knowledge and with basic social work values.

Insights from the women's movement have provided a new view of causality based on the processes of socialization and their effect on the personality development of women. As the facts of biology are gradually being separated from assumptions about gender, the relationship between role expectations and personality maladjustment is being reassessed. Furthermore, practitioners radically change their therapeutic goals and outcomes when they view a client differently. For example, a client who was previously seen as a castrating mother suffering the effects of an unresolved Oedipal struggle is now understood to be a talented woman whose artistic ambitions were thwarted by conformity to traditional feminine expectations.

Another important development has been the revival of support networks and the adaptation of self-help techniques to meet the needs of previously neglected populations, such as young mothers, middle-aged suburbanites, and elderly widows. Encouragement of helping systems that can ease the strains of everyday living holds promise for decreasing dependence on the medical model of helping that has often poorly served women.[13]

Female social workers have advocated on their own behalf only for about ten years. At that time, the first women's caucuses were formed in the National Association of Social Workers (NASW) and the Council on Social Work Education (CSWE). Participants in the caucuses were ridiculed and accused of maliciously diverting attention from the more important problems of racism and poverty. The notion that sexism was institutionalized, especially in social work, was dismissed as laughable. Women won some key victories, however, mainly by assertion, persuasion, and the power of numbers. Their battles produced the following results:

1. NASW and CSWE now have standing committees on women's issues.

2. NASW's affirmative action programs now require proportional representation of women in volunteer positions in the national offices and chapters. They also set guidelines for staffing.

3. Guidelines of the CSWE Accreditation Commission now require that women's issues be incorporated into the graduate and undergraduate curricula of schools of social work.

4. Women in the profession are now preparing themselves for leadership positions in unprecedented numbers. Although it is too early to document any substantial lessening in domination by men, the trend appears to be irreversible.

Moreover, female social workers are more and more coming to see their future as inextricably linked to that of all women. Cooperative activities are essential for broadening the base of women's participation and for achieving the power to preserve and win legislative and judicial victories. Individually and through NASW, social workers have stepped up active participation in coalitions working for the Equal Rights Amendment (ERA), freedom of choice in relation to abortion and other reproductive issues, legislation against domestic violence, and other goals.

THE LIMITS OF ADVOCACY

Advocacy is an essential component of the continuing struggle for justice and equity in the profession and in society. Many women are undergoing exciting transformations as they are helped to discover they are not isolated deviants and to cast off expectations of lifelong dependence in favor of self-images of competence and mastery.

However, in the current social milieu, individual women must fight the same battle again and again. Hence, the limitation of advocacy is that it deals with specific cases and issues. Battles are won, but the war still is being waged against persistent problems such as unequal salary levels for women; pressure on women to enter low-paying, dead-end jobs; and continuing political and religious opposition to new attempts to assure equality for all women. A series of victories does not always gain the concession of a principle or assure that the principle is put into practice. It is clear that redressing grievances on a case-by-case basis will not solve the underlying problems.

To move beyond advocacy, individual women must recognize that their problems are the problems of all women. They must engage in collective action on a vast scale to overcome the stigma of being female. The stigma may take the form of racial or ethnic bias or class or occupational disadvantage. The guise does not matter. Anatomy must cease to be destiny.

The social work profession is well suited to lead the struggle to establish true equality for all women by virtue of its professional Code of Ethics which affirms the principle that each individual has the right to achieve his or her maximum potential. Yet, members of the profession often have not practiced according to this principle. Moreover, women, who constitute two-thirds of the profession, have often participated in the oppression of the powerless, including other women, by accepting functions of social control in opposition to the professional ethos. Some of the "dirty worker" tasks have included keeping such undesirables as the mentally ill docile and under control, steering poor women into training programs for mental or nonexistent jobs, and policing the morals of welfare recipients. A woman's profession with its consciousness raised can no longer acquiesce in these or like assignments. But, at the same time, inconsistencies in social work only mirror inconsistencies in the world at large. It is to these contradictions that attention must be addressed if social work is to overcome the impediments to achieving its humanistic vision.

The failure of welfare workers and welfare mothers to recognize the essential commonality of their positions as women was mentioned earlier. Other paradoxes and examples of divided loyalties among women abound in the larger society. There are women who oppose ERA, women who embrace dependence, women who oppose advanced education for their daughters, and women in executive positions who sabotage the progress of other women.

Can common themes be discerned that throw light on these inconsistencies and point the way toward a reconciliation among women of opposing persuasions? Will women ever be able to answer with one voice Freud's exasperated query: "What do women want? Dear God, what do they want?"[14] Freud's answer to his own question unfortunately highlighted one assumption that plagues the helping professions to this day. He replied that women were genitally inferior. This idea, which is the starting point of "feminine psychology," relegates women to an inferior position because it views women as essentially deficient.

De Beauvoir explained the consequences of Freud's dictum: Woman's condition is to be forever the Other.[15] Man is the One, and in a world defined as male, woman exists only in relation to him, never as an independent being in her own right. Tracing the origins of this view is beyond the scope of this article, but evidence of the tenacity of the view abounds. For example, popular slang continues to be rife with allusions to women an inferior in such terms as "my old lady," "the old bag," "the ball and chain," and "that dumb broad."

Nevertheless, de Beauvoir acknowledged the advantages that women gain by remaining dependent. Women do not need to support themselves or succeed in any public arena or have their work judged by peers or reveal high aspirations. Powerful and successful men take all the risks inherent in action and independence. Although she did not deny the hazards of pursuing liberty and autonomy, de Beauvoir asserted women will be able to join with men to shape a destiny that is fully human only when they are free and independent. Failing this, "humanity" will remain strange and suspect, and the war between the sexes will rage endlessly.

Ten years before de Beauvoir wrote, Fromm examined the problem of freedom in the modern world.[16] He held that individualism—that is, the attainment of one's intellectual, emotional, and sensuous potential—must be achieved by spontaneous love and productive work. Isolated individuals become oppressed by feelings of powerlessness and insecurity. They experience a flight from freedom, which results in submission and dependence. In applying Fromm's analysis to the traditional position of women, one can argue that a similar flight from freedom is recognizable in the comfortable dependence of the status of the "little woman." Some women may perceive the women's movement's suggestions that women should seek greater autonomy more as a threat to what they already have than as encouragement to expand their horizons.

Horney's examination of such pertinent issues as distrust between the sexes and the problem of feminine masochism sheds further light on the dilemma of autonomy versus dependence. Horney thought that because love ". . constitutes a haven of peace in which women are spared the exertions and anxieties associated with the cultivation of other abilities and self-assertion in the face of criticism and rivalry."[17]

The observations of de Beauvoir, Fromm, and Horney help explain why many women reject women's liberation. The experience of these women tells them that they have more to lose than to gain by raising uncomfortable questions about the high psychological price they may be paying for security. The women's movement has not yet touched those who choose safety over freedom, but its leaders have begun to make significant attempts to appeal to the interests of all women.

Psychological dilemmas are not the only impediments to solidarity among women. Elitism, factionalism, antimale bias, excessive militancy, disputes about priorities, warring constituencies, and competition among charismatic leaders have also been divisive. The women's movement can profit from the valuable example of other social movements. Knowledge about the use of coalitions and alliances, political action, spontaneous leadership, charismatic leadership, rhetoric, and other such techniques has already been put into practice.

NEXT STEPS

In social work, advocacy can provide a base and an arena for the next steps in the process of liberating women and men. Many social workers see radical social change as necessary for the achievement of humanistic goals for all people, and they may well be correct. However, it is also necessary to build broad foundations of support for issues that a large number of women can support.

Beyond advocacy, women in social work, along with those in the women's movement, will need to help create alliances to achieve shared purposes. For example, they might ally themselves with other working women, including women who are members of labor unions, since all working women face similar problems. The statistics on women in the labor force are compelling: 34 percent of all married women with children work outside the home. By 1990, 75 percent of all women will work for pay. Four out of ten children born in the 1970s will live with a single parent, most likely a mother, at some time during their childhood. Working women report that support from their family, social circle, and workplace is often less than wholehearted.[18]

To an alliance of working women, social workers can bring valuable knowledge about human behavior, coping mechanisms, social systems, resources, and the needs of special groups such as mothers, divorced women, and single parents. They can assure that the unique needs of women who work are understood by counselors in traditional programs and that women are given priority in the rapidly expanding programs of industrial social work.

United, working women can assert their needs for overhauling the social security legislation, for setting state day care standards, or for organizing sessions on stress management in the workplace. Together, they can forge new personal, family, and social arrangements that could be of sweeping magnitude. But if women stay isolated and their endeavors remain fragmented, the problems are likely to remain insurmountable.

For those whose priority is the advancement of women in social work, opportunities exist for going beyond the early victories achieved through advocacy. Research findings on women from many fields may be used to build a data base about women in social work and to augment knowledge about how to make social systems more responsive to women. Data on the career patterns and life adjustments of professional women are contributing to knowledge about women's commitment to their careers, their work and career patterns, their dropout and return rates, the influence of childbearing and child rearing on the progress of their careers, and so on.[19]

Because such information is not available about women in social work, it is often difficult to combat the stereotypes that reinforce discrimination. For example, Etzioni said flatly:

> The public is less willing to grant professional autonomy to women than to men, and women are less likely than men to develop attitudes favorable to professionalism, because most of them are more oriented toward family roles.... this basic situation seems unlikely to change.[20]

However, results of recent studies of professional women indicate that Etzioni's conclusion is simply no longer true. On the contrary, many women go to extraordinary lengths to maintain their careers.[21] Documentation is needed to confirm whether these results hold for social workers in various settings, geographic locales, salary ranges, and age levels.

The personal, interpersonal, and organizational barriers to the advancement of women in organizations are widely known. Now the more difficult task is to find effective ways to break down those barriers. Social science researchers are delving into this issue too. For example, Epstein warned against too heavy an emphasis on the negative effects of socialization patterns that prevent women from having the self-confidence to achieve. She cited findings of women's inherent ability to master new knowledge and suggested conditions that can enhance the chance of success in new undertakings. Kanter discussed the uses and abuses of "tokenism," how to counteract tokenism, and how to move beyond it. Rubenstein reviewed a substantial body of research on women employed in organizations. She warned that unless male and female students in schools of social work are taught strategies for overcoming organizational barriers to the advancement of women, the field may lose many of its most able women.[22]

CONCLUSION

Social workers can play an important role in the further development of the women's movement. They must help break the endless cycle of case-after-case, experience-after-experience solutions that fail to affect the larger picture. Once again, the study of previous social movements will provide valuable lessons in the women's movement's attempts to become a full-fledged social movement. Rainwater's description of the functions of earlier social movements contains some terms that remain significant for current and future efforts. He defined those social movements as "collective behavior occasioned by social disorganization . . . and manifested in the organization of activities to accomplish a social end."[23] A movement is not tightly organized, as is the program of an institution or bureaucratic system. Rather, it arises here and there as critical incidents occur in different localities. Rainwater's description is an accurate representation of how the women's movement engages in various issues, with displaced homemaker legislation being a priority in one community and programs for battered women being emphasized in another.

Women in social work can help make the women's movement a social movement by the following five actions. First, they can become thoroughly informed of the new facts about women, mentioned earlier, that lay to rest old myths and introduce new concepts of what women are and what they can be.

Second, they can take deliberate steps to raise the consciousness of other women with regard to the new facts, the availability of new images, and the new possibilities for life and action.

Third, individual women should recruit an action system of like-minded persons and develop a constituency of supporters, including friends in other systems, rather than tackle an emerging local problem or issue by themselves. Doing so not only provides a "front" for the immediate task of confrontation, but also provides the shared experiences that create the body of precedents from which successful movements are made.

Fourth, women should thoroughly analyze any attempt to remedy a local situation so they may learn from the successes and failures and communicate the consequences to others. Doing so enlarges the body of shared experiences and provides valuable information to others as they confront subsequent critical incidents.

Fifth, women in social work should encourage and support the continuing development of women's networks and coalitions. These networks and coalitions are vital to the flow of ideas and information, buttress commitment through common cause, and provide a critical mass for action.

Some may raise objections that this article speaks almost entirely to women acting in their own behalf in various personal, professional, and political spheres, with only minimal acknowledgment of the participation of like-minded men. The author has done so because women must validate their own and separate-gender identities before men and women can contribute equally to the condition of being human. Beyond sexism, as rapidly as possible and for the long run, men must join with women and lend their support to the goals that women seek for themselves now, but eventually will seek for all people: the establishment of justice in social policy and in practice.

REFERENCES

1. Neil Gilbert, Henry Miller, and Harry Specht, *An Introduction to Social Work Practice* (Englewood Cliffs, N.J.: Prentice-Hall, 1980), pp. 28–32.

2. NASW Ad Hoc Committee on Advocacy, "The Social Worker as Advocate: Champion of Social Victims," *Social Work*, 14 (April 1969), pp. 16–22.

3. George A. Brager, "Advocacy and Political Behavior," *Social Work*, 13 (April 1968), pp. 5–15. *See also*, Paul Terrell, "The Social Worker as Radical: Roles of Advocacy," in Paul E. Weinberger, ed., *Perspectives on Social Welfare* (Toronto, Ont., Canada: Collier Macmillan, 1969), pp. 331–338; Richard A. Cloward and Richard M. Elman, "Advocacy in the Ghetto," in Fred M. Cox et al., eds., *Strategies of Community Organization* (Itasca, Ill.: F. E. Peacock Publishers, 1970), pp. 209–215; Armand Lauffer, *Social Planning at the Community Level* (Englewood Cliffs, N.J.: Prentice-Hall, 1978); and Charles F. Grosser, *New Directions in Community Organization* (New York: Praeger Publishers, 1973).

4. Cf. Elaine Norman and Arline Mancuso, eds., *Women's Issues and Social Work Practice* (Itasca, Ill.: F. E. Peacock Publishers, 1980); and Naomi Gottlieb, ed., *Alternative Social Services for Women* (New York: Columbia University Press, 1980).

5. Walter I. Trattner, *From Poor Law to Welfare State* (2d ed.; New York: Free Press, 1974); and Susan T. Vandiver, "A Herstory of Women in Social Work," in Norman and Mancuso, op. cit., pp. 21–38.

6. Mary Richmond, *Social Diagnosis* (New York: Russell Sage Foundation, 1917).

7. Trattner, op. cit., p. 211.

8. NASW Ad Hoc Committee on Advocacy, op. cit., pp. 16–18.

9. George Brager and John A. Michael, "The Sex Distribution in Social Work: Causes and Consequences," *Social Casework*, 50 (December 1969), pp. 595–601. One notable exception to the generalization is Frances Fox Piven. *See*, for example, Frances Fox Piven and Richard A. Cloward, *Poor People's Movement* (New York: Vintage Books, 1979).

10. Betty S. Johnson and Carol Holton, "Social Work and the Women's Movement," in Bernard Ross and S. K. Khinduka, eds., *Social Work in Practice* (Washington, D.C.: National Association of Social Workers, 1976), pp. 171–180.

11. Marjorie Moskol, "Feminist Therapy and Casework Practice," in Bernard Ross and S. K. Khinduka, eds., *Social Work in Practice* (Washington, D.C.: National Association of Social Workers, 1976), pp. 181–189; and Diane Kravetz, "Sexism in a Women's Profession," *Social Work*, 21 (November 1976), pp. 421–426.

12. Susan Amelia Thomas, "Theory and Practice in Feminist Therapy," *Social Work*, 22 (November 1977), pp. 447–453.

13. Patsy Turini, "A Mother's Center: Research, Service, and Advocacy," *Social Work*, 22 (November 1977), pp. 478–483.

14. Sigmund Freud, "Some Psychical Consequences of the Anatomical Distinctions Between the Sexes" (1925) in *Collected Papers*, Vol. 5 (London, England: Hogarth Press, 1950).

15. Simone de Beauvoir, *The Second Sex* (New York: Vintage Books, 1974).

16. Erich Fromm, *Escape From Freedom* (New York: Avon Books, 1941).

17. Karen Horney, *Feminine Psychology* (New York: W. W. Norton & Co., 1967).

18. Alfreda P. Iglehart, *Married Women and Work* (Lexington, Mass.: D. C. Heath & Co., 1979), pp. 81–82.

19. Alice M. Yohalem, *The Careers of Professional Women* (New York: Columbia University Press, 1978); and ibid.

20. Amitai Etzioni, *The Semi-Professions and Their Organizations* (New York: Free Press, 1969), p. 247.

21. Iglehart, op. cit.; and Yohalem, op. cit.

22. Cynthia F. Epstein, "Success Motivation and Social Structure: Comments on Women and Achievement," in Laurily Keir Epstein, ed., *Women in the Professions* (Lexington, Mass.: Lexington Books, 1975); Rosabeth Moss Kanter, *Men and Women of the Corporation* (New York: Basic Books, 1977); and Hiasaura Rubenstein, "Women in Organizations: A Review of Research and Some Implications for Teaching Social Work Practice," paper presented at the Annual Program Meeting, Council on Social Work Education, Los Angeles, Calif., March 1980.

23. Clarence E. Rainwater, *The Play Movement in the United States* (Chicago: University of Chicago Press, 1977), pp. 1–3.

ISSUES FOR WOMEN IN A 'WOMAN'S PROFESSION'

Carol H. Meyer

People respond to the expectations of their society. Despite the genetic, anatomical, instinctive, and intraphysical phenomena that are at work, people's feelings, attitudes, ideas, and behaviors are shaped by the expectations or mandates of their particular culture. A *New York Times* article on the United Nations World Conference on Women, held in Copenhagen, Denmark, in 1980, offered a poignant example of the intricate transactional relationships between people and the mandates of their culture.[1] As was brought out at the conference, women in some Third-World countries must undergo clitoral circumcision during latency, probably to keep them chaste before marriage. The chairman of the conference, herself, had experienced this sexual abuse and recalled screaming for her mother during the ritual "operation." She was horrified to see her mother among the onlookers, nodding benignly at this age-old ritual being inflicted on her daughter.

This incident is a stunning example of how human relationships are shaped by cultural mandates. Two further incidents at the conference that followed from the first one further illustrate this process. When the Western women heard of clitoral circumcision for the first time, they were horrified and wanted to petition the World Health Organization to outlaw what they viewed as the butchery of young girls in the Third World. To them, clitoral circumcision was a savage custom. However, an activist group of Third-World women, who had experienced clitoral circumcision, berated their critics for interfering with customs about which they were uninformed. Obviously, patterned social relationships, even when they entail physical pain and hardship, are necessary for individuals to maintain their personal and social integrity.

In this culture, girls do not experience any special rituals of physical abuse like clitoral circumcision or feet binding. In this culture, boys and girls are abused and neglected indiscriminately, they are denied public assistance in equal measure, and they suffer from a lack of day care and from inadequate education in a nonsexist fashion. The sexism practiced in this country is more subtle. But the principles drawn from the International Women's Conference remain: people's responses are shaped by their culture and inevitably they conspire to maintain that culture.

This article discusses the reciprocal transactions that occur in the tightly woven system of women, society, and social work. Before the system can be opened to change, women must first understand the reciprocity involved and must confront their complicity in keeping the system going. The article begins by examining women's responses to social expectations, goes on to explore the myths and issues involved in the role of women and of women in social work, and ends by suggesting ways that women can change the system.

WOMEN'S RESPONSES TO SOCIAL EXPECTATIONS

In general, women have responded to the stereotypes about how women "are" in ways that might be expected by those who feel powerless. Although all women do not feel, think, or behave in the same way or share all the characteristics supported or marketed by the cultural stereotypes, the following short list of "female characteristics" is all too familiar: women tend to act submissively, using accommodation, passivity, and responsiveness as opposed to aggression and assertive creativity. This section cannot explore the reasons for women being thus characterized, except to say that these stereotyped characteristics and behaviors have to serve some purposes in public and family life. Rather, it deals with women's responses to these stereotypes.

When a woman who is self-effacing and unthinkingly obedient to authority, as all women have been socialized to be, moves into professional life, she is expected to react characteristically to supervisors, administrators, teachers, and agency policies. Indeed, the woman who feels, thinks, and behaves in these expected ways is, or has been, an exemplar of the successfully socialized American woman. If her actions pleased her father and brothers, they will please her lover and husband—and her executive. One cannot forget that these actions pleased her mother as well; her mother had to smile benignly, for her daughter's socialization was her cultural imperative as well. Therefore, supervisors, teachers, and other male and female authority figures call forth stereotypical responses from female social workers who have not thought much about it or who are unable to change their response for whatever reason.

Cloward and Piven, in exploring women's "hidden protest," noted the lack of deviance among women, who tend toward privatism rather than group action. In women, deviance often takes the form of such self-destructive behavior as alcoholism and suicide, rather than crime or social activism. As Cloward and Piven wrote:

> We think that whether people respond to stress at all is socially structured. How stress is experienced is mediated by features of the historically specific social context in which people find themselves; by the interpretations they develop of the conditions they confront and by the assessment they make of their options in dealing with these conditions.[2]

To the extent that women view "culture as man and nature as woman" and persist in enduring and coping with the stress they view as an inevitable part of their lives, a private, self-effacing, and guilt-ridden behavior will characterize their coping.[3] Is getting along, going along? Social work clients, most of whom are women, in accommodating to social workers who exert power and authority, thereby cope with a reality that is often harsh and ambiguous. Clients who are creatively assertive or who engage in group action get into trouble with social agencies. Since the way "stress is experienced is mediated by the features of the historically specific social context," it is important to consider the contexts that social workers contrive for clients. This is an issue for women as much as it is a human issue.

That women as social workers and clients not only feel, think, and behave in socially defined ways but often have participated in defining the expectations (which could not otherwise have persisted) is one issue. Another issue is the view of social work as a "woman's profession." Social work is the context that elicits particular coping responses, so it is important to examine the properties of social work that impinge on women and create "issues for women."

A 'WOMAN'S PROFESSION'

Two myths are inherent in the idea that social work is a "woman's profession." The first myth is that social work is a woman's profession at all. By any criteria, women have not had control of the organization of social work, have not exerted executive leadership, have not carried the major responsibility for policy making, and have not earned the highest salaries.[4] Although women in social work like to call on Jane Addams, Mary Richmond, or the Abbott sisters as their models, these leaders have been exceptions, not the rule.[5] Yet the myth persists, probably because women are more numerous in social work than are men or than women in so-called men's professions.

The progress of women in social work can be measured by familiar, unpleasant criteria. Women are still perceived, judged, and paid in accordance with their personal characteristics and the "maleness" or "femaleness" of their vocational choice. It is not the intrinsic value of the work of the caseworker in child welfare or the administrator of a major teaching hospital that is looked at, but, rather, the so-called femaleness or maleness of the vocational context. It is the image of the caseworker in child welfare, not the hospital administrator, that leads people to the sexist idea that social work is a "woman's profession." It is sexist in both cases to define a professional by gender. Yet this is how social workers are viewed, not by such concrete measures as salary, power, and impact.

The second myth is more difficult to dispel because it cannot be subjected to tests of factual criteria or historical evidence. It has to do with the idea that the "nurturing" capacity of women naturally fits the "nurturing" function of social work. The idea suggests that men are not able to nurture. It is as dangerous and silly a notion as the idea that women cannot be decisive.

Furthermore, in a sexist society, any association of women's characteristics with a profession is pejorative. That is, there is intrinsic value to being a social worker, nurse, teacher, librarian, secretary, housewife, dental hygienist or whatever other profession or vocation has been associated with women. Society could not get along without any of these pursuits, yet they are denigrated and maintained as low-level jobs probably because they are associated with women. It is difficult to understand why women in social work persist in defining social work as a woman's profession because this deeply held conviction contributes to the low self-image and low public image suffered by social workers.

Moreover, medicine is probably the most "nurturing" profession, but in this country it is defined as a science and thus remains a male-dominated profession. Thus, it is the definition of social work as nurturing which has caused it to be considered a woman's profession. If social workers persist in using this definition, they will come back to the idea that if women perform a task, the task is viewed as what women can and should do naturally—mothering. Surely, all social workers are aware of the struggle by women in industry, banking, advertising, the media, and other nonnurturing vocations to prove their worth as individuals and to lay to rest the historical idea that women cannot wander from the literal or figurative hearth without social, psychological, physical, and economic risk. If social workers define their work as nurturing, they will have found security at the figurative hearth and will once again have met the stereotyped cultural mandate.

Furthermore, the assumption that nurturing is the most significant aspect of social work competes with other significant aspects, such as analytical thinking, clinical perceptiveness, the rigor of research, professional autonomy, and administrative decisiveness. Gender characteristics are so unclear and so stereotyped that to characterize any profession by gender can only serve sexism.

In keeping with the author's view that there is a reciprocity between women's responses and society's expectations, it would be helpful to see what an English scholar says about the implication of sexism and the choice of women's rules. Sharpe stated: "In a society in which obvious discrimination is condemned, 'normal' sex differences help to preserve the separation of roles and thus the inequalities upon which the economic system still depends."[6] Sharpe pointed out that the socialization of boys and girls into contrasting personalities and roles plays a significant part in the perpetuation of the social structure. Even the liberation of women through work has occurred primarily through jobs that have been as close as possible to and as undervalued as housework and monitoring. "It is a vicious cycle, in which women's work, like the status of women themselves, reinforces their own devaluation."[7]

It becomes clearer why women must persist in coping with pejorative titles, sex-role stereotyping, and ascription by gender. Women were not born to be an under class; there is too much evidence that they were made that way and that they have too often succumbed to external definitions of their worth.

The persistence of the idea that social work is a woman's profession evokes greater hazards in periods of social reaction and economic difficulty, as in the current period. Latent negative social attitudes about the liberation of women are strengthened by the threats of an abominable economy. These attitudes are expressed as concern about women working, especially in "real" jobs like industry, and crowding the employment market. The political reactions to the Equal Rights Amendment (ERA), day care, and abortion and birth control are not accidental; they are real and symbolic expressions of concern about the inexorable march of women toward liberation. Next to racism, in the minds of the powerful, sexism has become the most significant route to economic salvation.

Reactionary attitudes are especially directed toward the poor and the oppressed, among whom ethnic minorities and women are prominent. However, two options are available to women in social work that are not available to the poor, the oppressed, and ethnic minorities. That is, women in social work can assume a militant stance and claim that there is indeed a "womanishness" associated with social work—a nurturing quality that characterizes the profession. Or they can object to the stereotype, cease participating in the devaluation of social work as a woman's profession, and change their behavior from docility to decisiveness and competence.

This author would choose the second option, which is to "degenderize" social work and all other professions as well. Then change will come about through shifts in thinking and acting. The nonnurturing roles and functions that have been erroneously associated with "men's professions," such as appropriate aggression, analytic and critical thinking, craftsmanship and excellence in skills, and authoritative command of knowledge, would be far more successful than accommodation in changing society's prevailing attitudes toward women's issues and the role of women in the family. The issues should not be women's issues at all; they should be professional issues. The remainder of this article will propose some ways to move in this androgynous direction.

ISSUES FOR WOMEN IN SOCIAL WORK

The change from a "woman's profession" to an androgynous profession does not mean that women should be like men; it means that professional behavior would not be defined by gender. For all the reasons mentioned earlier, this change will not occur without problems. What is being sought is a no-fault image—one that goes beyond sexist definitions. Let us explore the possibilities as if sexism were not an issue at all.

Solomon wrote that she looked forward to "a future in our profession and in our country when restrictive prejudices based on race, sex, or class will not be important and therefore will not require 'special' attention."[8] Clearly that future is not yet here, but the hope remains in areas where women in social work who are in charge of their attitudes and actions will be able to defy the prejudices, define their own terms, and put the lie to the stereotypes. There is no external force in society that will help; women have to remember that they are locked into this system through mutual agreement. The only way to change the system is to shift at least one of its components—women's feelings, attitudes, and behaviors. The rest will follow; in any system, it has to.

After women's awareness is raised, the next change is in self-image and a fearless approach to every issue and situation. Challenging what is viewed as wrong, unethical, or irrational—whether agency policies, supervisors' suggestions, or organizational behavior—is not a male characteristic, but a professional requirement. Looking for novel ways of dealing with recalcitrant situations is not male or radical; it is the hallmark of professionalism. And although seeking higher office in agencies or schools of social work is aggressive, to be ambitious is American as well. This decade is going to be hard for women who make the effort, but, as a consequence of present efforts, in the next decade quality, not gender, will be the determinant of worth.

But rhetoric is not sufficient. There is work to be done. Brown made the ecosystems point that individual competence and effectiveness require an enabling environment.[9] This idea suggests that since social work is riddled with the same sexism as the rest of society, it will not enable its professional women to demonstrate their competence any more than will any other social institution. Therefore, women who are now in decision-making positions—senior women who are supervisors, full professors, executives, and deans—will have to open up new paths. Opportunities for growth and advancement, for experiment, and for competence have to be created so in the new generation the professional social worker will be defined in a nonsexist way.

Furthermore, all social workers need to consider the importance of helping their clients to develop competence through mastery and independence. Low expectations of clients because they are clients is patronizing and a form of sexism. Female social workers are as inclined as the rest of society to carry out the cultural mandate that demands dependence and submissiveness in female clients. It is time for women to stop looking on benignly.

In addition to shifting their thinking, behavior, and approaches to promoting competence in women clients, all social workers can use their knowledge and practice theory to mitigate sex-role stereotyping and sexist practices in the environments of clients, be they housing, schools, jobs, hospitals, clinics, social agencies, or governmental bureaucracies. Direct intervention in environments must be part of the social worker's repertoire, whatever the theoretical commitment; otherwise clients will continue in the same sex-related cycles.

Nonsexist social work is good practice. To avoid sex-role definitions of health, to seek an open nondeterministic behavioral theory, and to be thoughtful, critical, and discriminating about practice approaches are sound professional ideas. Although they allow for the level of practice that will enhance the lives of clients and the real status of women, they go beyond "issues for women." Benefits will accrue to men, women, and children, which is the highest human and professional purpose.

There is more to social work than direct practice, although women have been slow to move into policy and organizational roles. There is some irony in the fact that female social workers have decried their lack of power while avoiding the very positions that provide the context, direction, and goals of practice. In the 1960s, social workers were told that women's characteristics were better adapted to direct practice than to policy and administration, which were defined as the province of men.[10] How many female corporate executives were once led to believe they were better suited to be secretaries? Today women have sufficient models in politics, the media, the sciences, and other professions to disbelieve the stereotype expectations that once entrapped women in "women's jobs." Policy analysis and administrative leadership are too vital to social work to be left only to men.

Intellectual rigor and analytic thinking are not inherently male characteristics; they are the consequence of differential socialization that can be mediated through self-awareness and changes in attitudes supported by communal efforts. Women in social work should be able to give up their "doing good" and nurturing roles and to return these functions to clients and their families, friends, and self-help groups. Professional knowledge and skills, whether used in psychotherapy or social change, are more complex and demanding than are caring for and loving clients.

At least one illustration is needed to avoid the idea that this author is proposing that female social workers should exchange empathy for computer behavior. In child welfare, a field that is filled with unloved children, it is insufficient professional behavior to love a foster child when attention is not paid to the social policies and organizational behaviors that have placed him or her in foster care. Critical analysis and aggressive action related to untangling the policy mess are the professional tasks. They require extensive knowledge, political sophistication, and craftsmanship; love is not enough. Love is not enough for the foster child, and it is not enough to characterize women in social work.

True liberation of women in professional work will take place when roles and functions are not always defined in personal, family, or maternal terms. These are terms for personal, not professional lives. That is the issue for women in social work. Can professional women in social work come to feel so secure that they can practice their craft in an androgynous fashion? Can female social workers "hang tough" in a tough world? The liberation of women in social work, if successful, will result in the liberation of social work as well.

TOWARD A NEW 'OLD-GIRL' NETWORK

The awareness by women that there is a reciprocity between their responses and society's expectations for their behavior, their choice to "degenderize" their profesional behavior, and their progress in sharpening their clinical practice and organizational expertise are ongoing tasks. But there is another level of important activity in which women have not typically engaged—politics. One consequence of the socialization of women has been their avoidance of politics, in this case professional, personal, women's politics. Politics, more than all the other new roles and functions being tried by women, flies most savagely in the face of women's upbringing. "Good" girls do their best and are rewarded for carrying out the mandates of their culture. These rewards will not be forthcoming when women change and challenge these mandates. That is the concern often expressed by such opponents of ERA as Phyllis Schlafly who think that passage of ERA will mean women will lose traditional rewards like having men pull out a chair for them.

Empowerment will indeed shift things around, especially now. While change is in process, women will need support from each other at least.

Women know little about group solidarity; yet, solidarity on issues that are important to women is exactly the course women must follow during the lonely times to come. Each woman must seek her own network. Once she is part of a network, she must reach out to others, be active, and make issues for women a personal and professional priority.

REFERENCES

1. Georgia Dullea, "Female Circumcision a Topic at U.N. Parley," *New York Times*, Friday July 18, 1980, Sec. B, p.4.

2. Richard A. Cloward and Frances Fox Piven, "Hidden Protest: The Channeling of Female Innovation and Resistance," *Signs: Journal of Women in Culture and Society*, 4 (December 1979), p. 662.

3. Sandra M. Gilbert, "The Revisionary Imperative," *Columbia*, (Summer 1980), p. 35.

4. Jeanne M. Giovannoni and Margaret E. Purvine, "The Myth of the Social Work Matriarchy," *Social Welfare Forum, 1973* (New York: Columbia University Press, 1973).

5. Susan T. Vandiver, "A Herstory of Women in Social Work," in Elaine Norman and Arlene Mancuso, eds., *Women's Issues and Social Work Practice* (Itasca, Ill.: F. E. Peacock, Publishers, 1980), pp. 21–38.

6. Sue Sharpe, *Just Like a Girl: How Girls Learn To Be Women* (London, England: Penguin Books, 1976), p. 62.

7. Ibid., p. 173.

8. Barbara Bryant Solomon, "Is It Sex, Race, or Class?" Editorial Page, *Social Work*, 21 (November 1976), p. 420.

9. Prudence Brown, "Women and Competence," in Anthony N. Maluccio, ed., *Promoting Competence in Clients: A New-Old Approach to Social Work Intervention* (New York: Free Press, 1981).

10. *See*, for example, George Brager and John A. Michael, "The Sex Distribution in Social Work: Causes and Consequences," *Social Casework*, 50 (December 1969), pp. 595–601.

Social Work Values and Skills to Empower Women

When the possibility of a special issue of *Social Work* devoted to women's issues was explored in the early 1970s, serious questions were raised about whether there was enough sexism in social work or scholarly material dealing with unique concerns of women to warrant a special issue. However, since then, the rapidly expanding literature has documented the various forms of discrimination against women, as well as the efforts of social workers to eliminate or at least reduce them. Some of the topics covered have been the denial of job opportunities or promotions to women because of their sex, the inappropriate treatment of women for depression, and the insensitive responses of the medical, law enforcement, and judicial systems to rape victims and battered women.[1] Other topics have included the overburdening of women with household responsibilities despite full-time employment, the overprescription of drugs to and the unnecessary performance of hysterectomies on women, and, what is perhaps most poignant, the fate of women "displaced" by husbands and threatened by social policies that leave them unprotected.[2]

The literature has also informed social workers of the obstacles they will face if they attempt to engage in nonsexist social work practice. For example, efforts to develop adequate treatment programs for young female offenders have often been given a lower priority than such programs for young male offenders, efforts to treat alcoholic women have been hamperd by such stereotyped assumptions as the tendency to consider alcoholic women psychologically sicker than alcoholic men, and efforts to assist displaced homemakers have been resisted by those who think that women enter the employment market to supplement the family income rather than to be breadwinners.[3] Two themes have emerged to characterize the profession's stance on women's issues. The first is the profession's acceptance of sexist value orientations in its practice; the second is the relevance of social work skills and strategies for dealing with characteristic problems encountered by women.

It would be fitting to subject these themes to a critical analysis in an effort to capture more vividly the implications for practitioners. Therefore, two questions will be addressed in this article: How can social work resist more effectively the tendency for a profession to reflect the attitudes of society, either good or bad? Which skills have the greatest potential for a social work strategy to empower women?

CONFLICTING VALUES

There are several excellent reviews of the literature on the social work profession's efforts to deal with women's issues and the contributions made by female practitioners and scholars.[4] These reviews reveal an interesting paradox. On the one hand, in the nineteenth and early twentieth centuries, social work provided the opportunity for intelligent women—not always feminists but with a strong social consciousness—to be involved in the charity and reform movements in behalf of the poor, the mentally ill, dependent children, racial minorities, and women themselves. It should be added that black women (only a breath away from slavery themselves) were also active in organizing services for disadvantaged groups in their oppressed communities—a fact often ignored in standard texts on the history of social welfare. On the other hand, the early volunteers were predominantly upper-class white women who believed the poor were largely to blame for their low social status and who considered themselves to be superior to the people they were helping. Those volunteers who sought training in the emerging social work profession still counseled women to adjust to society's views of the roles of wife and mother, including the expectation that women should be passive and dependent. To some extent, this paradox may be explained by the fact that in the early days of the profession, most social workers were either not married or were not living with their husbands or children.[5] In those days, women could not have careers and be wives and mothers, since society perceived these roles as being in conflict. Thus, these female social workers could work toward eliminating biases against women but evidently could not bring themselves to counsel other women to fight rather than adjust.

Obviously, some gains have been made in expanding opportunities for women since that time. However, the society's value orientation is still sexist. That is, society still conceives of women as passive, nurturing, and emotional rather than aggressive, decisive, and rational; society often prefers that women hold certain jobs and not others; and society often prefers to deal with women's physical complaints by attributing their origin to emotional problems and prescribing tranquilizers rather than exploring other possible causes. Feminist values are antithetical to these conceptions. At some times and in some places, social work has supported feminist values, whereas at other times and in other places it has supported the sexist values of society. Moreover, whether another set of values is supported does not seem to be determined by whether the social worker works for an organization that has adopted a sexist stance; rather it seems to be determined by the viewpoints of individual social workers.

Parenti stated that no belief system can give equal accommodation to all human preferences; rather, certain beliefs are pursued at the expense of others.[6] Therefore, American society has incorporated a hierarchy of values in dynamic flux rather than a closed system in which some values are included and others excluded. As a result, social reformers and professional practitioners alike are continually confronted with the phenomenon of a social policy or program emanating from their value orientation that is modified or distorted by those who hold a competing or conflicting value orientation. For example, the efforts of legislatures to respond to demands for a redistribution of wealth through the graduated income tax became laughable when gaping loopholes were left in to placate more powerful corporate interests. And humanistic efforts to provide health care to the elderly have been sabotaged by the excesses of the providers. Furthermore, victories won by women and minority groups in affirmative action may well be hollow victories in that as women and racial minorities move up the organizational ladder, the power in the organization often rises to the positions just above those held by them. Thus, the issue is not whether social work reflects the values of society, since there are many conflicting values in the society. The issue is whether social workers can exert the power required to have their professional values prevail.

Those readers who are likely to snicker at this picture of social work locked in combat with the purveyors of nonhumanistic values should be reminded that despite the exploitation of Medicare by some greedy physicians, the elderly are better off with Medicare than without it. Despite loopholes in the tax laws, Americans are better off than when the robber barons were unchecked in their hoarding of the country's resources. Despite the limited success of affirmative action programs, women and minorities have more educational and occupational opportunities than they would have if no affirmative action laws had been passed. Despite the fact that landlords and contractors have increased the cost of housing the poor, the poor are far better off with subsidized housing programs than they would be with no programs at all. There is no cause for apathy because social workers cannot win all the battles with those whose values are, too often, given priority in this society. Winning the whole war can occur only with radical reform of the society. In the meantime, the intense involvement of social workers can win the little battles and often minimize the negative consequences that would surely come about if nonhumanistic values were uncontested.

Boulding suggested that protest is usually effective if a majority of the population supports the goals of the protesters even if that support has not been articulated.[7] This is one reason given for the success of the sit-ins that protested segregation of public accommodations in the late 1950s and 1960s and for the relative lack of success of the demonstrations against the Vietnam War. That is, most Americans considered desegregation to be a joint demand but were not opposed to war.

The same point was made in regard to the fight for the Equal Rights Amendment (ERA) in an article titled "Who Killed E.R.A.? Women Did." The article clearly states that the major opposition to ERA has come from women—not men. Many women consider ERA as a threat because they are afraid it will reduce the moral and cultural pressures that often have kept men in a marriage. Women who want their husbands to stay in the marriage out of a sense of duty may seem pathetic to liberated women, but, in this society, women depreciate faster than men. Furthermore, divorce can give a man the opportunity to choose a younger woman. For the wife, however, divorce may symbolize the end of the life she chose—an unfairness that even ERA will not remedy. As the article noted:

> Even if the wife at home has never seen the statistics, she knows that if she finds herself divorced at the age of 40, her own chances for remarriage are less than 1 in 3. This realization is hardly one to align her with women who seem ready to give their husbands a second stab at life.[8]

But are not women who are opposed to ERA in the minority? The answer is no—not among women who vote. According to Hacker, fewer than half the single women in this country vote in most elections, whereas close to two-thirds of the married women do. Moreover, about 60 percent of the women aged 45–64 usually vote, whereas less than 40 percent of the 25–34 age group vote—and that is the group most likely to support ERA.[9]

Thus it is clear that an accurate assessment of the majority's pivotal concerns and preferences will indicate when the values of social work are more or less likely to be supported. When social workers find less support for their values, they need to make a major effort to create support for their values among the masses. Their emphasis must be on raising the consciousness of those who do not think that the concerns of social work are relevant to their own lives and on encouraging communication with nonsupporters to reduce the force of mutual myths. When the pendulum inevitably swings back toward increased support for liberal, humanistic concerns, social workers must be prepared to take advantage of the more accepting social context and put into operation the strategies for empowering women and other minorities that were not possible in more repressive times. Whether creating mass support or implementing innovative programs, specific social work skills are crucial. The author has identified the following five skills that may be used to combat sexism in practice and in society.

SKILLS TO EMPOWER WOMEN

The first skill is *assessment of complex, interactional systems*. This skill requires the mastery of the systems perspective and a consideration of how the various parts of the client's ecological system (people and their social and physical environments) affect each other. For example, if the supporters of ERA had recognized that ERA posed a threat to a certain group of women and that the opposing group had the power to create and stimulate opposition, they might have used other strategies to obtain ratification of the amendment. The importance of accurate and comprehensive assessment for developing effective intervention strategies cannot be overestimated.

Feminist social workers have discussed many ways to improve the quality of life for women, such as "upgrading" the homemaker role by obtaining "fringe benefits" for housewives, including social security and income tax deductions, and insuring the availability of twenty-four-hour-a-day affordable child care programs for children of working women. Another such goal has been to upgrade the foster care program, to professionalize it with standards and fringe benefits in accordance with the highly specialized services it renders. Yet, the complex interrelationships among these emotionally charged goals are rarely appreciated. For example, the well-documented push to move women into nontraditional occupational roles in business and industry has brought many benefits to women.[10] However, it has also meant that a smaller pool of women is available to work as foster mothers. Similarly, the Children's Defense Fund has emphasized the need for policies aimed at strengthening family ties to counteract the tendency of child welfare agencies to engage in unnecessary out-of-home placements.[11] Kadushin, on the other hand, urged less criticism of the foster care system and the implementation of policies directed toward improving the delivery of such services to those children and families for whom foster care is indispensable.[12]

Obviously, these issues are related, and the adoption or failure to adopt any one policy could well affect one or more of the others. Yet the proponents of each policy are not likely to be concerned about the other proposals when they are competing for scarce resources. The mistake made by supporters of ERA could well be made again, that is, pushing for change without considering and understanding the consequences for those with related concerns.

It may seem irrational or an unnecessary expenditure of energy and resources for feminist social workers to consider the concerns of those who may be on the other side of the feminist issue. However, one may learn a lesson in that regard from the persistent problem of school integration. Those who fought against busing often stated that the schools should not bear the burden of solving all the ills of society and that the more critical problem was residential segregation. They urged that the schools should be left alone and that neighborhoods and workplaces should be integrated. Proponents of school integration usually ignored this "diversionary tactic." However, a far wiser move might well have been to insist on the simultaneous implementation of residential and school integration.

The second skill is *consciousness raising,* which is a specialized form of information giving. Consciousness raising involves heightening the awareness of the self as an individual and in relation to others.[13] In their traditional roles, women often have not had the opportunity to explore with other women issues related to their personal and collective identities or to relate these identities to the larger political and economic world. Facilitating this process so women can evolve a more realistic view of the world, engage in actions to influence it, or take advantage of opportunities to increase their potential requires a skill that social workers have begun to develop. Since this skill involves an assumption that the issues for the client are political and social rather than intrapsychic, it cannot be effectively implemented without a consideration of multiple systems.

A third skill is the *mobilization of resources.* This is a basic social work skill—one that clients value most and social workers prize least. Most social workers have had to deal with the massive needs of clients for so long that they have become adept at mobilizing all types of resources: connecting widows and displaced homemakers to resources for vocational counseling, career planning, and training; developing cooperative low-cost housing arrangements for groups of single mothers; creating a network of comprehensive services for rape victims; and encouraging the development of mobile maternal and child care units in isolated poor communities without medical services. These services, among many others, represent the application of a high-level skill in mobilizing resources—a unique component of professional social work services.

A fourth skill is the *creation of support systems,* which is related to the mobilization of resources but is more specialized in that the resources mobilized are interpersonal rather than material. A major problem for any oppressed group is the difficulty involved in engaging in collective action—one of the few ways in which those who have little power can increase it. Cohesiveness and trust in these groups are prerequisites to successful collective action. However, oppression often breeds mistrust because individuals in the oppressed group are forced to compete for the scraps of goods and services that are made available. Thus, there are women who do not develop peer networks with other women because they are convinced they cannot trust other women; they believe that if they trust another woman they will suddenly find that the woman has stolen their promotion, their reputation, or their man. It is important to be able to reduce this mistrust so women may develop the ability to deal with women's concerns through collective action. Thus, the ability to create new support systems and to promote greater effectiveness of natural support systems is a skill that social workers, particularly those working in ethnic minority communities, have developed and that can be utilized in work with women.

The fifth skill is in bringing about *organizational change*. The effective social worker (according to the feminist perspective) is skillful in modifying the organization in which she works to remove impediments to nonsexist practice. Knowledge of organizational behavior can serve as the basis for a number of strategies that Pawlak referred to as "organizational tinkering."[14] For example, social workers may more readily gain expanded services for women when a form of organizational instability is created because the agency administration is undergoing change. In some cases, resistance to altering treatment services for female clients may not be due to deep-seated sexism but to a reluctance to make large-scale changes when the consequences are unpredictable. In such a case, a pilot program may be accepted to test the viability of the approach.

CONCLUSION

Social workers who apply these skills frequently and competently in the interest of feminist goals can be an effective force in changing the status of women. But application of technical skills is not sufficient for achieving full empowerment. For example, the medieval physician may have been competent in the technical skill of bleeding a patient, but the patient was rarely cured of the disease for which he or she was being treated. Similarly, the social worker may be effective in analyzing complex systems, but if she does not try to address all parts of the system, she is minimizing her potential impact. If the social worker helps women to develop a greater understanding of their rights but does nothing to change policies that do not protect or that abrogate these rights, she minimizes her impact. If she mobilizes resources in the community to provide shelters for battered women but does not provide equal access to minority women because of the location, policies, and programs of the shelters, she minimizes her impact. If she creates new support systems for women and ignores existing natural support systems, she minimizes her impact. If she overcomes opposition to the development of a rape treatment center in a hospital but does not attempt to influence the law enforcement and judiciary systems with which the center must interact, she minimizes her impact.

No one ever said that social work is easy. Social workers have mastered many skills that have been creatively organized and applied to complex problem situations, such as the characteristic problems of women in a sexist society. Such mastery requires energy and intellect. However, as has been amply demonstrated by the innovative efforts of a growing number of social workers throughout the country, it also requires a vision, a set of countervailing values, and a determination to overcome.

REFERENCES

1. *See*, for example, Cynthia Epstein, *Women's Place: Options and Limits in Professional Careers* (Berkeley: University of California Press, 1980); E. Mostow and P. Newberry, "Work Role and Depression in Women: A Comparison of Workers and Housewives in Treatment," *American Journal of Orthopsychiatry*, 45 (July 1975), pp. 538–548; Louise S. Bakke and Jean B. Edson, "Women in Management: Moving Up?" *Social Work*, 22 (November 1977), pp. 512–514; Marjorie D. Moskol, "Feminist Theory and Casework Practice," in Bernard Ross and S. K. Khinduka, eds., *Social Work in Practice* (Washington, D.C.: National Association of Social Workers, 1976), pp. 181–190; Anne Seiden, "Overview: Research on the Psychology of Women. II.: Women in Families, Work and Psychotherapy," *American Journal of Psychiatry*, 133 (September 1976), pp. 995–1007; Gail Abarbanel, "Helping Victims of Rape," *Social Work*, 21 (November 1976), pp. 478–482; and Doris A. Stevens, "Rape Victims," in Naomi Gottlieb, ed., *Alternative Social Services for Women* (New York: Columbia University Press, 1980), pp. 235–251.

2. *See*, for example, Herma H. Kay, *Sex-Based Discrimination in Family Law* (St. Paul, Minn.: West Publishing Co., 1974); and Merton C. Bernstein, "Forecast of Women's Retirement Income: Cloudy and Colder, Twenty-five Percent Chance of Poverty," *Industrial Gerontology*, 1 (Winter 1974), pp. 1–13.

3. *See Little Sisters and the Law* (Washington, D.C.: Female Offender Resource Center, National Offender Services Coordination Program, American Bar Association, 1977), pp. 4–19; Elaine M. Corrigan and Sandra C. Anderson, "Training for Treatment of Alcoholism in Women," *Social Casework*, 59 (January 1978), p. 43; and Dona Lansing Bracht, "The Displaced Homemaker," in Naomi Gottlieb, ed., *Alternative Services for Women* (New York: Columbia University Press, 1980), pp. 320–321.

4. *See* Janet Saltzman Chafetz, "Women in Social Work," *Social Work*, 17 (September 1972), pp. 12–18; Diane Kravetz, "Sexism in a Woman's Profession," *Social Work*, 21 (November 1976), pp. 421–427; and Susan T. Vandiver, "A Herstory of Women in Social Work," in Elaine Norman and Arlene Mancuso, eds., *Women's Issues and Social Work Practice* (Itasca, Ill.: F. E. Peacock Publishers, 1980), pp. 21–38.

5. Vandiver, op. cit. p. 24.

6. Michael Parenti, *Power and the Powerless* (New York: St. Martin's Press, 1978).

7. Kenneth E. Boulding, "Towards a Theory of Protest," *ETC: A Review of General Semantics*, 24 (March 1967), pp. 49–58.

8. Andrew Hacker, "Who Killed E.R.A.? Women Did!" *Washington Post*, September 14, 1980, Sec. C, pp. 1–3.

9. Ibid.

10. Gladys Harbeson, *Choice and Challenge For the American Woman* (Rev. ed.; Cambridge, Mass.: Schenkman Publishing Co., 1971), p. 47; Nancy S. Barrett, "Women in the Job Market: Occupations, Earnings and Career Opportunities," in Ralph E. Smith, ed., *The Subtle Revolution: Women at Work* (Washington, D.C.: Urban Institute, 1979), pp. 31–61; and Alan Pifer, "Women Working: Toward a New Society," in Karen Wolk Feinstein, ed., *Working Women and Families* (Beverly Hills, Calif.: Sage Publications, 1979), pp. 13–33.

11. *Children Without Homes: An Examination of Public Responsibility to Children in Out-of-Home Care* (Washington, D.C.: Children's Defense Fund, 1978), pp. 15–36.

12. Alfred Kadushin, "Children in Foster Families and Institutions," in Henry S. Maas, ed., *Social Service Research: Reviews of Studies* (Washington, D.C.: National Association of Social Workers, 1978), p. 105.

13. An excellent discussion of consciousness raising as a social work technique is in John Longres and Eileen McLeod, "Consciousness Raising and Social Work Practice," *Social Casework*, 61 (May 1980), pp. 267–276.

14. Edward J. Pawlak, "Organizational Tinkering," *Social Work*, 21 (September 1976), pp. 376–380.